C000293395

BAGGAGE OF EMPIRE

Baggage
of Empire

**REPORTING POLITICS AND INDUSTRY IN
THE SHADOW OF IMPERIAL DECLINE**

MARTIN ADENEY

Biteback Publishing

First published in Great Britain in 2016 by
Biteback Publishing Ltd
Westminster Tower
3 Albert Embankment
London SE1 7SP
Copyright © Martin Adeney 2016

Martin Adeney has asserted his right under the Copyright, Designs
and Patents Act 1988 to be identified as the author of this work.

All rights reserved. No part of this publication may be reproduced,
stored in a retrieval system or transmitted, in any form or by any means,
without the publisher's prior permission in writing.

This book is sold subject to the condition that it shall not, by way of
trade or otherwise, be lent, resold, hired out or otherwise circulated
without the publisher's prior consent in any form of binding or cover
other than that in which it is published and without a similar condition,
including this condition, being imposed on the subsequent purchaser.

Every reasonable effort has been made to trace copyright holders
of material reproduced in this book, but if any have been inadvertently
overlooked the publishers would be glad to hear from them.

ISBN 978-1-78590-083-9

10 9 8 7 6 5 4 3 2 1

A CIP catalogue record for this book is available from the British Library.

Set in Dante and Clarendon by Adrian McLaughlin

Printed and bound in Great Britain by
CPI Group (UK) Ltd, Croydon CR0 4YY

MIX
Paper from
responsible sources
FSC® C020471

In memory of Ann.
Wife, partner, enabler.

Contents

Introduction

My generation was the last to be born while the British Empire still existed. I suppose we could be called 'twilight's children'. But imperial attitudes, imperial nostalgia and imperial consequences have continued to shape us and resonate throughout most of our lives.

I have had a particularly strong appreciation of it as the child of parents who sought their vocation, if not their fortune, in imperial climes, as well as through the opportunities offered to me as a journalistic observer. Much of what I experienced, however, is little different to my contemporaries. We heard the same stories, read the same books and newspapers and encountered the same attitudes.

As history slips by, this book is an attempt to share some of those experiences in part to clarify my own recollections, in part to explain how it was and where we have come from. For that reason, I have quoted at some length from my contemporary articles and diary entries. However ill-phrased they may be, that was what I thought or wrote at the time.

Much of my experience has been associated with industry and

business, but what I have watched and reported has been driven and shaped by all sorts of underlying currents – political and international realignments, great movements of peoples, changing social attitudes and mores, new ways of work and leisure.

And what has happened to British business and industry has reflected and illuminated those forces in turn.

I am tempted to see it as a journey through the ruins, rather like bumping through the middle of a vast inner-city construction site of the kind familiar in our great northern cities in the 1960s. The old is crumbling or being torn down, and the new remains under development but is never quite finished, in a shifting variety of styles, some of which are then themselves demolished. The reality, however, is more complex or, in a word now popular but scarcely used in the twentieth century, more nuanced.

Vocabulary has been under reconstruction too. As I look through publications of the period, and my own reports and diaries, words and phrases have changed their meanings or have passed in and out of fashion. The slang of my childhood has been replaced by the language of my grandchildren. Railway stations have now almost universally turned into train stations, while words like flawed and forensic have become over-used clichés at some distance from their original meaning.

I have used the imperial prism to interpret the events of these three score years and ten, but I have applied it to a series of different, if interlinked, imperial experiences.

First, there is the experience of my family and myself of the empire as it still remained in my early years, both abroad and back home where it was reflected and affected us in our homes and schools and the traditional workplaces of British industry.

Patriarchy marched with empire. Its imperial attitudes were still in the ascendancy in my four years at Cambridge University, although the challenges were beginning to mount with the decline of defer-ence, which I helped to chronicle among the generation that came to adulthood in the '60s; my own generation.

My time in a Birmingham factory and two and a half years of reporting across the once-mighty industrial cities of northern England brought me face-to-face with the decline of the great indus-tries and cities which had benefited from imperial trade. In step with that came a great retreat of the newspaper empires from the north to an almost exclusively metropolitan viewpoint, a shrinking of the ambition for a world view. At the same time, we were witnessing a huge and unexpected consequence of our imperial spread, the reverse flow, as more and more Commonwealth immigrants sought to make their homes and their living here with very visible effects on our cities.

It was a subject that increasingly preoccupied me as I moved to '60s London as a reporter, before an all-too-short exposure to south and Southeast Asia. In the India and Sri Lanka of those days, the footprints of the empire were still clearly imprinted, sometimes in almost comic ways, in exaggerated flummeries, inappropriate hotel food and a devotion to niceties of the English language fast disappear-ing at home. As an Englishman, the imperial overhang meant that I was treated with a respect and care now unimaginable in these days of terrorism and mass tourism. It was, it is now clear, an interlude.

Back in London, the imperial fabric of the city, even Piccadilly itself, was under siege from developers and I found myself lending my shoulder to attempts to achieve sensible solutions that did not trample on the needs of residents and preserved treasured fabric.

Finally I immersed myself in the world of labour and industry, which showed most clearly the effects and symptoms of imperial decline. I reported on the rise and fall of the trade union empires which dominated political discourse from the end of the '60s to the mid-'80s. Concurrently I charted the struggles of the industries that had been at the heart of the imperial project – coal, steel, shipbuilding and, latterly, motor manufacturing – as they were affected by the growing competition from overseas. Sadly, too many of those empires crumbled.

Repeatedly in my reporting I had complained about the unwillingness both of trade union leaders and, even more so, industrialists, to come out and speak frankly about their concerns and intentions. Whether you call it an English reluctance or a traditional imperial snobbery that has affected many of our institutions, British business has consistently failed to make its case in public and often to engage in public discussion at all ('none of your business'). I believe that this failure has not only wrecked its reputation with the public, but has kept it from playing its proper role in society. It has also prevented it from discovering how it could perform better.

So, when in 1989 the opportunity came to join a company I respected and which understood that it needed to make a better case for itself, I was tempted. It helped that the company was Britain's leading exporter, a major spender on research and had a reputation for enlightened labour relations. It mattered. So I joined the ultimate imperial icon: ICI, Imperial Chemical Industries, to manage their media relations and later the rest of their communications.

Once more, however, I found myself amid crumbling empires. Traditionally structured companies were under siege from financially driven predators challenging the spread of their businesses and looking to sell off parts of their empire at a profit. At ICI, we resisted an incursion by Lord Hanson but as time went on it became clear that British, and international, investors were no longer prepared to finance the kind of big investment projects that major industries like ICI required. The stock market was looking for quick returns and the rather charmingly named 'patient money' was less and less available.

As a result, the industry was increasingly dominated by private companies often belonging to a single family, usually from the Far East but sometimes from the US. New empires had risen. ICI successfully floated off the life science interests, which its brilliant scientists had developed as Zeneca, now Astra-Zeneca, one of the world's leading drugs companies. But its traditional heavy chemical empire was then sold off piece by reluctant piece. The baggage of empire.

I have tried to write this study as far as possible from my personal experiences without too much consulting of reference books and other people's recollections. It remains a personal view but inevitably I have had to check some dates and facts.

I have written two books that deal with some of the issues I cover – on the miners' strike and the motor industry. I stand by them and have tried not to go over the same ground again, although some repetition is unavoidable. As for analysing the decline of British industry, mine is an anecdotal story and for a full consideration of the issues I would refer to detailed academic studies.

This book is, of course, a memoir – a catalogue of personal experiences. The most appropriate words are those my friend and colleague John Cole chose for his autobiography, 'As it seemed to me'.

Chapter One
Imperial beginnings

I was born as the British Empire tottered, in a region at the very eye of the storm – the Middle East, at the moment in 1942 when Rommel was poised to break through demoralised British defences. It was a few weeks before the battle of Alamein.

My parents, children of the empire, were living in Egypt where my father was port chaplain at Port Said, the Mediterranean gateway to one of the empire's most celebrated symbols and its lifeline, the Suez Canal. A few days earlier, so dire the risk of defeat was adjudged to be that my mother had been evacuated with other women and children. But, unlike many others sent to await ship to India from Suez, at the southern end of the canal, my mother had managed to stay close by (dangerously close by if the Germans had broken through) with friends in Jerusalem. There, as Marjorie Blagden until her marriage, she had been vice-principal of the Jerusalem Girls' College, which had prided itself on teaching both Arab and Jewish children.

Just how tense a time it was is illustrated by a letter written by my mother to my father a few days before I was born.

> I got a bit shaken yesterday by a man and his wife talking about immediate evacuation to South Africa; their visas had just materialised. Then Alec [her host] announced that he was convinced that Rommel would get Alexandria. However I thought of your quiet confidence and by having an evening on my own while they were at a cinema, I got myself straight.

The news of my birth was telegraphed to my father together with the words 'eight wounds'. Fortunately, in close contact with seamen and the military, and an active Boy Scout leader, he knew enough Morse code to understand how similar the symbols were for 'p' and 'w'. Three weeks later, my mother and I joined him in Port Said.

My parents were no great figures of the empire, but they were part of its warp and weft, like thousands of their compatriots. They came from what one mid-Victorian grandee typed as 'what we may call the non-commissioned officers of English society – the clergy, the lawyers, the doctors, the country squires, the junior partners in banks and merchants' offices, men who are in every sense of the word gentlemen though no one would class them with the aristocracy'.[1]

That they were in the Middle East at all owed much to the all-pervasive climate of empire and its handmaid, evangelical religion, and its influence on their families. Similarly, although I have spent almost my entire life in England after being transported there in a wartime convoy, the legacy of my parents and their generation have in turn shaped the prism through which I and my generation has viewed events. Our over-riding experience has been of institutions

---

1   Stephen Fitzjames, *Edinburgh Review* (April 1859), p. 557

and corporations struggling to adapt or even to survive in a climate formed by imperial assumptions, in a world in which they have been progressively dismantled.

So how had my parents come to be in the Middle East amid the baggage of empire on the cusp of history?

In the case of my father, Jack Adeney, the answer is simple, although the story goes back some generations. You could label it 'religious imperialism'. He was essentially the product of the powerful evangelical awakening of the late eighteenth and early nineteenth centuries that stirred the likes of Shaftesbury and Wilberforce to political reforms and also to the importance, indeed compulsion, to convert the heathen wherever in the world they were to be found.

At the turn of the nineteenth century, my great-great-grandfather William found them close by, among his employees. A tailor in Sackville Street, off Piccadilly in central London, he was the most devout of Christians, preaching to his workers in their lunch break but, in fairness, paying them to attend his homilies. The family still possess the wooden bowl from which the pence were distributed. After work, proselytism continued. He was thrown off an omnibus by the conductor for attempting to convert the upper deck and in the evening might be found ministering to fallen women on Rochester Row some years before Mr Gladstone. He was briefly arrested for his open-air preaching in the West End.

A flavour of the proceedings is provided by his brother, John, in describing the 'congregation' William held at his own house at eight o'clock on Saturday mornings, for

> all the slums of the neighbourhood to hear first an earnest address
> from him as he stood on the staircase; and then to receive each
> of them a penny, and children a halfpenny and a religious tract.
>
> At the original gathering of this ungainly group, the police

were startled and immediately interfered, but retired on my brother's explanation and entreaty. The neighbours too liked not to have such a mass of outcasts in their immediate propinquity.

John admitted that they might have reason:

It was necessary to secure everything moveable, even to the stair rods. One of these 'town Arabs' thinking the time occupied by the address lost to his profession, busied himself in taking off and carrying away with him some small portions of the fastening and furniture of a door near which he stood, to the display rather of his industry and ingenuity than of his gratitude or of his moral or spiritual improvement.

In general however they were all exceedingly well-behaved and attentive. The upturned faces and gleaming eyes, exhibiting every phase of squalid misery and vice, constituted a group for an artist's pencil. The sickening reek and fumes from their breath and from their bodies and garments were almost overpowering and rendered on their exit an immediate ventilation from open windows and outer doors, a matter of first necessity.

Who could tell, he wondered, 'whether any or what good this act of mercy and true charity may have been the means of effecting?'[2]

William's descendants spread their net farther afield. His eldest son chose to get away and emigrate to Australia at eighteen. The memoir of William does not say why but records his anguish. His son would in his turn found a line of evangelical clerics.

But it was one of William's London grandsons, Frederick, who decided to join the Church Missionary Society, which his grandfather

2   *Wearing not Rusting: A Brief Memoir of Mr W. Adeney* (W. H. Dalton, 1860)

had supported, and who began what would become a flood of missionaries. He was posted to Jerusalem, a backwater then still ruled by the Ottoman Empire, in 1892. He found it a city of 'dead churches and dying creeds'. Diagnosed with tuberculosis, he was soon transferred to Egypt where the climate was drier and his sister, Helen, joined him as a missionary.

In 1897, it was the turn of their younger brother, my grandfather, to arrive in Jerusalem. A printed postcard with Turkish franking records his concerns – the safe arrival of a catalogue from England and the task of conveying his feverish sister back to her missionary posting in Egypt.

My grandfather had a particularly defined objective. He had joined the London Jews Society, later to become the more aptly named Church Mission to the Jews, whose long-hallowed goal was the conversion of Christ's own people. As my grandfather noted, the Jewish community in Jerusalem was surprisingly small. After three years he left Palestine for a post in Romania where he would spend the next thirty years among a populous Jewish community, founding successful schools.

He met my grandmother, Emma Webster, at an evangelical convention. She in turn came from an Anglican family in Dublin and had joined the CMJ as second best, having failed the medical for the more illustrious and wide-ranging Church Missionary Society. Posted to Hamburg, she sent an anguished plea to the society for a move. In a touching biographical note, she explained how her name and description had been circulated. Servants were warned not to admit her. Potential converts saw her coming and locked their doors.

A friend told her how her visits had been discussed at a gathering of one large Jewish family with 'roars of laughter and many expressions of indignation and anger'. 'One gentleman asked Mrs K why she had not turned you out. "I would have done so", she said, "but she was a lady and I had to treat her as such."'

Tragically, she died a few weeks after the birth of her only child, my father. He was sent back to England to be brought up by his uncle and aunt. Uncle Arthur had taken the civil service route and was to become Deputy Controller of the London Post Office region. There was little doubt, however, that my father would enter what was effectively becoming the second family business after tailoring.

So, after public school and Cambridge, he was duly ordained into the Church of England and in 1932 he sailed for Egypt as assistant port chaplain at Port Said and Suez. Technically he was joining the Jerusalem and the East Mission but in practice he was in Egypt to minister to the British community, and, through his work for the Missions to Seamen, to the crews of British ships sailing through the canal.

They called it 'the Gateway to the East'. The idea of gateways was a popular metaphor, and imperial voyagers passed from one to another. Southampton, where we would settle later, proclaimed itself 'the Gateway to the Empire' as you entered the town, while the gateway to India is still realised in brick and stone on the waterfront at what was then Bombay, now Mumbai.

Through the Suez Canal heaved and hissed the great steamships of the P&O and the Orient lines, smaller British India vessels, regular deployments of the Royal Navy and oil tankers serving the fledgling industry of the Persian Gulf. My father would set out to board the ships from his hired launch with a Muslim boatman, who would regularly pause to say his prayers. He estimated that he boarded nearly 5,000 ships in seven years at Port Said and in the Persian Gulf where later he became chaplain at Basrah.

He specialised in the growing numbers of oil tankers plying to Abadan, returning laden five weeks later, but only pausing for two or three hours. He would supply books to the English officers and try to cheer invalid sailors in hospital. In the evening, a chaplain's job could be the organising of dances and entertainments in the Mission Hall for visiting naval squadrons and passing merchant ships. My father recorded without apparent irony that 'it was not easy to get enough girls, mainly Greek or Maltese, to come to them'.

Essentially it was a service industry job: supporting the empire and its servants far from home; encouraging young cadets on their first voyages; entertaining service personnel who had got leave from camp to come to church; visiting the engineers developing the early oilfields in the Gulf; observing the established Anglican calendar of festivals and events; preserving the familiar forms of the UK.

So, when my father later travelled down to Bahrain or Kuwait, he would as often travel by the Sunderland flying boats of the RAF's 203 Squadron as by the civilian flying boats of the BOAC. And when he stayed in Bahrain after taking services at the new oil prospecting camp at Kuwait, it would usually be with the British advisor to the sheikh.

Back in wartime Port Said as chaplain from 1942, with bombing raids and ships being mined in the harbour approaches, there was a new manifestation of the empire as African pioneer troops arrived to join the battle, with their own Christian padres. Groups came for recreation to the church – tea, games and a short service – and my father was struck by the baptism of thirteen Ugandan soldiers. 'It was most impressive to see them baptised in new names and then advance to the front of the church with the other Christians, singing "Onward Christian Soldiers".' It was a reminder of the reach and the cultural control exercised by the empire. Imperial or otherwise, it struck a chord with my father. He would keep a 'school photo' of himself with the African troops on the mantelpiece wherever we lived.

The attitudes of the British community (relatively small in Port Said compared with Cairo, the seat of the British ambassador and military headquarters) are illuminated by a programme for the Victory in Europe Ball held at the Casino Palace Hotel at Port Said on 26 May 1945. 'You can', it announced, 'dance until 2 a.m. and with a gay and carefree heart for the war in Europe is won.'

Its centre spread carried a message from the British Consul declaring 'Never has victory been so cleanly won ... we fought not only for freedom but that the highest values of the human spirit might endure'. For him these were 'truth, light and justice', contrasting with the 'lies, hate and ignorance' which would have been 'the fate of tortured humanity' had Britain gone down to defeat.

He exhorted his readers to prove worthy of the victory by the way they lived – 'only thus can we show that the ideals we fought for are not mere words but permeate our daily lives'.

The programme solicited donations to the Victory Thanksgiving Appeal. Tellingly, it went only to support British institutions in Egypt – primarily hospitals and schools, 'to make more fully available to British children the kind of education which would be theirs at home, and to give to those parents of other nationalities, who wish it, increased facilities for educating their children in the British manner'. That done, the consul concluded, 'Let us go forth, gay and confident, yet sober, to face our future.'

But the Britain to which the former White Star liner *Britannic* would convey my father a few weeks later, for a reunion with my mother and myself, would turn out far from gay.

Like many returning expatriates and service people, my father struggled to find a place in post-war Britain. We stayed with my grandfather for a while, then went to live in a flat in Portsmouth for six months while he did effectively the same modest job as he had done before leaving for Egypt. Finally, in 1947, he found a job as a vicar of an industrial parish on the outskirts of Birmingham at Tyseley, the home of a famous railway depot.

It was an industrial setting. Not so much of satanic mills as the boxy industrial factory estates of the 1930s. The street names were workaday. We lived at 469 Reddings Lane. Opposite the church ran Foreman's Road, with Foreman's Road School, while lining the streets were a series of modest factories with prefabs beyond. One of the factories was the Lucas Battery factory, condemned years later for the poisonous lead it had emitted for years.

I remember one day a car driving past it, turning too late, colliding with the church fence and toppling onto its side. A group of men rushed up; the driver, wearing a long mac, was pulled clear and with a metallic scraping the car was simply pushed upright. The driver got in and drove away. Another evening we were called from our beds to the pavement to witness a great red umbrella of cloud as the distant BSA factory, a manufacturer of motorcycles that went all over the empire, dissolved into flames.

Cars were hard to come by. Steel was rationed and the government was giving exports priority. To get a car, it was said, you had to know someone in the industry. Fortunately, this was Birmingham and in due course my father did, and a small black Austin Eight turned up outside our door.

Food and clothes rationing continued and strange foods appeared on the table. In the butcher's they hung red and black rings of polony, but we rather liked fried-up Pom, a sort of early version of Cadbury's Smash: potato powder to which you added water. In the winter of 1947 when we watched the snow piling up in the backyard, we got used to blackouts as electricity supplies failed for want of coal.

My father worked hard, laying out a memorial garden beside the church for those killed in the war and regularly visiting the factories and the railway depot, but the tides of the Middle East continued to flow through our living room.

My parents would speak Arabic at the dining table, particularly when they did not want us to understand. I remember their dismay when the news came in 1946 of the bombing by Jewish nationalists of the King David Hotel in Jerusalem, which housed the British HQ. They debated events, not exactly taking sides, although I sensed my mother was more pro-Arab, my father working hard to see the Jewish view.

When we went on holiday, to a cousin's house in Bournemouth, I found them swotting up on Swahili grammar in the evening, apparently in anticipation of a new life in Africa. For whatever reason it did not happen, but nevertheless my parents were warned that they had to make a move. My youngest sister had suffered a bad bout of pneumonia. Our doctor warned that she might not survive another winter in the polluted air and habitual fogs of industrial Birmingham before the Clean Air Act. Instead, my father managed to get a move to a bigger parish, and a bigger house, in Southampton.

Chapter Two
Gateway to empire

It was as the road sign said as we drove into Southampton, 'The Gateway to the Empire', and it displayed a suitable sketch of an ocean liner. Four years on, reminders of the war were everywhere. Almost my first memory is seeing two DUKWS, the amphibious vehicles used on the Normandy beaches, driving round a roundabout in the centre of town. A few years later the dock beside what was inevitably called the Royal Pier (originally the Royal Victoria Pier) was clogged with orderly lines of shattered military vehicles that had been salvaged and shipped back from the invasion beaches. We inspected them with little understanding, and there were no obvious signs of the human carnage that had accompanied their destruction.

Not that the town needed any reminders of the war from outside. We became accustomed to taking shortcuts across bomb sites, with fireplaces and flapping wallpaper hanging off exposed upstairs walls, on the way to the shops with our ration coupons. If you went east where the Woolston chain ferry clanked across the River Itchen you could see the burnt-out shell of the Spitfire factory. And in the heart of the old town, within the medieval walls, all was devastation from the bombs.

From the shattered tower of Holy Rood to the miraculously preserved ancient church of St Michaels, where the vaulted undercrofts of old wine cellars and a Norman warehouse still survived nearby, there were row on row of damaged and derelict ancient houses. I poked around in one, the seventeenth-century home of Isaac Watts, who penned the appropriate hymn 'O God our help in Ages Past, our hope for years to come. Be thou our guard while troubles last'. The Civic Centre clock chimed its tune every four hours. Nearby, in the creaking attics of the Tudor House museum, a layout of the docks still displayed models of ships lost in wartime naval service.

But the battered port itself was booming, still recognisably the Gateway to the Empire. As air travel remained difficult, scarce and expensive, it was bursting with hastily patched-up passenger ships of all sizes, their times of arrival and departure recorded every day in the local newspaper. An adjacent column entitled 'Round the Port' provided nuggets of information about visiting steamers, their history, their previous ownerships. One entry logged the arrival of a sister ship to the *Athenia*, the first British passenger vessel to be sunk by German submarines in 1939 while transporting children evacuees to Canada. My cousins had been evacuated on the same route.

Our house and garden still showed the marks of wartime use by the Home Guard. In a dark corner of the loft, beside the rolled-up blackout blinds labelled in case of the need for reuse, the sun's rays picked out the silhouette of a .303 rifle. When we eventually plucked up the courage to venture through the shadows to inspect it, it turned out to be a Dad's Army dummy, used for drill training, or maybe to make it look as if the Home Guard post-Dunkirk were better armed than they actually were. It was a useful addition to our games, although rather heavy.

In the garden we could play on a large sandbank that had been the back of a firing range, or a store for extinguishing fires. In an old wooden garage marooned in the vegetable patch we found to our delight a tin helmet and a working stirrup pump used to project a spray of water from a bucket, to help douse a fire. Mixed up with them were lawn tennis nets that pointed to a more expansive, more luxurious, vanished past.

We picked through the jumble at the nearby church hall. The frequent sales brought in a gallimaufry of strange objects, many of them relics brought back from imperial service and journeyings. There was the stuffed alligator that was dumped under the stage and we pored through a complete set of *Sixty Years a Queen*, the collectable part-work published for Victoria's jubilee with its accounts of the great conquests of her reign. We swapped cigarette cards illustrating the different regimental uniforms of the Indian Army.

But it was also a disconcerting time. You had only to look at the rusting chocolate vending machines on the platform of the central station to know that things had been sweeter before the war and while there would be brave talk of a new Elizabethan era, the news was full of difficulty and retreat.

Deference abounded. As Wolf Cubs, we were taken to parade before Lord Louis Mountbatten, a sort of local hero, not so long returned from the shambles of Indian independence. We were supposed to perform a forward roll in his honour as he sparkled distantly in a tangle of gold braid. Our ragged performance would not have passed muster in North Korea.

But then the news from Korea was bad, as we learnt of the brave last stand of the troops we knew as the 'Glorious Gloucesters' at the battle of the Imjin River, with the imprisonment of many of the survivors.

And the empire was crumbling. After Korea, there was the Malaysian emergency. Then the papers were full of the Mau Mau and the Kenya emergency. A few years later it would be Cyprus and EOKA. All were seen as rebellions to be dealt with rather than struggles for independence, or, in EOKA's case, for Enosis, union with Greece. National Service remained a fact of life and elder brothers or friends, who had been at school a few weeks before, were among the troops sent out to deal with the trouble.

Opposite the vicarage, the houses were large and rather dilapidated. Through their rented rooms passed both the old empire in the persons of a retired District Commissioner and his family (shorts and thick white socks) and those who would shape its future; West African students arrived to study at what was then the University College of Southampton. Some were Muslim Nigerian in their bright robes; some Christian. But they were the first black faces we had seen. 'Nice black chaps,' said my mother, and set about inviting one to lunch.

He was a Christian called Ade from the Gold Coast, which became independent Ghana. We felt particular affinity with him because his name started with the same letters as our own surname, which originates from a Saxon village in Shropshire. We were soon to discover how many West African names started with 'Ade'. Years later I received a letter from a London lawyer offering help if I wanted to deal with the immigration of, I presumed, my Nigerian relations.

On 6 February 1952, we were called into the school assembly hall – a corrugated wartime Nissen hut. The headmaster (whose name, Mr Savage, was not actually bestowed from his habit of beating whole classes of boys one after the other) intoned in a voice full of portent, 'His Majesty the King died in his sleep early this morning.'

Sports were cancelled as a mark of respect and we were sent home for the day. It made a change from having to decide which famous battle was being commemorated on the days when Percy Wilson, our history master and a gunnery veteran of the First World War, wore his Royal Artillery tie.

Over the coming weeks we sat silently at our desks while solemn music played on the radio and we learnt words and phrases like 'cortege' and 'slow march' and 'muffled drums'. Then we did it all over again when Queen Mary died.

After the coronation, watched in a house where neighbours owned a television, we had another repeat. The school took us to the cinema to see it all over again and later *The Conquest of Everest*, which had been dramatically announced on the morning of the coronation.

The town had its own royal connections and its pride was what we called simply 'the Queens' – the *Queen Mary* and *Queen Elizabeth*, the two largest passenger ships in the world.

The *Mary* held the Blue Riband – the record for the fastest Atlantic crossing wrested back from the French in the 1930s. The fabled weekly service across the Atlantic carried every sort of celebrity, from kings and queens to prime ministers and Hollywood stars, and would be met by legendary hard-bitten reporters at the New York pier. 'Will you be visiting any nightclubs in New York, Bishop?' ran the Southampton joke. 'Are there any nightclubs in New York?' Cue headline: 'Bishop's first question in New York'. Told by a local alderman, it was my first introduction to our ambiguous relationship with the press.

People would still line piers to greet arriving liners. But, in 1952, the newly completed American liner, the *United States*, secured the Blue Riband on her maiden voyage, striking a blow to local and national pride. As I stood with my parents on the shore to watch her steam in, a long streak of rubbed paint along her waterline where she must have brushed against a quay, a man beside me, clutching at straws, said, 'She may not last long. She is welded together – American cruisers broke up in the war because they weren't riveted.'

It was all of a piece with our conversations at school. The father of a friend of mine was a BOAC pilot. He had flown bombers in the war. He used to bring back clockwork toys from Japan. My friend explained how they were much cleverer than British toys but they always broke down. British was more long-lasting. British was best. It was a theme and attitude that ran through the country.

The advent of the *United States* was a symbolic moment – liners were seen as national champions. Increasingly there was a recognition that the Americans, the 'Yanks', were taking over first place in all sorts of areas. 'How is the world's second largest navy?' the American officer is supposed to have asked his British counterpart when US military tonnage overtook British. 'How's the world's second best navy?' came the reply in the cheer-up joke of the time.

Soon the government would subsidise the building of a replacement for 'the Queens', the *QE2*, just as it had poured money into her predecessors in the 1930s, although it resisted the idea of competing again for the Blue Riband. The French joined in with the completion of their champion, the *France*, in 1961, deliberately longer than the Cunarders but still not quite as fast as the *United States*, dashing the hopes of President De Gaulle, who expressed at her launch that she too would compete for the Blue Riband.

It was the final days; the closing chapter for the 'greyhounds of the ocean'. In 1980, I filmed for the BBC in a dry-dock at Bremerhaven as two of the *France*'s four propellers were sawn off and she was converted to a slower moving, more economic, Norwegian cruise ship – an emblematic end to the express seaborne Atlantic crossing that had been an international virility symbol for the past half century and more.

In the '80s I came back to Southampton to film a news piece about the decline of Britain's merchant navy. Behind me a giant supertanker was laid up on the old Union Castle liner berths, eventually to act as a storage ship in the Far East. Its tonnage, I reported, accounted for a fifth of the entire British merchant navy.

But back in the early 1950s we were still writing essays in school about whether sea travel or air travel was more effective, with a presumption in Southampton that the answer could still be sea travel. The custom sheds at the Ocean Dock where the great Transatlantic Cunarders docked were replaced by the grander Ocean Terminal.

There was still time for plenty of last goodbyes. Besides the transatlantic departures, at 4 p.m. every Thursday a Union Castle liner with a distinctive lilac hull would cast off from berth 101, the most visible in the docks, and steam past the recreation ground and Royal Pier. Every year, it seemed, a new P&O or Orient liner would make its appearance before departing for all places east; their names echoed their destinations – *Canton, Himalaya, Chusan, Cathay* and, as times changed, *Canberra*. From an inner dock every night the yellow and black funnelled steamers of nationalised British Railways would set out across the Channel for Normandy and the Channel Islands.

Shipping was in short supply and while the northern shipyards struggled to build enough new tonnage, all sorts of vessels were pressed into use. In 1949, I watched a last voyage of the four-funnelled *Aquitania*, which had been designed long before to compete with the *Titanic*. Sadly for its owners, Cunard, it had been so exhausted by its wartime efforts that it failed its Ministry of Transport inspection, part of the deck collapsing when the inspectors were actually eating their lunch.

But other stalwarts sailed on. Supplies to the Isle of Wight went by the grandly named *Lord Elgin*, a nineteenth-century coal-fired paddle steamer that puffed and struggled to breast the tide on its way up Southampton Water, overtaken by everything in sight. No Elgin marbles but plenty of building materials. Cars had to be transported on a converted landing craft.

On the way they would pass the charred hulk of the *Monarch of*

Bermuda, once a three-funnelled liner delighting the luxury American tourist market. Soon, with engine exhausts trunked into a single funnel and a stubby tripod mast from which smoke billowed, she emerged as the *New Australia*, fit enough to transport the subsidised immigrants who paid just £10 for their voyage to Australia.

Round a corner, in the suitably named Empress dock, were moored even more basic transport, the troopships. They were painted white with yellow funnels like cruise liners and a broad blue band round their hull. Although they took their grand names from English rivers, they were mostly prizes of war, converted from captured German liners. One had served as a U-boat mother ship; another as a supply vessel to the battleship *Tirpitz*.

But now the *Pretoria*, *Potsdam* and *Ubena* had become the *Empire Orwell*, *Empire Fowey*, and the *Empire Ken*, servicing the garrisons of the Suez Canal Zone and taking troops to Port Said for the 1956 invasion. Ironically, some would end as pilgrim ships to Mecca.

Then, of course, there was the *Empire Windrush*, a regular visitor. Formerly the *Monte Rosa* of the Hamburg-Sud-Amerika line, she had written her name into history in 1948 transporting the first shipload of West Indians to work for London Transport in labour-starved Britain. That historic moment – the word iconic had not been invented – had not registered with us then. We were much more interested in the newspaper reports when the ship later caught fire and sank dramatically in the Mediterranean.

The docks harboured a nod to the importance of air travel, although it was soon to be obsolete technology; a terminal for flying boats that still plied the long-haul routes to Africa and Southeast Asia, landing on convenient lakes and rivers mostly under imperial control. In 1949, we went down there to welcome back my uncle, another missionary, expelled by the new communist government of China. He was unwanted baggage of empire.

Farther down Southampton Water, if you were lucky you might catch a sight of what was supposed to be the ultimate commercial flying boat – the *Saunders-Roe Princess*, the largest all-metal flying boat ever built – taking off on a test flight or landing in a cloud of spray. An impressive sight with its distinctive 'double-bubble' hull and room for more than 100 passengers, it joined a line of famous UK white elephants, unwanted by the airlines, and, as it turned out, too large for its under-powered propeller engines.

Port activity made its presence felt at home. A regular line of friends and acquaintances would be given a bed for the night on their way abroad: a bishop returning to Bombay, an American couple travelling on one of their grey-funnelled troopships and others.

It did nothing to settle my parents – a constant reminder for these children of empire of life outside Britain. They must have planned it for months, but it seemed that only days after I had secured a place at my father's old boarding school they announced in 1955 that they were, in the words of my father's sermon, 'launching out into the deep'. My father had been appointed Archdeacon of Cyprus.

What that meant was that he was once again a chaplain to the British community abroad. As he made clear, perhaps rather too firmly, it was the smallest archdeaconry in the Anglican communion; he only had one other priest to supervise on an island with just five Anglican churches. It was an appointment, however, that would pitch him into the heart of post-imperial politics.

Chapter Three
Colonial hard truths

The year was 1955. On 1 April, the Greek Cypriot organisation EOKA had signalled the start of a terrorist campaign against the British colonial government by launching a series of armed attacks on military targets and the Cyprus Broadcasting Corporation. It announced its objective of 'throwing off the British yoke' and achieving its long-cherished goal of Enosis, union with Greece.

In the months that followed, the terrorist campaign ratcheted up. My parents had been invited to spend their first few days at Government House as the governor's wife had been a friend of my mother's at Oxford. (Imperial links.) But, by the time they arrived in October, the security situation had become so bad that the governor had been replaced by a military man, the former head of the British Army and one of Montgomery's tank commanders, Field Marshal Sir John Harding. His attitude to EOKA had not been improved by the discovery one morning of an unexploded bomb under his bed, apparently planted the previous night by one of his service staff.

With their previous Middle Eastern experiences, particularly in Palestine, my parents were no strangers to violence. Even in the 1930s my father had a military escort when he was taking boys to a mission school for Jews and Arabs in northern Palestine. He said baldly, 'My wife and I had been used to "troubles" in the Palestine years so we preferred [to leave England] to take on the task on the beautiful island.'

As for the concern of friends and relations in the UK when they heard reports of bombings or shootings, my parents' standard, if rather gung-ho response, echoed by many other veterans of the empire, would be that such and such a place – Palestine, Iraq, Jerusalem, Basrah, Nicosia – covered a large area and they were usually at a distance to any trouble.

It also helped that the bombs planted in Cyprus were, by today's standards, small affairs, and, as Harding's escape demonstrated, not always reliable. Plastic explosives were scarce and car bombs were not employed. It was not yet Northern Ireland or Iraq. But the violence was not just directed at the military: it also targeted British civilians, as well as soldiers' wives and teenage children picked off at close quarters on the street. One of my first memories in Cyprus was attending a viewing of Olivier's blood-soaked film of Richard III in the house of a woman whose husband had been shot down in Nicosia's main shopping street, Ledra Street, with two companions a few weeks before. It became known as murder mile.

Every Sunday, the governor, a brisk, compact presence, came to church, driving from Government House down past our house on Canningos Street, named for the British Foreign Secretary, George Canning, who had supported the Greek struggle for independence from Turkey. His car would be preceded by an armoured car, commander in the open turret, with another following.

I don't recall that he ever came under fire, but I vividly remember the faces of other members of the congregation who were later picked off by gunmen as they went about their commercial business.

My father found himself in a curious position. As a priest and chief Anglican representative on the island he was supposed to foster good relations with the autonomous Greek Orthodox church in Cyprus, with whom the Church of England was in communion. Indeed, he was entrusted with a florid letter of formal greeting from the Archbishop of Canterbury to deliver to Archbishop Makarios. The problem was that the Archbishop was not just the spiritual but also the political leader of the community, a legacy from the days of Turkish occupation when the pashas would only deal through the priests. It was an open secret that Makarios was backing EOKA.

My father took a bullish view of his own safety, judging that his ecclesiastical status and links with the Orthodox church would protect him from becoming a target and also using his British position to disregard the increasingly frequent curfews and bans on travel. These were employed by the authorities to aid their security sweeps and penalise areas where terrorist attacks had occurred. House-to-house searches were often roughly conducted.

The one area we did avoid was the Troodos Mountains, the forest stronghold of Colonel Grivas of EOKA, where some of the most intense guerrilla activity and anti-terrorism skirmishing took place. It had been the summer seat of the administration, a sort of mini-Shimla. It had its own English church and chaplain's house, but these were now strictly out of bounds.

Otherwise, my father roamed widely, taking services in unmanned churches and among expatriate communities. These included mining engineers at the Skouriotissa copper mine complex, whose excavations were cheek by jowl with old Roman and Phoenician spoil heaps, as well as isolated groups of police officers and warders and prison officers at the detention camps for EOKA suspects and Communist Party supporters.

He also paid regular visits to Greek Orthodox monasteries, whose abbots gave him a spectrum of welcomes, from the very friendly to the distinctly chilly. EOKA weapons were frequently hidden in monasteries and with Greek priests.

Relations with the local Greek community remained difficult. Terrorists or freedom fighters came from unexpected members of the community including police and journalists. Bitterness was stoked up by anti-British agitation in mainland Greece. After incidents at Athens airport, aircraft flying from the UK to Cyprus had to avoid Greece and find other refuelling stops.

My first flight to Cyprus was on an aircraft chartered by expatriate parents to bring out children who were at school in England (as I was) for the school holidays. The aircraft, a stubby, twin-engined Viking, a poor British equivalent to the American Dakota, was used extensively for troop-carrying. Eventually airborne trooping would lead to the phasing out of the troopships familiar in Southampton.

We flew from the Eagle Airways base (nowadays it would be called a hub) at the old wartime aerodrome of Blackbushe in Hampshire. On our first visit, the wreckage of another Viking that had ploughed off the runway and into the trees was still visible. It was a none-too-encouraging start for those of us who had never flown before.

Flying was a lengthy business, requiring frequent stops. It took us two days to reach Nicosia. Our first hop allowed us to refuel at Nice. Then we landed at Malta, the home of the British Mediterranean fleet, whose destroyers were moored in Sliema Creek close to the hotel where we were accommodated for the night. (No night flights in those days.)

The following day saw us cross over to North Africa and refuel again at El Adem, an RAF base in pre-Gaddafi Libya. Then finally to

Nicosia, where we were greeted by the sight of the burnt-out fuselage of a much bigger plane blown up by EOKA a few weeks before. Welcome to Cyprus.

My father's own confidence in his safety, though vindicated, was perhaps misplaced. Returning from a visit to the mine, he drove over a bridge on the main road only to be told at the subsequent checkpoint that there had been an unexploded device beneath it.

His continuing demonstration of imperial sangfroid, though, meant that as children we were able to travel all over the island to classical and Crusader ruins, Venetian ramparts, and gothic cathedrals converted into Turkish mosques; a graphic introductory lesson on the rise and fall of occupying powers, however supposedly benevolent.

In Kyrenia, the little port town less than an hour's drive from Nicosia and the favoured escape for British families in the extreme of summer heat now Troodos was out of bounds, the Wiltshire regiment had actually made its headquarters in the old castle flanking the harbour, past which Richard the Lionheart's contingents had passed six and a half centuries before.

The town had once been called the city of the dreadful knights. It had now been nicknamed 'the city of the return of the dreadful knights' because of the large number of retired colonial civil servants who had made their home there, though their numbers were diminishing as the scale of the violence increased.

Beyond the castle and a securely guarded beach was the Club, an institution familiar throughout the empire. Here in a cliff-top villa that would not have been out of place in Guildford, English manners and cuisine held sway, natives were discouraged and the lounge was well-supplied with weekly editions of the UK tabloids.

Farther out of town, however, an English farm, with animals to pet and a milk bar to enjoy, soon had to close because of security fears. Higher up in the mountain foothills was the picturesque village and gothic abbey of Bellapais with its tree of idleness made famous in Lawrence Durrell's *Bitter Lemons*. Durrell, too, briefly and uncomfortably a government information officer, had now departed.

Kyrenia harbour, like almost every other port in Cyprus, was too small and shallow for serious shipping to dock. The only harbour where ships could berth alongside was at Famagusta, where the Venetians and Shakespeare's Othello had come ashore. Elsewhere ships anchored offshore and were supplied by lighter. There seemed to be few plans to improve the situation.

There was no merchant shipping at all at Kyrenia and fishing was restricted in order to prevent arms being smuggled. But it was regularly visited by Royal Navy frigates and destroyers of the Battle Class, *Agincourt*, *Lagos* and *Corunna*, commemorating famous British victories, which swung at anchor offshore.

On one visit, my father, revisiting his Missions to Seamen days, offered to entertain the junior ratings ashore. Unfortunately there was confusion about the timing and we arrived late at the quayside by which time another generous expat had stood them all drinks; quite a few drinks. I don't think they appreciated their cultural visit to the mountain-top castle of St Hilarion up a series of steep inclines and hairpin bends. As others vomited, I listened to one homesick sixteen-year-old pouring out the miseries of life in the Royal Navy.

My father's ambiguous status would briefly propel his name onto the front pages in January 1956, when there was a first attempt at peace talks with the Greek community. The search for a neutral venue settled on the Anglican Archdeacon's house. My parents received just an hour or two's notice that Harding and Makarios would be arriving and taking over the parish meeting room and my father's study.

A subsequent note from Harding thanked my father for the use of the house and continued:

I hope that you and your wife have not been upset by the inevitable publicity and that you will not be worried by newspaper correspondents. I feel myself that it is most appropriate that attempts to bring peace to this island should be made at the Archdeaconry and I am sure that this view will be shared by everyone who wants to see an agreement.

In the event, the talks failed and Makarios was exiled, in line with imperial precedent, to a distant island in the Seychelles, not returning to Cyprus until after talks involving the Greek and Turkish governments in 1958.

In the meantime, the place was filling up with troops. The final departure of British forces from the Canal Zone in Egypt was completed in April 1956 and with President Nasser aggressively promoting Arab nationalism, Cyprus was the obvious holding point for the displaced troops. When Nasser nationalised the Suez Canal in July, even more troops were sent. They outstripped the existing military facilities and large tented camps started to appear.

The French arrived and a detachment of paras set up camp. My father, recalling the demand for books by British troops in Egypt during the war, put together a collection of French language books. I went with him up to the hilltop camp, where a bemused French colonel, a veteran of the fighting in Vietnam, received them with puzzlement.

Throughout the summer, the build-up continued, and as we drove round the island we noticed a growing number of army lorries with a large white 'H' painted on their cabs. We played guessing games for what it stood for. The answer, we later discovered, was that these were the resources earmarked for the disastrous Anglo-French Suez invasion of Egypt that took place that October.

By then I was back at school in England. My concern when I learnt that the bombing of Egyptian airfields had come from RAF planes based in Cyprus was not so much the rights and wrongs as whether Cyprus, and my parents, would be bombed in response. The destruction of the Egyptian air force spared them but weeks later they found themselves with another sort of fallout.

Following the eventual withdrawal, British citizens resident in Egypt were expelled and many of the refugees washed up in Cyprus on their way to a UK which some had not seen for years. My parents found themselves consoling old acquaintances.

My mother wrote:

> Last week 500 or so folk from Egypt arrived. The English and some of the Maltese were in Kyrenia so we went down. We knew almost all of them. They were our Port Said folk who had been able to bring most of their stuff with them – even a grand piano. They told me how sad the Egyptians were to see them go.
>
> The Maltese, in spite of being Roman Catholics, were almost pathetically glad to see your father, and I got kissed on both cheeks by one old lady whom I remembered.

It was a reminder of the different communities swept up for good or ill in the imperial experience, but too often seen by the newly independent as a part of the imperial legacy to be expunged; collateral casualties, whether Maltese in Egypt or, later, the Ugandan Asians I would greet off the first evacuation plane into Stansted.

It also pointed up the widening split between the colonial trappings and European atmosphere of Cyprus and the increasing Arab nationalism of the states to the south and east. When my father and I briefly visited a very peaceful Beirut in 1957 on the way to the enthronement of a new Anglican Archbishop in Jerusalem, speeches by President Nasser resounded from radios throughout the markets.

The EOKA troubles significantly worsened in 1957 and it became clear that a military approach was not going to work for the British. My father had still hoped to extend his stay. However, when I returned to Cyprus for the school holidays, the atmosphere was sharply different.

As part of the emergency, detention camps had been set up for EOKA members and convicted terrorists, as well as, separately, for their political rivals, the communists. Somehow or other, perhaps through his contacts with the warders for whom he used to take services, my father received information about ill-treatment of prisoners.

I do not know whether he tried to take it up through official channels or not, but he referred to it in some way in a sermon, with, of course, Sir John Harding sitting a few feet away. Knowing my father, it was probably a none-too-specific reference, perhaps that we should not ourselves be corrupted by violence and should treat prisoners fairly.

Harding, who was himself under pressure and would resign late in 1957, erupted. He demanded that the diocesan bishop (of Jerusalem) sack my father. The bishop declined but it was agreed that my father's term would not be extended.

Ironically, by the time the moment for extension would have arrived, Harding was gone and a new governor, Sir Hugh Foot, much more to my parents' liking, had arrived with a brief to find a political settlement and a determination to build bridges with the Greek community.

Eventually a settlement was reached in 1958, although it would perish in inter-communal violence in 1969.

But, by then, my parents were back in England. Again, they found problems with re-entry. My father acted as an assistant priest in other people's parishes for several months before becoming, to his great delight, the rector of the rapidly growing market town of Witney in Oxfordshire. Cyprus ended his imperial service but he kept his overseas connections with a series of summer chaplaincies in various European cities.

In 1968, a decade after my father had left, we all returned to Cyprus as he had a month's locum in his old job. It was just pre-partition and it was still possible to travel all over the island. I was struck by the way development had followed independence. At Kyrenia, the harbour entrance had been rebuilt with a new sea wall, transforming the approach, while we passed an agricultural research station that had been established, apparently with international support. I doubted that either initiative would have happened in colonial times.

But, again, we were on the cusp of unhappy history. We caught up with our old gardener, Charilaos. He was Greek and had been a mounted policeman in colonial days. The café he owned in the centre of the old city of Nicosia was now derelict because it was on the Green Line separating the Greek and Turkish communities.

He sat on his balcony overlooking the Mediterranean in the northern village of Lapithos. He leant forward to make a suggestion to my father. A marriage between myself and his granddaughter. The dowry; the village coffee shop. It was a good thing it did not happen. A year later Turkish invasion forces came ashore at almost exactly that spot. The Greeks were expelled.

Back at school in England, the presence of the empire was palpable. The school had been founded by a nineteenth-century vicar who accommodated pupils whose parents were abroad, usually as missionaries, and the tradition continued. Two honours boards dominated the dining hall: one for the winners of university scholarships, the other for those who had become missionaries, a steady stream of whom returned to preach in Sunday chapel. The school calculated that something like one in ten of its old boys had become missionaries or ministers of religion. I recollect only a single black face among my schoolmates, a boy from Ghana. But there were plenty of missionaries' children.

The atmosphere was conservative. Concern about the success of the Suez invasion; little discussion of its pros and cons. When later in Harold Macmillan's 'Never had it so good' election I stood for Labour in our light-hearted imitation, I gathered just ten votes. When I erected a mildly worded poster, 'Vote Conservative for muddle-headed bungling; Suez, Hola, Cyprus', I was asked to take it down as muckraking. Hola was a detention camp in Kenya, where guards had bludgeoned inmates to death for refusing to work.

The senior master, Alfred Lace, had commanded detachments of East African soldiers in the war and held the rank of colonel. When he retired he went out to Tanganyika, now Tanzania, as a headmaster. A brisk man with a quick-fire manner and a rapid delivery, he was puzzled by the way the Africans responded to it even less enthusiastically than we did.

A letter he wrote to me reflects the mixture of genuine concern and rather patronising incomprehension of the way things were moving.

> Up to a point in class the Africans work very well. But they are not good at oral work. I don't think this is mainly due to language difficulty; it is rather that they are naturally rather inert. So my custom of quick question and answer has so far not been successful. It will be interesting to see if I succeed in quickening them up.
>
> They have their eye on their next exam and little else seems to interest them. I am trying to run a weekly evening variety session – debates, discussions etc. with the top class. And two of the brightest boys after the first time came and asked leave not to come again as it was 'no good' to them.
>
> Politically Tanganyika is on the move. The great cry is 'Freedom'. It is no use our expecting the African to be logical and to be grateful to us for what we have done and are doing.

Nor does he stop to think whether he is capable of governing himself. Nor probably does he understand what a bad example of self-government Ghana is.

My classmates at school included the children of missionaries and of a civil-service advisor to the Sultan of Brunei, as well as the sons of an Egyptian contemporary of my father. A succession of Sunday preachers and letters from school old boys 'serving in the mission field' made sure our attention was routinely focused on the old imperial footsteps still evident in the world outside Britain.

South Africa and Apartheid were a particular focus. The charismatic monk, Father Trevor Huddleston, whose work among the slums of Cape Town had ended in expulsion, came to talk about his book, *Naught For Your Comfort*, and was invited back to give Lenten addresses. We vigorously debated whether black enfranchisement in South Africa could be achieved without violence.

Rudimentary military training in the Combined Cadet Force prepared us to play our part in defending our remaining imperial possessions. Since the start of the war and continuing through subsequent peace time, boys of eighteen had had to spend two years in the services. National servicemen had been relied on to play their part, and give their lives, in successive imperial emergencies, from Palestine to Cyprus.

But a couple of years before it was our turn, national service ended. We were about the first boys to have what came to be called the 'gap year' option.

The year 1958 saw the founding of VSO, Voluntary Service Overseas, under which school and university leavers spent a year or so doing community work, often teaching, in developing countries. A classmate, Tim Lankester, departed on it.

I stayed on to take university scholarship exams. I had visions of spending a year teaching in Africa, even with Mr Lace, but the nine months left before going up to Cambridge were short of the full year required.

Instead I found myself transported to another great empire – the world of British industry, itself beginning to feel the tremors of imperial change.

Chapter Four

From the workshop of the world to imperious academe

At the end of 1960, I left my boarding school in the lush valleys of Somerset for the oily grime of Birmingham and an introduction to British industry from the inside. It was an opportunity to assess the health of the industrial muscle that had traditionally powered the British Empire since the days of the Industrial Revolution.

I had had ideas of joining the family business – going into the church – and my father thought it would be a good idea for me to get a taste of industrial life. Through his continuing contact with Canon Stevens, the industrial chaplain to the bishop of Birmingham, I found myself lodged with seven other potential ordinands in a vicarage of a slum parish in the city's decaying inner ring.

We were a mixed bunch. Two were recent graduates and a couple had recently completed national service. There were public and grammar school boys alongside a Scunthorpe steelworker and a salesman from a menswear shop. Of the three clergy in the house, two would become bishops and the other the vicar of St Martin-in-the-Fields.

By day we worked in factories; in the evenings and weekends we helped in the parish with services and youth clubs. Over communal supper, there was some vigorous argument and good knockabout, often provoked by one of the curates, Geoffrey Brown, who had been a member of the Footlights at Cambridge and took delight in challenging our pretensions.

We were generously befriended by the small band of local parishioners. They welcomed us into their often damp terraced houses, soon to be condemned. We chatted in the back room where the television was usually permanently switched on. On special occasions we might be invited into the front room for tinned salmon sandwiches. Sometimes there was a piano, but they were becoming fewer and fewer. There was a glut of unwanted pianos. When we held a parish fête, one of the popular sideshows was to break up a piano to the satisfactory accompaniment of much twanging and banging. Lavatories were almost always outside, ranged along a wall in a communal backyard alley. (Best to have a lock and key.) A few years later, our friends were scattered to high-rise flats elsewhere in the city.

My experience in Birmingham was formative. From my restricted, imperial upbringing, it encouraged me to appreciate a broad range of people regardless of their background. It also fostered an interest in industry, fundamental to my future journalistic career. Watching the experiences of my own friends, and our children since, it is striking how important, and frequently unexpected, the experiences of the gap year are on shaping the direction of people's ensuing lives.

Birmingham was nicknamed 'the city of a thousand trades'. Walking to work in the morning from Springhill through Summer

Hill past Soho to the city centre, you passed through streets lined with small metal-bashing workshops. They beat out all kinds of items, from cutlery and kettles – I remember Swan Brand as one of the smarter premises – to the specialist parts for the motor industry, for which the city was known worldwide.

It was a time when unemployment was virtually unknown, and I was found work in the jobbing factory of a company called M. Mole and Son. It was situated in Charlotte Street in the very centre of Birmingham, only a few streets away from the City Art Gallery and the Museum of Industry.

In truth, M. Mole's was a bit of a museum itself. The company had opened a newer factory in Newport, Monmouthshire, I presume because of the regional grants available. It would eventually move there entirely. But at the time it was still conducting its gallimaufry of operations over three or four floors of an old redbrick factory building, with, I seem to remember, a curious open-sided top floor.

It produced or processed a bewildering array of objects, from the chromium-plated door handles for cars to the protective housings of washing machine motors to brass fittings for the helmets of deep-sea divers.

Materials were brought in on the ground floor where the very particular reek of oil mixed with metal scrap seeped into your skin as you pushed through protective rubber curtains, before punching your card at the time clock to record your arrival. Beyond it, a stamping shop started the long process of turning raw materials into finished products and there were long rows of power presses, the classic Birmingham workhorse.

It was not much different to the systems to be seen in old film of First World War munitions production. Long spinning axles were suspended overhead throughout the shops and driven from a central power supply. James Watt had developed his steam engines to drive a similar system at his Soho factory a few hundred yards away a century before. The presses in turn were driven by belts fed down from the overhead spindles.

The function of the presses was to trim the various metal castings, deposited beside them in great crates by forklift trucks. Using a basic up and down motion, controlled by the operator, they freed the castings of the thin frills of metal left around their edges through their pressing or stamping action or else they drilled and shaped them. Operatives were provided with gloves to protect themselves from the sharp metal edges. These would be replaced, gouged and scratched, at the end of the shift.

Metal guard-rails were fitted on the machines to prevent operators putting in their hands as the press punched downwards. The number of people you encountered with parts of fingers missing showed the guards did not always work. Sometimes the presses repeated. Sometimes workers disabled the guards in the interests of speed.

We wore overalls on the ground floor but on the first floor (where my roommate Roger was working) the workers wore brown coats and stood at benches. His job was to file the irregularities off chrome car door handles, which were manufactured separately from the doors. They were placed by hand into a vice and then scraped with a common or garden file – pretty rough and ready it seemed to me.

Above them worked the toolmakers, the skilled workers who produced the fabled Mole wrench, an adjustable wrench that had been patented by the managing director, Mr Coughtrie, whose office was on one of the floors above. It was Mr Coughtrie, a man with a record of enlightened factory management, who had agreed to our placements. When Roger and I left at the summer holiday break he presented us each with one of the wrenches.

Years later I found his obituary. One of the fascinations of obituaries, whether you read them or have to research them, is the extraordinary resourcefulness of the people that they record and how seemingly unexceptional people turn out to have lived exceptional lives. It is particularly true of wartime service. In Coughtrie's case, he was credited with securing the success of the Mulberry floating harbours employed during the Normandy invasions by his pains-taking inspection of their individual components, while later his invention of the Mole wrench – the DIY enthusiast's delight – had turned round the company's fortunes.

Birmingham ran on piecework, the favoured system in the Midlands, apparently easy to operate and understand but whose complications and rigidities were effectively to destroy British Leyland in the years to come. The idea was simple. Every job was allocated a price per item; so you were paid for what you turned out. Payment by results in theory provided an incentive for workers to produce as much as possible as quickly as possible.

Obviously it raised questions about quality, but the complica-tion of fixing a rate for every item also meant that changes were difficult, particularly when they involved reorganisations and par-ticularly when trade union power was as strong as it became in the motor assembly plants. Negotiations became interminable. Change was expensive.

From an individual's point of view it meant you were always count-ing your output and watching the clock. You knew exactly how much per gross you were being paid.

I worked on the ground floor; in the hot stamp shop where we started the long process that would eventually turn steel rods into the valve caps of motor car engines. My job was to cut up the rods on a press and then heat the pieces to white heat in a gas fired 'muffle', a small, shoulder-height box furnace, before stamping the hot cylin-ders into discs under the press. If you allowed the cylinders to cool too much, the press laboured and could slip the belt off its spinning overhead axle. Then you had to wait for the maintenance team, and your payment was reduced to the much lower day rate.

It was a scene to captivate Joseph Wright of Derby; a dim, greenish atmosphere, with the drive shafts noisily spinning in the half light above, illuminated by the flickering glow of flames and heated metal from the muffles. Arrows of sparks erupted regularly as the presses hammered the glowing steel into a new configuration.

At one end, where the light was brighter, benches topped with dented metal supported a process that shocked me by its crudity when I was allocated to it in my first few days.

Among our products were electric conducting pieces for tube trains – at that point a basic bronze 'L' shape. After they had been stamped out, they retained a thin frill of waste metal on their outer edge. The way of removing this was to place them under an old-fashioned hand-press weighted down by what appeared to be cannon balls at either end of the handle and then to whizz this heavy arm round by giving it a good push. The price, as I remember, was a few pence a gross. But, much more shocking was that this exhausting manual job was normally carried out by Isobel, a middle-aged working mother, much smaller than me, at a differential rate of pay which was about half what I was getting for exactly the same operation.

So, after some days on the hand-worked press I was pleased to move into the hot stamp proper, even though the heat from the flaring gas would send me on my first journey to the water fountain within an hour of start-up.

We worked from Monday to Friday but the factory had only recently stopped working Saturday mornings as well. There were forty-five minutes for lunch with a ten-minute tea break in both morning and afternoon. At one point in the morning the loudspeakers were turned on for half an hour as the BBC radio programme *Music While You Work*, a wartime innovation, sent band music echoing through the shops. It linked us with factories and workplaces throughout Britain, supposedly cheering us up and increasing our productivity by keeping an even tempo. In the hot stamp it was drowned out by the crash of the hammers.

I spent the tea break a few feet away from my muffle, its gas jet turned down to a quiet hiss, sitting on a component box with Billy. He operated one of the heavy hammers in the stamp shop and was also the shop steward. I suggested that I should join the union – then the Amalgamated Engineering Union – but he dissuaded me, arguing that it was not a closed shop and the organisation was too weak to bring me any benefit.

His concern was whether the factory would be closed and operations concentrated on Newport, as it turned out they eventually were. Roger and I raised the issue with Coughtrie in our valedictory meeting; he had little trouble in deflecting the enquiry. Billy was proud of his Birmingham roots and told me with pride that his father had been responsible for all the tiling of the large public lavatory at nearby Snow Hill station.

Wally, a younger, more athletic man, worked on the next machine to Billy. When he had to change the tool pieces on his press to carry out a different process he would knock out the supporting wedges with a cold chisel, inviting me to hold it with my bare hands while he swung a hammer at it. My main sensation was relief that it was not me swinging the hammer.

The third press, a little way off, was worked by Sam. The group was completed by Fred, the labourer. A small man with a cloth cap and a fondness for snuff, still working at seventy, he weighed the completed jobs, swept the floor and acted as a bookie's runner, conveying bets to illegal bookies outside the factory.

It was a disciplined operation. There was a pub on the next corner, but nobody drank during the day. We had a small celebration there when I left and they presented me with a fountain pen. Later, in an exchange you would blush to invent, Sam said to me, 'When you are out of here, think of us, wishing our lives away.'

It was a time when Commonwealth immigration, predominantly from the West Indies and the Indian sub-continent, was beginning to become a political issue and later in the year, the government would announce a restrictive Commonwealth Immigration Bill. It was just becoming apparent from where we were. The factory was overwhelmingly white, as was the city, but some West Indians were beginning to find jobs in the press shop. There was a lot of comment among white workers about a West Indian man who brought two women to work in a large car. They called them 'his women' and complained that they operated the presses badly.

In the outside world, the fascist Oswald Mosley was sensing a new opportunity and starting what would be his final run at political influence. He was billed to speak in Handsworth, a destination for early West Indian immigrants, and I bicycled over to his meeting one evening.

He spoke in what I remember as a school hall. A few policemen lingered in nearby streets but there was no activity or demonstration outside and inside the hall was not much more than half-full. The speech was not memorable apart from an extraordinary reference to Africa. He indicated a great north–south line, a road running, as Cecil Rhodes dreamed, from Cairo to the Cape, and suggested a geographical division of the Continent between black and white. 'We don't want much,' he said. 'Just one third.' It was a measure of just how out of touch Mosley and the empire romantics had become.

It was with this background that I arrived in Cambridge in 1961. After Birmingham, it felt like going on an extended holiday.

It was a bastion of privilege; once again old traditions were being challenged but this empire was certainly not fading away. There was, however, change in the air; the most obvious to the university authorities, the shift from rather older and mature students who had been through the crucible of two years' national service in the services, with its imperial traditions and evocations, to a younger group, many fresh from school, with a different outlook and more limited experience.

The outward flimflammery was quaint and pervasive, but also somehow rather enticing. Suddenly your elders and betters – tutors or college staff – were addressing you as Mister, in an unexpected measure of formal respect. Your college room would be tidied and your bed made by a college employee – they called them 'servants' – who was known as a 'bedder'.

In the evening, you were required to eat your dinner in a medieval hall under the gaze of historic worthies and always wearing your academic gown. At night, a proctor, a don in full fig, mortar board clamped to his temples, gown swirling behind him, would patrol the streets with two bowler-hatted 'bulldogs' to make sure that all undergraduates were properly dressed in their gowns, distinguishing them from ordinary townspeople. The bulldogs, college porters in real life, had the job of pursuing and apprehending undergraduates without gowns, who were duly fined the sum of six shillings and eightpence – a third of a pound.

College gates were locked at midnight and those caught outside were subject to discipline. If you were in digs outside the college, as I was in my first year, your landlady was expected to report you if you returned after the witching hour.

We were conscious of the private school/state school divide, but for us it was more the difference between those educated at public schools and those from non-fee-paying grammar schools, many of them, like Manchester Grammar, with formidable academic reputations. Comprehensive schools had barely been invented. Every so often someone would do an estimate of the breakdown – my memory is that it worked out as about 55 to 45 per cent in favour, if that is the word, of public schools.

And then there was the gender question. The university was overwhelmingly male, with about two and a half women's colleges to more like twenty male colleges – Girton, Newnham and the small if growing New Hall. The imbalance between the sexes was partly made up by female students from outside the formal university precincts, Homerton, the teacher training college, and the large numbers of foreign students, mostly from Europe, who came to Cambridge to attend language schools, but it remained an unhealthy ratio. I would find myself arguing later in the pages of the university newspaper that the next college to be established should be a mixed one.

An indication of how sexist attitudes remained was provided by the Cambridge union, the debating club with its old Victorian premises and chamber, where would-be politicians pretended that they were already in the House of Commons.

The union did not admit women members, although this regime was under challenge. A ballot in my first year came out against the admission of women, but the following attempt was successful. My father had presented me with two gifts which he believed important to my standing – membership of the union and a dinner suit tailored by the same Cambridge shop who had provided his own, an unconscious nod, perhaps, to his own tailoring forbears.

I rarely attended union debates but followed its activities in the pages of *Varsity*, the university student newspaper, whose offices occupied the twisted floors of an old wooden-framed house next to the union itself. Later, as a reporter and editor of the paper, I would have more to do with the union, and chronicle its declining membership. Its fading aura was more apparent inside the university than externally, where memories of the famous pre-war Oxford union debate 'This house would not fight for King and Country' still coloured perceptions of the great university debating houses.

But, while one might mock the self-importance of the debates and the way nineteen- and twenty-year-olds mimicked the behaviour and pomposities of MPs, a serious number of my fellow students did indeed find themselves in the Palace of Westminster before too long and reach senior Cabinet rank, almost every one a Conservative and none, that I recall, from Labour.

My first encounter was with Ken Clarke, who would go on to be Chancellor. He came to expound the virtues of the Conservative Club to freshmen at my college, Queens', and I remember him, improbably, for his sartorial sense. He was the first person that I recall wearing a striped shirt, ironically for someone who would later be known for his baggy suits and scuffed shoes.

Clarke sparred in the Conservative Club and on the floor of the union with Michael Howard, who would later lead the Conservative Party, and John Gummer, another future Cabinet minister, while my exact contemporary was Norman Lamont, another later Chancellor. I had more to do with Norman, as he struggled to reform the union. With an early understanding of the power of the media, he invited me and my predecessor as editor of *Varsity* to act as honorary tellers for his final debate as union president.

I stayed in touch with Norman, rather desultorily, as his career developed and he progressed through the junior ministerial ranks. I remember once asking what department he had enjoyed most – regardless of rank. He smiled and said he thought that it was the rank that mattered. Full marks for honesty.

The union's position was suffering from the more general decline of deference to old-established institutions. In the wider political world, the Conservative government under Harold Macmillan was collapsing under an extraordinary tide of scandal. We laughed as the

Prime Minister was mocked in our recordings of *Beyond the Fringe*. In the summer of 1963, we sunned ourselves as we turned the pages of the Sunday newspapers with increasingly lurid accounts of the Profumo scandal with its story of prostitutes and espionage and bad behaviour in high places. On a Saturday evening, the college's common room would be crammed with, not especially political, undergraduates lapping up the unfamiliar ridicule being heaped on our leading politicians by the sketches in the television sensation *That Was the Week That Was*.

The most dramatic incursion of international, or new imperial, politics into our cloistered lives, however, had come with the Cuban Missile Crisis of 1962. I can still remember the moment around midnight when my roommate and I placed a transistor radio on the window sill of our college bedroom to hear the distinctive flat delivery of President John F. Kennedy warning the Soviet Union against supplying missiles to Cuba and placing a military embargo around the island. It was chilling; nuclear war, its possibilities never too far from our thoughts, seemed genuinely conceivable within a few hours. We were right to be scared. Just how close it got, we would find out much later.

The following evening we crowded onto Parker's Piece, a large green adjoining the University Arms Hotel, to make our indignant and frightened voices heard at a 'Hands Off, Cuba' rally. In pubs afterwards we debated the wrongs and rights of Kennedy's ultimately successful realpolitik with students who took a different view and saw it as robust strategy.

At most other times, we saw ourselves as living in a rather separate universe. We felt that we were undergraduates, belonging to a great university, not part of the generality of students. There was no effective branch of the National Union of Students (NUS) at Cambridge, although we became interested in travelling on student trains and transport to Europe when the vacations came.

It was a time when universities were expanding and new ones were being founded. While I was editing *Varsity* we went over to Norwich to see how the first thirty or so students at the new University of East Anglia (UEA) were faring. I later wrote an editorial urging Cambridge dons, who were holding a special vote, to allow their UEA counterparts to have access to the Cambridge University Library. For the record, they did so.

Questions about university discipline came up sporadically, but were given a major push when the Home Secretary, Henry Brooke, arrived to give a speech. A noisy demonstration climaxed with an egg being thrown at him and hitting the mark. It was front-page national news. In the aftermath, there was controversy over whether the egg-thrower should be subject to university or police discipline or both. I argued in another editorial that if students wanted to be treated as adults, they should be subject to the law of the land rather than rely on university justice.

Lurking somewhere behind it was the question of student representation and involvement in university administration – a demand increasingly in tune with the times but comfortably ignored by the authorities. In 1964, a group of students came together to propose the formation of a student representative council, with representatives from every college and six elected by the university as a whole. Among those who sat round the table at the first council meeting in a room at the Union Society was Vince Cable (another future Cabinet minister), Lisa Jardine, Anthony Barnett of *New Left Review* and others who have gone on to become distinguished academics.

I had stood successfully for election from my college, although there was not a lot of interest, and found myself chosen as chairman as a middle-of-the-road figure.

Gaining recognition posed an interesting challenge. The university declined any formal acknowledgement, so with advice from some sympathetic dons, including Lord Noel Annan, the Master of Kings, we set out to establish our credentials. A report on university discipline seemed the obvious starter. It seemed a bit too predictable, however, and though we decided to start work on it we let it follow something more comfortably academic, a report on university libraries which I largely wrote. It contained a few good lines – the highest rate of theft occurred in the Theology department, for example – and its principal recommendation was that the university library and others should be open in the evenings and on Saturday afternoons, and that gowns should not be required. Other recommendations were welcomed by the university's own librarians.

It wasn't until 1975 that the SRC, renamed the Cambridge Students' Union, achieved a place on the University Council and 1985 before it was formally recognised by the university. Today all students are members and regular elections are held for student representatives on faculty boards and other university administrative bodies.

The university prided itself on its imperial alumni – the graduates from countries of the empire who had returned to lead their nations. But, among the 120 or so who appeared on our college freshmen photograph, there were hardly any dark faces.

They included Winston Oh from Singapore, defiantly named at a crucial point of the Japanese advance in the war, who became a consultant surgeon. And there was Eddie Laing, who would become my close friend and roommate, from Belize (then British Honduras), whose father was a newspaper editor and would become his country's ambassador to the United States and an international judge before his early death.

Later, some older serving East African civil servants joined us but just as we were getting to know them their course was cut short. They had to return because of the army mutinies, put down with British military help, in 1964.

By then this was a story for me to break in *Varsity*, the university newspaper, run by undergraduates, where I had tried my hand as a reporter in my third term. The first piece I wrote in the summer of 1962 covered the introduction of parking meters to Cambridge. Some things do not change.

A year and a half later I became editor of the paper and in the summer of 1964 spent three months in the USA under a scheme where, in the interests of international understanding, holiday jobs were provided to Cambridge students through the Junior Chambers of Commerce in the north-west states of Oregon and Washington.

For two months I worked in KIMA, a local broadcasting station in Yakima in Washington, before spending another month completing a circuit of the country by Greyhound bus.

It was the year after Kennedy's assassination. The civil rights issue was boiling and three American students on a voter registration drive in Mississippi had recently been shot dead. Later that year the Civil Rights Act would be passed. We watched the party conventions on television as the right-wing Republican challenger for the presidency, Barry Goldwater, made his famous declaration, 'Extremism in the defense of liberty is no vice. And moderation in the pursuit of justice is no virtue.'

Given this background it was natural that I, and a fellow Cambridge student also working at KIMA, Gill Carruthers, should seek out the black community in Yakima to learn more. In fact it was tiny. The town was overwhelmingly white but the black community leaders gave us time to explain the national situation and recommend the books to read, notably Martin Luther King's *Why We Can't Wait*.

I don't remember them making too much of problems in Yakima. But I do remember being chided by one of the managers at the station for leaving Gill alone in the company of a black lawyer who was a friend of both of us. It was indicative enough.

Later I travelled with another friend through the south on Greyhound buses. Segregation had been outlawed, but black people still sat at the back of the bus. In Birmingham, Alabama, I stayed with a charming young white family, relations of Yakima friends, who explained to me how 'nigrahs' were just different.

But what they and others repeatedly said to us was, 'Never mind us. Haven't you got a problem with your race relations in England too?'

We returned to Britain to the general election of 1964, when Labour under Harold Wilson won a paper-thin majority, and race, for the first time, had become an election issue. There had been an unabashed racist (we called it racialist then) campaign in the Smethwick constituency on the outskirts of Birmingham, where a Conservative, Peter Griffiths, had defeated the Labour choice for Home Secretary, Sir Frank Soskice. The campaign had been famous for a slogan: 'If you want a nigger for a neighbour, vote Labour.'

At the time, Cambridge boasted an occasional single-issue magazine, the rather grandly named *Cambridge Opinion*. On my return, I approached its academic sponsor, the distinguished anthropologist Edmund Leach, with the idea of an issue devoted to race relations in Britain. He put me in touch with a fellow student, Tim Sparrow, who had a similar interest, and the project was agreed.

Reading it now, it is striking how the thrust of the issues has stayed the same over half a century. Our editorial, when it was published in the spring of 1965, was critical of an 'obsession with immigration control'. We argued that it meant that the position of the 'coloured' community already here and 'the sort of problems they have been creating and facing' have largely been kept out of serious discussion. We should deal with 'empirical problems'.

We referred to a speech Griffiths had subsequently made at the Cambridge union, quoting his suggestion that 'at some stage, the people of this country might well be asked whether they want a multiracial society'. Instead we argued:

> Britain is already a multiracial society and the clock cannot be turned back by stopping the flow of immigrants. We live in a multiracial world and as Sir Alec Douglas-Home [the recently defeated Conservative Prime Minister] has pointed out, divisions and hostilities are likely to be formed increasingly along racial lines.

We emphasised the importance of the second generation, the children of immigrants, who were Britons in their own right, and featured an article by Paul Stephenson, a British-born black youth worker in Bristol, on the richness of black heritage. Paul had led the 1963 Bristol bus boycott when the local bus service had point-blank refused to employ black people.

The publication included a table showing how frequently immigration issues featured in the press, an interview with the chief officer of the National Committee for Commonwealth Immigrants and a long article on education. This included an interview with a headmaster who had a school which was now 40 per cent immigrant and a number of case studies of children in a London secondary school supplied by another. We spoke to careers officers, some of whom warned against excessive expectations, although we do not seem to have interviewed any employers directly.

In the course of our research, I went back to Birmingham to speak to community leaders and school teachers and look at a particular initiative, the Sparkbrook Association. My friend Patrick Eagar, later to become the prince of cricket photographers, generously came with me to take pictures to illustrate the magazine. Our cover showed a black bus conductor on the platform of his bus with a wall behind showing racist graffiti.

I used material from the magazine in my application for journalistic jobs later in the year. I chose to take the one I had most hoped
for, as a trainee reporter on *The Guardian* in Manchester.

But, before I joined, I took three weeks of my summer break to
work as an interviewer for the wide-ranging Survey of Race Relations
in Britain, set up by the Institute of Race Relations, later published
as 'Colour and Citizenship'. I was based in Bristol, where my eldest
sister was at university.

The job involved knocking on doors in every street of the survey
area, the poor and multi-occupied St Paul's district, to chart how
many households lived there. Every five households or so, we admin-
istered a more detailed questionnaire.

It was a wonderful sunny summer and looking back I am amazed
at what a friendly reception we received. I remember in particular
one mixed road of about seventy houses. At one end they were very
crowded, with the most populous households being Irish. Some were
rough lodging houses for single Irish men who came over as seasonal
labour. Then there were West Indian families. Older people included
a former soldier, living alone, who showed me the bayonet scar he
had received fighting in a British unit supporting the white Russians
against the Bolsheviks at the end of the First World War. There were
a few chatty white prostitutes, too, who sat with me on an outside
wall to fill in a questionnaire.

When I reached the more respectable end, a man opened the door
to me and said, shaking his head, 'You know there are seventy people a
house at the other end of this street?' 'No,' I said, 'no more than thirty
at most; I have just been at that end.' 'Do you hear that?' he called to
his wife. 'There are thirty people living in some of those houses at
the end of the street.' It was a lesson in preconceptions.

A couple of weeks later I joined *The Guardian*.

Chapter Five

Vanishing glories

On 13 September 1965, I joined *The Guardian* in Manchester as a graduate trainee. It became another excursion into departing empires.

The first empire was that of nationwide newspapers, then at the apex of their reach. The second was the historic *Manchester Guardian* itself. In 1900, Alfred Harmsworth, the later Lord Northcliffe, had started to print his newly founded *Daily Mail* in Manchester as well as London. It initiated a process that would see newspaper offices established in the city for all the major papers, with populous reporting staffs. The most dramatic belonged to the *Daily Express*. Double-storey, plate-glass windows framed its printing machines as it churned out its publications in full view of passers-by on the pavement.

From Manchester, reporting teams fanned out across the north of England with subsidiary offices in major centres like Leeds and Newcastle-upon-Tyne. It was taken as a given that the papers would attempt to cover the major regional news stories as they occurred; many of them were by now dealing with the challenge of encouraging regional development to arrest a decline of the regions, which the demise of these journalistic bastions would soon starkly illustrate.

The regional principle was also upheld by the National Union of Journalists (NUJ), although it would prove a losing battle. The reason I was in Manchester in the first place was the union rule that new journalists should serve their time in the provinces (a phrase that now strikes oddly) before being permitted to work in London, then as now the destination of choice for most aspiring journalists.

The paper I had joined was moving in the opposite direction, however – a sign of decline of the power of regional centres and its own lack of self-confidence. The trend would accelerate as the century wore on.

In 1962, the *Manchester Guardian*, world famous for its liberal values in the nineteenth century and in the twentieth for its opposition to the Boer War and more recently the Suez invasion, had decided that it could not be a genuinely national voice unless it moved its headquarters, and main editorial base, to London.

Ghosts still stalked the Manchester offices. The bust of C. P. Scott, the legendary nonconformist editor, surveyed the front stairs. The leader writers' panelled corridor still housed a few editorial writers, although the coal fires were no longer stoked. In an effort to maintain parity with London, all foreign news was transmitted to Manchester, and feature pages were laid out and rather clumsily sent down to London by train.

A glass screen partitioned off the foreign sub-editors. Pasted on it were memorable despatches. My favourite, from the United Nations correspondent, read, 'If this story is too long, please cut from the beginning.' Across the room was the cotton desk, once exclusively devoted to the facts and figures of the cotton industry, where elderly subs, who had grown up when Manchester was the capital of the cotton industry, still plied their trade.

On the top floor, a canteen stretched the length of the building and remained open all hours to accommodate the printers. It offered a magnificent menu of regional specialties. There was cow heel pie, tripe and onions, Irish stew with great ribs sticking out of it, sheep's hearts and lamb fries, chip butties and, of course, Lancashire hotpot.

The paper was delivered free by arrangement with a local news-agent but, as he explained to us, its peripheral sales were reduced because of one major omission. It covered no horse racing; a relic of Scott's anti-gambling views. The story went that he had once offered a cup for greyhound racing. When his amazed staff urged second thoughts, he brushed them aside with the information that he knew perfectly well that the hare was not live.

The reporters' room was a schizophrenic place. There was a mix-ture of experienced, mainly northern, journalists who had learnt their trade on regional papers, mostly the two Manchester evening titles, *The Chronicle*, recently extinct, and the *Manchester Evening News*. The *MEN* was quartered in the same building. Its editorial line was well to the right of *The Guardian*, but its profits subsidised it, as its reporters took pleasure in reminding us.

Alongside the local men, we trainees sat with a few younger aspir-ing journalists. We had a lot to learn about the disciplines of accurate reporting and clear writing but our sights were generally set on what we regarded as the bigger canvas of London and beyond.

One strand of our education was the night reporter's shift. Arriving as other reporters left, the night reporter was on hand in case anything significant occurred. It rarely did. The job had largely degenerated into ringing a string of police and fire stations across the north-west to enquire if there was any news; an attempt to pretend a greater local connection than the paper by now enjoyed.

The yellowing list of contact numbers was glued to a piece of crumbling cardboard that resembled pressed straw. Oddly for a newspaper, the telephone system in the reporters' room, or 'The Room' as it was known, was a mess. There were not enough telephones to go around and they were routed via a switchboard. But, at the far end of the office, under two greasy plywood hoods, were what, from memory, were the only direct-dial telephones. Now, as night reporter, one took the list over to them and laboriously went through the typewritten numbers at two-hourly intervals. There was usually little result.

One evening the police reported a car crash in Derbyshire and I wrote a couple of paragraphs for the local edition explaining that the car had hit a tree. The night news editor pursed his lips and reached for the red pencil. Nothing must be assumed, he explained. The car was 'in collision' with the tree. Basic learning but an indication of the rigour with which stories had been traditionally scrutinised.

Another night, news came through that a famous shipyard trade union leader was on the point of death and an obituary urgently needed. I scrabbled through paper cuttings in a brown cardboard folder excavating what personal information I could and added a few colourful phrases. When he died a few years later, I was amused to find that the official obituary still contained a large selection of the epithets from my hastily spatchcocked composition. The pattern still continues. Once words, or pictures, get into the system, they have a life of their own; a tendency that the advent of the internet and electronic media has infinitely multiplied.

Our night shifts were filling in for the regular night reporter. And here the baggage of empire cast a more sinister shadow. Tony Pearson, the night reporter, brought raffishness to the office. Arriving at seven o'clock, billycock hat tipped to the back of his head, front teeth missing and with a pronounced Derbyshire accent, he would deliberately position himself at the end of the room next to the door that led to the backstairs. It was an escape route.

Tony engaged us about his problems with his landlady and his creditors. I never saw him more upset than when he had agreed to write an article for a brewing magazine with a colleague. When the promised cheque took a long time coming, he found that it had been delivered to his equally hard-up and hard-drinking colleague and promptly spent. He had cause to use the backstairs more than once.

But his great daytime enthusiasm, for which the night shift set him up perfectly, was fishing. He was very accomplished and for some years wrote a popular column about it. But Tony, it turned out, was not what he seemed. He had reinvented himself after traumatic beginnings.

He had actually been brought up in Kenya. When the bitter and bloody Mau Mau rebellion had occurred, Tony had been drafted as a very young man into one of the most difficult and terrifying secret operations – the pseudo-gangs. These were teams of Kikuyu and members of the security services, usually led by Mau Mau informers, who went and lived in the Kenyan forests alongside the real Mau Mau groupings with the aim of tracking them down and killing them. A gap-year experience to leave anyone traumatised. I don't think Tony ever recovered. One understood the appeal of fishing.

Tony actually returned to Kenya after persuading the *Sunday Times Magazine* to stake him to write a piece on fishing. He set out to line fish from Mombasa but failed to catch anything satisfactory. Unabashed, he bought a large specimen from the market, had himself photographed with it, and claimed a record catch. A few days later, after similar lack of success on Lake Victoria, he cut out the shape of a fish so it could be photographed on his hook in the shadow of the setting sun. He was upset when the *Sunday Times* did not publish.

Tony contrasted with the long-serving Manchester reporters,

who tended to be men of steady habits and respectability – George Hawthorne was a dedicated countryman who later bought his own smallholding and became a lay reader, while Baden Hickman's Episcopal manner complimented his eventual appointment as religious correspondent. Others had long and careful service on local papers.

Mostly we got on well. Our older colleagues were generous with their advice and friendship, as well as, it has to be said, rather amused by us.

The problem was the lack of stories. In choosing *The Guardian* and its Manchester base, I had been looking to be worked hard and to gain experience in what we jokingly called 'the school of hard knocks'. It did not quite work out that way.

The news editor, Harry Whewell, was a fascinating and fascinated man, whose sharp intelligence always sought out the difficult or intriguing question, and he delighted in the quirky. If you were to be locked in a pub all night, it was Harry you would choose as your companion. He had just started to write a droll and perceptive Saturday column. A committed Mancunian, he addressed the north/south divide and in the course of lunchtime research at the pub he asked me – an obvious southerner – what people in the south thought about the north. I replied that I didn't think they actually thought about the north. Noticeably surprised, he promptly put it into his column.

Harry, however, had lost an empire and was struggling to find a role. He had been offered the job of news editor in London but had opted to stay close to his roots. The job had by now gone to John Cole, the labour correspondent, later to become a household presence as the BBC's political editor.

Although the telephoned news conferences that shaped the paper engaged both London and Manchester, it was clear that major news

was being covered from London. We in the north were covering breaking news north of Birmingham but otherwise providing
regional material and sometimes case studies and colour to illustrate
major national issues.

Not much happened in the reporters' room in the morning
until close to lunchtime or the early afternoon, when Harry would
emerge from his office with a small handful of frankly desultory
press releases. Seasoned reporters with their contacts in the town
hall would be preparing material for the Manchester edition while
the young graduates would be encouraged to go off to review plays
in the evening.

An idea might emerge over a drink with Harry at lunchtime; at
Epiphany, where could one actually buy myrrh? Just how many hoops
did you have to go through to close a railway line? What exactly did
the development plan for Boggart Hole Clough mean? But too often
we were scratching.

The problem was obvious to the new northern editor, who
had started in the same month as I did. He was the ebullient Brian
Redhead, later to be better known as a BBC Radio 4 *Today* presenter.
By then he had already been a *Guardian* reporter, planning correspondent and features editor along with a brief but memorable stint
on the celebrated *Tonight* television programme, where he had told
them, inter alia, that they knew nothing about news.

On our first meeting, I explained the survey work I had been doing
in Bristol. His characteristic response was to ask whether I thought
surveys produced anything that a good journalist could not find out
in much less time. His view was obvious.

Now he called us all into a meeting to explain that he was going to
disperse the reporters' room. Liverpool, Sheffield, a reinforced Leeds
and Newcastle-upon-Tyne would all have a permanent presence and
the man there (it was a man in every case) would be as important as

the correspondent in Paris. It was a quintessential Brian overstatement. It fooled nobody.

The connection between Manchester and *The Guardian*, though ebbing, still remained strong, sometimes touchingly so, even though the city's name had been gone from the masthead for some years. As we still scrambled and scraped to find Manchester stories, I was sent with a photographer to a scrap yard where the first machine in the city to crunch scrapped cars into rectangular blocks had just been installed. Some days later, the owner appeared in the office, so delighted to have been in the paper that he had bought us each a bottle of Drambuie.

During the Seamen's Strike that famously blew the Wilson government off course in 1966, I went down to the National Union of Seamen's offices on the still-functioning Manchester docks. As members swirled around him, the union secretary advised them to look in *The Guardian* the next morning to find out what was happening. I didn't say he had given me nothing to write about.

One of the biggest lessons I learnt was of people's instinctive loyalty to their organisations, and pride in them, something which management too often overlook. My teacher was Mr Gaunt. He worked for the Manchester Ship Canal company that ran the docks, doing some kind of manual job. He would arrive at my flat to deliver Labour Party leaflets on his bicycle wearing a blue cotton working suit and clumping boots with no socks. When he learnt I worked for *The Guardian*, he arranged for the company to send me a pack of information about the Canal company and checked that I had received it.

However, for all Mr Gaunt's pride in it, the Ship Canal was just one of the cornerstones of Manchester that was crumbling, as containerisation and the remorseless rise in the size of vessels left it unable to cope with the latest ways of shipping cargo. It was another fading empire. Elsewhere, whole areas of the city were strange eerie deserts pockmarked with occasional piles of scattered bricks. As I drove to work each morning through the district of Hulme, for half a mile or more in each direction there were no buildings at all, apart from a few isolated pubs that still stood on street corners and to which old residents, often now disorientated, would return at weekends. It was a surreal experience to stop at traffic lights with not a building in sight.

In Manchester, as in other big cities at the time, the received wisdom was to sweep away slum housing and relocate people to tower blocks and estates on the edge of town. Councils all over the country boasted of their progress. My friends in Springhill in Birmingham had experienced much the same. A couple of years later working in Leeds, again little different in its practice, I saw the beginning of a rethink, when attempts were made to redevelop some of the old, but more solidly built, back-to-back housing by selective demolition and the introduction of green spaces in-between. But the high rises kept on coming.

It led to strange contrasts. In the centre of the city, Piccadilly, a prominent square, had been redeveloped with a dominating '60s modernist hotel. But a few streets away in one of a swathe of smoke-encrusted railway offices, I entered an unroofed wooden lift with sides no more than a metre high to make enquiries about the proposed closure of a rural line. An old man sitting on a stool pulled on a rope to take me to the first floor. It was scarcely even nineteenth-century technology.

Not far from there a fine shopping arcade stood derelict and doomed and soon after I left Manchester, *The Guardian*'s historic home on Cross Street was pulled down to make way for the elevated monster of the Arndale Centre, which swallowed that part of Manchester like a giant blind-eyed lizard.

With his commitment to the north, Harry encouraged us to get out and about in the region. One day I found myself in a field near

Preston where a new method of tagging cattle was exhibited which entailed blasting a hole in the animal's skull. Another time I was freezing on the dockside at isolated Barrow-in-Furness ('Nobody comes here by accident,' said the security man) to greet the first shipment of foreign nuclear waste arriving for reprocessing at Sellafield. It was a symbol of the new Britain, although the reprocessing story went terribly and expensively wrong, as technology and supervision proved inadequate. The frailties of Sellafield would occupy me to the end of my career.

As would the mining industry. I had my first encounter with its issues and its trade unions at Clock Face colliery – named for the local pub which sported a large clock – near St Helens. In October 1965, its closure had been announced but with the assurance that all its workforce would be found work in neighbouring collieries from which Clock Face's coal reserves could also be reached. The neighbouring pits were short of miners. Eight months' notice was given but in November five men had staged a sit-in, in vogue with students at that time, at the bottom of the pit, in protest against the immediate transfer of 200 men. With the miners incommunicado at the pit bottom, it was not an easy story to write. It was a symbolic protest. They returned to the surface after forty-eight hours.

Criss-crossing the region, it was not just industrial dereliction that struck me but also the state of the rivers around and within Manchester. For someone used to seeking out riverside pubs in Cambridge or Oxfordshire, it was shocking to visit their counterpart on the outskirts of the city to find a reeking and polluted Mersey in discouragingly close proximity. In retrospect, and as I was to experience later with ICI, one of our most reputable companies, it was astonishing what wastes industry had been permitted to discharge into watercourses.

Conferences were a frequent source of copy. There were plenty of them. There were a lot of worthy regional development ones, where I learnt to buttonhole speakers to extract their precise names and initials, and where planning was the buzzword; it was, after all, the time of Harold Wilson's ill-fated National Plan, the attempt to map out the economy, a wish list derailed by the economic downturn of the mid-'60s.

Others brought national organisations to conference venues in the north, often at the seaside. At one in Scarborough for educational executives, my story, with the headline 'Drinks while you read at the public library', reported a minister's suggestion that libraries should be a place 'for people to eat and drink, meet and talk' – then an apparently bizarre idea. Harry, of course, found this suggestion highly amusing and suggested in his column that you should be able to select a particular vintage appropriate to the book you had chosen. The idea would return with a vengeance at the turn of the century and now scarcely any institution can afford to be without its café.

The greatest conferences were the political ones. A team of Manchester reporters, their shorthand honed by years on evening papers, provided reports on every debate. Some of us youngsters were allowed to join them and although we struggled to keep up, it was a tremendous introduction to the national scene and to figures we would follow and interview for years to come.

The 1965 Labour Party conference, the first since Labour's victory after 'thirteen wasted years', was a triumphant celebration in Blackpool, with minister after new minister arriving to announce new initiatives to build more houses or comprehensive schools or to boost industry while the small shrunken figure of Clement Attlee watched from the end of the podium table. It is interesting to recall how popular Harold Wilson was, particularly in the north. In the 1966 election, a local Manchester poster simply carried a picture of his pipe with the words 'Vote Labour'. The closest parallel I found was at Berlin Railway Station in 2013, which displayed a vast illuminated close-up of Angela Merkel's (safe) hands. I don't remember Mrs Thatcher's handbag being used to impart such a sense of security.

At conferences, we benefited from the advice and experiences of the paper's long-serving political editor Francis (later Sir Francis) Boyd, who took care regularly to join us for dinner. He was a kindly Eeyorish figure who, like many journalists, had a chip on his shoulder about being insufficiently appreciated by the hierarchy, though he could not have been more helpful and encouraging to younger reporters as he joshed us about our supposed future glittering careers.

From him we learnt to attend the gatherings of party agents at the Conservative conferences for the shrewdest feel of what was happening. At one conference, *The Guardian* displayed a poster, inspired, I think, by Harry, which read, 'Not Blue but True'; at another we watched the suits on the platform crowding round an intense, thin-faced young woman on the Treasury team as she wiped away a tear after delivering her first conference speech, to applause. Her name was Margaret Thatcher.

Meanwhile, the flames of a fundamental challenge to the old imperial order were just beginning to flicker on the edges of our reporting universe.

The Manchester office remit also covered Northern Ireland, which would become of central importance a few years later when a team from Manchester, powerfully supported by Harry, bravely and brilliantly reported the Troubles and made the reputations of Simon Winchester and Simon Hoggart.

But these were the years just before the violence broke surface and troops were sent in. Gerry Fitt, the heroic Social Democrat MP, was a frequent visitor to Manchester. I remember him at one meeting warning gnomically of the dark things that were being prepared, and hinting at consequences if reforms were not enacted. But it scarcely made a story.

Ian Paisley was already on the stump, but still primarily a church-man, not formally a politician. I was sent to write about him. He refused to see me and brushed me aside when I tried to ask a question after a church service. A helpful journalist arranged for me to view his police file. I turned up at some Nissen huts on the outskirts of Belfast with anticipation. Someone brought me a cardboard folder. Inside were about four newspaper cuttings. So much for police intelligence. It was a pallid profile.

There was even restiveness and a demand for independence from the Isle of Man. The concerns of its ancient Parliament, the Tynwald, were taken so seriously that a junior Home Office Minister, Lord Stonham, was sent to defuse their complaints about British government interference. We flew in too.

One of the main issues centred on the local Manx Radio, Radio Manninagh. In an illustration of just how far communications have changed, it was then the only local radio station on British soil, only permitted because of the island's special status. Its format was a blueprint, copied from the USA, for the stations that would later emerge on the mainland. In this case a mixture of music (50 per cent), advertising (not more than 15 per cent) and speech. 'We will do literally anything to bring the Manx man onto the air and get him to talk about himself,' the manager explained to me.

The station, and the Manx government, wanted a stronger signal that would allow it to reach its island listeners better, but would also mean that it was audible in parts of north-west England. Permission resided with the UK Postmaster-General, who was unhelpful, and, to add insult to injury, the provisions of the new Act outlawing pirate radio, broadcast from ships off the UK coast, had now been extended to the Isle of Man.

The talks ended in more talks, with the Tynwald agreeing to a working party with the Home Office. The arguments over Manx

Radio were overtaken by the arrival of local radio stations in the rest of the British Isles. Little more was heard of independence.

We witnessed another demonstration of fast-changing communications technology in February 1966. The Russians had landed the first rocket, Luna 9, on the moon and the speculation was that it was transmitting back the first ever pictures of the surface. The radio telescope at Jodrell Bank, near Manchester, was attempting to gatecrash the party and intercept the transmissions. With my fellow trainee, Jonathan Steele, later *The Guardian*'s chief foreign correspondent, I was despatched to the observatory a few hours after they began to pick up some signals.

Soon an excited Sir Bernard Lovell, the director, was holding up the first close-up stills ever seen of the moon's surface and declaring 'a historic moment'. The pictures, he said, 'seem to destroy the theory that the moon's surface is covered with dust several feet thick … the pictures tend to confirm the view of the moon's surface as a hard, sponge-like, pumice-stone substance. It would be perfectly satisfactory for landing not only heavy vehicles but also men.' The Russians had kept the pictures secret, and Jodrell Bank had scooped them.

We rushed for the phones. No mobiles of course and while the observatory could receive signals from the moon, it could not provide landlines for reporters. None were available, except for the benefit of the ExTel news agency reporter. He carried a large black plastic handset, about the size of his boots, which he plugged into a rented socket. The rest of us queued up to feed coins into a public telephone box down a lane.

Worse was to follow. As we watched the first edition being delivered from the press, our story my first ever front-page lead, we noticed that two of the first lines of type were upside down. It was, after all, the days of the Grauniad, famed for its misprints.

Later, Jodrell Bank made a discovery of their own. They had indeed intercepted and deciphered the first pictures from the moon's surface, using a standard fax machine borrowed from the *Daily Express*, as it happened. But they had not appreciated that the Russians were not on the recognised international standard and were using a slightly different horizontal/vertical ratio, so the shapes of the rocks on the moon's surface were actually distorted. The Russians did not let them forget it.

The big challenge for an aspiring reporter was to find issues of national importance. I found one in the questions of race relations, both in my reporting and in my own spare time as an activist in the Campaign Against Racial Discrimination (CARD). As the black population of Britain grew in the 1960s, we looked for our models to the American civil rights movement – voter registration and securing the evidence of discrimination, which astonishingly was still being denied by large sections of the establishment.

With Jonathan Steele, who had experience of the US civil rights movement while studying in the States, and others, I helped set up a Manchester branch of CARD. It brought together a mix of long-established middle-class immigrants – the proprietor of Manchester's first IndoPakistani restaurant, West Indians who had served in the forces, an Indian doctor, together with younger people; Sikhs, a few more West Indians and some Trotskyist activists.

We began house-to-house electoral registration in Moss Side and attempted to probe the extent of discrimination with black and white pairings, making the same applications to estate agents and employers and comparing the results. The objective was to demonstrate the need for effective legislation to outlaw discrimination, for which lawyers in London like Anthony Lester were lobbying the Labour government.

The first Race Relations Act was introduced at the end of 1965, but was plainly inadequate. It outlawed discrimination on the 'grounds of colour, race, or ethnic or national origins' in public places, but specifically exempted shops and excluded housing and employment. Extending the law became the objective.

As a journalist, I covered different aspects of the growing immigrant population, particularly in education, an early frontline, which was forced to deal with the new realities of large numbers of children from different cultures and often unable to speak English. It had been a key part of our Cambridge Opinion survey. I went to Bradford where some schools were just becoming more than 50 per cent immigrant, and to Leeds where a special university unit was devising classroom schemes and aids, including bingo games, to help with language learning.

In a bizarre postscript, following my article we received an offer from Spain to set up bingo centres throughout the country to teach English, if we would send the writer the material.

But, while educationalists were keen to talk about their problems, employers and unions were not. In one instance I got wind of a story in Huddersfield. A local engineering company, it was said, had established a separate (segregated) workshop for its Asian workers, by agreement with its union. I spent twenty-four hours in the town and found the place; it opened onto the street and about half a dozen men worked here. They would not talk. Neither would the company. I went to the office of the local union secretary. From memory it was the AEU, the Amalgamated Engineering Union, the union for skilled engineering workers. I asked my questions. The official sat back in his chair. 'You can ask me what you like,' he said, 'but you are never going to get an answer from me.'

I decided to concentrate on youth employment and investigate the opportunities for black school-leavers who had had the benefit of an English education and could not be rejected on the basis of their ignorance of English ways. My report, 'Breaking the jobs barrier', appeared in early 1965 following interviews and research both in Manchester and in Notting Hill in London. It makes shocking reading today, evidence of the complacency that existed at the time.

In these two areas of well-established immigrant settlement, I wrote:

> Youth employment officers say that shortage of labour enables them to find employment of some sort without trouble but it is difficult for coloured children to get jobs corresponding to their ability. They usually compare the problem to that of placing a handicapped child: it is possible but takes longer than it does for others.
>
> Jobs which they say are specially difficult to find are those involving trade training and leading to supervisory positions, white-collar jobs and those which mean coming face-to-face with the public – for example as shop assistants. Places in banks and white hairdressing salons are said to be virtually impossible to get. One reason often given by employers for not taking coloured workers is the feelings or the prejudices of their customers or staff.
>
> Mrs S. Lemoine, who was a youth employment officer in Manchester until last year, said that she found it was difficult to place girls in companies dealing with the public, and almost impossible to place them with chartered accountants and small financial firms. But the more European-looking a girl was, the easier she was to place.

I quoted a Sheffield youth service study which had found that hardly any coloured girls were employed in stores in the city. Immigrants and educationists felt that there was an 'unofficial colour bar'.

In the face of this, the Commonwealth Immigrants Advisory Council, a quango, had concluded a couple of years before that there was no evidence that 'immigrants' who applied for apprenticeships and had the necessary qualifications did not have equal opportunities of getting them. I quoted Manchester Central Youth Employment figures: of sixty-three 'coloured' boys who had used the service, eight had found apprenticeships.

I concluded:

> The coloured leaver depends largely on the exertions the youth employment officer is prepared to make on his behalf. Some officers try to persuade firms that may discriminate to try a well-qualified applicant, and this is officially encouraged in some areas. Instead of not telling the coloured child about the vacancy to save him hurt or embarrassment, they let him try for it in an attempt to break down prejudice. It does not always work. Other officers try to extend the field by looking for enlightened employers who might take coloured workers.
>
> But it may be, as one officer said, that although youth employment staff help by doing their best to enlarge the circle of jobs, the real need is for a stronger lead from the government, perhaps an extension of the Race Relations Act to cover employment.

That extension came in 1968 and the powers were continued in the subsequent 1976 Act. The argument at the time that the Act would have an educational effect on changing behaviour, without leading to an avalanche of cases, has been borne out.

One of the noticeable features of my report, apart from the use of the word 'coloured', which was usual at the time (we also spoke of 'racialism', which later became 'racism'), was its background assumption of full employment. But that started to change as the glad, confident morning of the new Labour government became clouded by the economic difficulties that led to the 1967 devaluation.

I got a taste of what was to come in the summer of 1966, when I was doing a stint in the Newcastle-upon-Tyne office and the closure was announced of the shipyard at Blyth; a relatively small, antiquated yard, some miles from the bigger yards which were concentrated on the Tyne itself. The liquidator had been called in.

The mixture of despair and incomprehension among the workforce would become all too familiar. Many of the 1,200 workers had been on holiday and first heard the news on television. One of them, Bill Hart, explained that he had been asked to work during the holiday; now the yard was closing. For many it was the only job they had known.

I wrote:

> It seems clear that there will be few jobs available at Blyth itself, a straggling curl of brick terraces cut off from the sea by the shipyard and an elevated railway which carries coal from the colliery to the docks. Its unemployment rate is 2.6 per cent, compared with 2 per cent for the northern region and the national average of 1.1 per cent.

The figures now seem astonishingly low.

Over the next quarter of the century, I would travel to one northeastern shipbuilding yard after another to witness a switchback progression of flag-waving launches and desperate new initiatives until not a single yard remained, and the collieries had gone as well.

A few months later it was *The Guardian*'s turn. The management of the move to London had been a financial disaster. As the economy stumbled and advertising contracted, not just *The Guardian* but also *The Times*, owned at the time by Canadian newspaperman Lord Thomson, was in trouble. Plans were secretly discussed to merge the two papers.

They stuttered. There were questions about which company and which editor would be in charge but it was blindingly obvious, to us at least, that in any merger it would be *The Times* brand that would prevail. We held urgent union meetings to oppose. The talks collapsed only to be revived by the advent of a Welsh entrepreneur, Claud Morris, who had rescued a threatened south Wales regional title. Somehow he managed to convince the *Guardian* chairman, Laurence Scott, that he was a player of substance, and a deal could work. In our union meeting, the children's author John Rowe Townsend warned colourfully of the idiocy of relying on what he called 'hedgerow armies' for our salvation.

Matters were referred to the Competition Commission. In a graphic cross-examination, the claim by Mr Morris to have serious City backing just melted away. The battle was over but the fallout continued.

The paper retrenched. It announced cuts of 25 per cent in all departments, including editorial. There would be compulsory redundancies if not enough volunteers came forward. We all started to sound out alternative possibilities. The result was that some of the best left and even some who stayed were soon on their way as a result of the feelers they had put out during the period of uncertainty.

One of the feature writers, Bob Waterhouse, transferred into the reporter's room. Harry gloomily observed his fashionable leather tie and groaned, 'We have got enough to do to save the paper without having to start a bloody sartorial revolution as well.' Bob subsequently became a great advocate of northern-based reporting but sadly the north-west paper he managed to found only survived for a few issues.

For me, the changes meant a move away from Manchester across the Pennines to Leeds. My predecessor had found a berth on the *Sunday Times* in pursuit of his ambition to drink in the most celebrated bar of every city in the world. He had previously succeeded Bernard Ingham, who was now in London as a *Guardian* Labour reporter, but continued to write a column for the city's weekly Labour Party paper, the *Leeds Weekly Citizen*. He had a suitably four-square byline, Albion, with a rock-solid derivation. Its middle letters spelt out BI and the *Guardian* offices were in Albion Street. Bernard still made occasional visits. I would stay in touch with him and appreciate his advice for years to come.

Leeds had many similarities with Manchester – an emblematic town hall, an extensive textile industry (but based on wool not cotton), and an obvious position as a regional capital. But it had a more diverse industrial base, and it had an enormous hinterland in the huge agricultural estates which extended north. The *Yorkshire Post*, owned by 'Yorkshire Conservative Newspapers', used to run pictures in its social pages of tenants being entertained to annual dinners by the landlords of their farms. The tenants were themselves of senior military rank.

The city still boasted a music hall, the City Varieties, whose shows were televised weekly. When I was looking for a flat, I found an advertisement for a bedsitter in a boarding house patronised, it explained, by performers from the City Varieties. Harry was disappointed when I did not take it.

For a reporter, the region offered the delights of the Dales and historic buildings like Fountains Abbey and York Minster (in danger, as I reported, of collapse), alongside grittier realities of the thriving coalfields, the docks and fishing fleets of Hull and the steel industry of Sheffield, which had recently banished its smogs by an active and progressive campaign of smoke abatement.

One of the first stories I wrote, urged on by my colleague Mike Parkin, was about the changing face of energy. Mike was the most charming of writers, with a whimsical turn of phrase, who relished nothing more than an amusing update on the dialect phrases newly uncovered by his friends at Leeds University.

My piece, though, was about the emergence of the giant power stations looming like anchored battlecruisers along the edge of the Yorkshire coalfield. Ferrybridge and Eggborough were coming on stream and Drax, the biggest of all, was rising. The new merry-go-round trains that shuttled the coal from pithead to power stations on a continuous loop were making their appearance. It was becoming the engine room of the nation.

The coalfield, by and large, was at peace. For the year I spent in Yorkshire, 1967, it was the dog that didn't bark. The reasons were various. Prospects seemed buoyant, with the new power plants and talk of new mines near Selby. Relations between the National Coal Board (NCB) chairman, Lord Robens, and the union, led by its conscientious communist General Secretary Will Paynter, were good. Hundreds of miners from less well-endowed coalfields in Scotland and Wales had been transferred to more secure jobs in Yorkshire, and were still to spread their radicalism widely.

There had been an extraordinary feat of social engineering that saw the industry reduced from 698 pits and 583,000 employees to 292 pits and 283,000 people in a decade. Many miners were dispersed to pits in other areas. It was facilitated by full employment and manpower shortages and by the Coal Board's stock of company-owned houses. It was much greater than the reduction under Mrs Thatcher. It went off without major disruption but the strain eventually showed, with the first national miners' strike for nearly fifty years beginning in 1972, the year after Robens stepped down. Paynter had retired two years before.

Robens stood out from most of his contemporaries as an astute PR operator. He made sure that he was a regular visitor to the coalfields. When he came to a pit, he would invite the local press and talk in an informal way about the issues, both local and national, confronting the industry. Even if there was not really a national story, it was an educative experience. It made his failures over Aberfan, delaying his visit and trying to wriggle out of both responsibility and the costs of clean-up, the more surprising.

The NCB provided one of the first examples of good professional media relations that I came across. I would come to appreciate it even more over the coming years. The NCB's media relations were the best in the business. There was a widely spread commitment to clarity and honesty among its press officers, which lasted until the first months of the 1984 strike. It was exemplified and fostered by the determined but unassuming figure of Geoffrey Kirk, who was the NCB's Director of Public Relations from 1960 until his resignation and death in the middle of the strike.

However, accessibility was not all. Another high-profile business leader I encountered was T. Dan Smith. His activities were mostly covered by my colleague John Ardill, who was based in Newcastle-upon-Tyne, and I first met him while I was relieving John. Smith went to jail for corruption in 1974 and his relations with contractors, John Poulson, in particular, were pilloried in the play, later a BBC series, *Our Friends in the North*. In the '60s, though, as leader of Newcastle City Council and then chairman of the Northern Economic Planning Council, a Labour initiative to revive the regions, he was a dominant and popular figure.

It was a grim time for the north-east. I remember being taken to a new industrial estate, planned as a beacon for new investment. We drove round it to find a single small distribution depot. In spite of closures like the Blyth shipyard setting recovery efforts back further, Smith, accessible to the press, a great talker who even had his own PR firm, painted a future of hope and took vigorous action to secure it. His chosen vehicles were redevelopment – Newcastle

had one of the first planning departments – and encouragement of
the arts.

While his artistic ambitions now look far-sighted, however, with
later developments like the Sage and the Baltic delivering an attractive
profile to the city, his large-scale redevelopment and accelerated slum
clearance, which he styled as creating 'The Brasilia of the North',
resulted in serious damage to the city's historic centre, while parts of
the new housing became modern slums, and have since been demolished. It was not a story, it is fair to say, unique to Newcastle.

Smith and Robens posed a conundrum for journalists. Just because
they explained themselves well and made themselves accessible, could
you believe them? Were they more effective than their peers in other
places for whom the old adage that 'an empty vessel makes the most
noise' was a guiding principle?

The sensible if stock answer is that a measured judgement needs to
be made. Results should be reviewed over an extended period and journalists need to be cautious about the prominent figures whom they
report and with whom they may have close professional relations. The
importance of figures like Robens and Smith, though, lay in the fact
that they raised the debate. They explained themselves at a time when
many of their contemporaries, particularly in large industries and
organisations, simply expected not to be questioned and be paid due
deference. As British industry was increasingly challenged and driven
into decline, its failure to explain compounded its problems and lost
it both public attention and support, as I shall argue in detail later.

Back in the cities, the strains and stresses of immigration and
the integration of new minorities continued to build up. In Leeds, the
Campaign Against Racial Discrimination was led by an energetic and
challenging Irishwoman, Maureen Baker, who became a close personal friend. We found ourselves logging the same problems we had
found in Manchester and North Kensington.

In a newsletter I reported the case of a Ghanaian dentist trained at the city's medical school who was refused a job because 'he was coloured and the patients might not like it' and a typist in a national-ised industry who was asked to resign when she had a new manager. She was told that she would be given a recommendation to a private employment provider and 'would be happier with other coloured people'. With our assistance, she kept her job.

We organised a conference to discuss extensions to the Race Relations Act; a Home Office Minister, David Ennals, agreed to speak. He ignored the subject and delivered a speech about the need for tough immigration controls. It was a lesson on realpolitik.

Another visitor was the so-called Michael X. In the 1960s, we were all looking at the US for models for race relations on this side of the Atlantic. Michael de Freitas, a Trinidadian, who had been one of the enforcers for Peter Rachman, the notorious slum landlord in Notting Hill who had evicted many of his tenants, had subsequently embraced the Black Power movement. He renamed himself as Michael X, after meeting the American Malcolm X in London. Later, echoing the Black Muslims, he changed his name again to Michael Abdul Malik. In 1975, he was hanged for murder in his native Trinidad after returning to start a commune, two members of whom were later found murdered.

In 1967, he would be sentenced to a year in jail under the Race Relations Act for advocating the instant killing of any white man caught 'laying hands' on a black woman, but earlier that year he sud-denly appeared in Leeds. It was not clear whether it was a fact-finding visit or a serious attempt to spread the reach of what he claimed was a significant Black Power grouping.

Michael, who had various celebrity supporters, including John Lennon, made a series of visits to immigrant groups in Leeds and Bradford over a weekend. He had lunch at a Sikh temple and then returned as mysteriously as he had come. He would not speak to the press and continued to cultivate an air of mystery. Nothing seemed to eventuate.

Our paths crossed again later, but a promised interview – 'that would be nice' – never materialised and when I met him at Swansea jail on his release from his sentence, he again declined to speak. He knew how to make the cult of celebrity work in his favour, even being styled by one journalist 'the true voice of black bitterness'.

At the end of 1967, I was offered a job in *The Guardian*'s London office and left Leeds. But my wife, Ann, whom I married later, came from Manchester and I returned to the north routinely in the years to come, as a correspondent for *The Guardian*, the *Sunday Telegraph* and the BBC. There was scarcely a seaside town I did not visit for some union conference or another and I filmed at more coal mines, shipyards, steelworks and factories than I care to count.

The empires continued to crumble. When I covered a fatal train crash near Thirsk, I found myself competing with teams of four or five from the *Daily Express* and the *Daily Mail*. Today the offices from which they came in northern England are closed. The first to go was *The Sun*. It had been intended as a brighter replacement for the plodding Labour-supporting *Daily Herald*. It was a decent but scarcely a sparkling effort.

When Rupert Murdoch bought it in 1969, in his first excursion into British newspaper publishing, one of his first moves was to close the Manchester office. Steadily, the process started by Harmsworth unwound. Even *The Guardian* eventually reduced its staff to a single northern correspondent.

Today the metropolising of the British press means that everything is seen from a London spectrum and reporters rarely venture out of the capital except in the company of politicians or to visit crime scenes. The only organisation that attempts to stand against it is the BBC, which still maintains large regional establishments although their news output is largely dedicated to local programming.

On a wider canvas, the large initiatives to encourage regional development had mostly disappeared before George Osborne's 'Northern Powerhouse' attempted to reverse the trend. The regional grants that enticed firms to locate in areas of unemployment were greatly diminished. While central government had some successes in relocating its activities – the Royal Mint to Cardiff, pensions administration to Newcastle, the Inland Revenue to Bootle or Bradford – industrial activity simply went south, in both senses of the word.

Some industries – mining, shipbuilding and textile weaving, for example, and now maybe steel – have simply disappeared. On the other hand, the biggest success has probably been the Nissan plant in Sunderland, where workers from the shipyards and pits whose closure I logged now have Europe's most productive car factory on their doorstep; a lasting achievement of Mrs Thatcher's government. On the other side of the country, the remnants of Jaguar and Rover, so long supported by taxpayers as British Leyland, have found success again under the ownership of the Indian group, Tata.

Steady accumulation of government control over local government spending has eroded the powers of local administrations and their perceived importance. It has not been helped by the metropolising of media coverage. In the '60s, in the big cities like Manchester, Leeds or Newcastle-upon-Tyne, dedicated reporters effectively camped in the town halls, chronicling their activities. Their focus spread into the reporting of national newspapers through their regional correspondents. No more.

Now there are attempts by government to restore some power to local centres and the BBC has made a major attempt to shift staff to Salford in the old Manchester docklands. But too many BBC staff simply travel up from London for only part of the week. It remains to be seen whether Chancellor George Osborne's attempts to establish a 'Northern Powerhouse' are more successful than the series of regional initiatives by successive governments that failed to convince the communities they were supposed to empower.

The central arbiter of media coverage remains cosmopolitan London. And, in 1968, that was where I headed.

Chapter Six

The challenging '60s

The year 1968 was an angry one. Protests against the Vietnam War, another legacy of empire, reached a crescendo and, in London, anti-American demonstrators rampaged across Grosvenor Square. In Paris, student riots came close to overthrowing General de Gaulle. In London, dockers downed tools and marched in support of Enoch Powell's warnings on immigration in his 'Rivers of Blood' speech. Protest became the bread and butter of my reporting.

In the UK universities, there was talk of serious trouble. Late in the previous year, a sit-in at the London School of Economics (LSE) had resulted in a brawl and suspensions. Now a series of protests and sit-ins spread round the country – Leicester, Essex, Manchester, the Hornsey College of Art, and elsewhere. It was an eclectic drum roll but the patterns were similar. Complaints about student facilities would lead to angry confrontations, but then the argument broadened out to encompass the unwillingness of university authorities to engage with students in the running of the colleges. The final stage was a challenge, often with heavy political overtones, to the values and assumptions of the institutions, with demands to amend the curriculum and introduce new ways of teaching.

A case in point was the occupation of Hornsey College of Art in north London. When it began I had spent time talking to the occupying students, had got a confused response, and filed a piece saying it had all started about facilities like a billiard table. So it had, but my article provoked an angry response from some of the students, who insisted it was far more than that and went on to challenge the whole basis on which art education was being run in the UK.

Another view, however, saw the student protest as an incipient challenge to accepted institutions. Some of the commentary was apocalyptic, particularly when those accustomed to analyse found themselves as participants on the receiving end. No less an observer than Asa Briggs, the vice-chancellor of Sussex, after red paint had been thrown over an American diplomat and his daughter in a Vietnam protest, talked of a possibility of perpetual conflict between the student age group and other age groups, amid worry about their dissatisfaction with authority and 'a lot of general malaise not clearly defined'.

Other left-sympathising academics found themselves, if temporarily, conflicted when they found picket lines barring them from their offices.

To me, though, as I reported from one college after another, it seemed more a natural development from the thinking that had led us to set up the very moderate Student Representative Council in Cambridge – a desire to be taken seriously by the university authorities; to be included in decisions about our tuition and treatment.

It was still miles away from the attitudes of the twenty-first century, when students, with a new sense of entitlement, could complain that university staff were not providing their money's worth. But it was part of the death rattle of deference that was becoming apparent across wide sections of British society – the arts, the trade unions, the church, the establishment.

In universities that responded imaginatively, sensible accommodations were reached. I reported from Southampton, where a left-wing student president had sent a deputation to support LSE students and even paid for a public advertisement in support of the Vietcong, and praised the university's readiness to talk.

By contrast, the more politically moderate students I met at Leicester were outraged by their treatment by the university and later by the pillorying they received from some of the press when they staged a sit-in and prevented the vice-chancellor from entering his office.

I noticed a psychological characteristic that I was to find later in covering industrial strikes, where it was often associated with what were dubbed 'virgin strikers'. It was often the more moderate and reasonable of the students who were most upset by the uncompromising treatment of the authorities. They then proved the most unyielding. The more savvy or cynical were less surprised by the reaction and dealt more pragmatically with the consequences.

The apocalyptic chuntering focused on a few incidents – the sit-ins, the noisy protests, and also those that were specifically connected with Vietnam. The Foreign Secretary was shouted down at Manchester; there was the red paint at Sussex; and students walked out of a speech by a US presidential aide at Canterbury.

In the background were some more militant noises. An anti-university was set up in London, to avoid the structure of a normal university. One of its supporters, an American, described the current educational system as 'producing parts for the factory system which owns and runs them'. A group of activists founded the Radical Students Alliance; a good title which got them probably more publicity than their membership warranted. A supporter at the Regent Street Poly declared 'examinations in their present sense should be abolished'.

The issues were played out to a struggle for control of the National Union of Students in which the RSA was engaged. The choice was between the existing leadership, inevitably tagged as establishment, and a radical alternative led, unlikely as it may seem now, by the Leeds University president, Jack Straw. Jack had been a congenial acquaintance of mine in Leeds and seemed a notably non-threatening and fair minded, if earnest, presence. But he knew how to make the right alliances, and the right noises.

He struck an attitude. 'There should be less public criticism of responsible militant action; students need no apologies.' At the same time, he insisted that the NUS should stick to educational issues rather than unrelated national political issues. He was elected, and the NUS turned left, but not very.

We tried to sum it up in a *Guardian* enquiry, 'The British student: democrat or layabout?': 'There is a deep division between those who are eager for more power within universities and want to press their political views, and those who choose to tread more softly. The first group – the minority – sometimes slips into violence but on the whole the vote must go to the democrat.' It was a very *Guardian* conclusion.

The bitterest incidents centred on national, or rather international, politics and overwhelmingly the Vietnam War. It was enflamed by visits from high-ranking but now largely forgotten American officials like McGeorge Bundy (people walked out when he spoke to the University of Kent at Canterbury) and a concern that Britain would be drawn in and send troops to Vietnam.

In retrospect, it seems a tribute to the sometimes derided Wilson government that, facing what was no doubt fearsome pressure from Lyndon Johnson and the USA, they kept us out.

The key emblematic confrontation, which I reported, was the pitched battle at Grosvenor Square in front of the US embassy on 17 March 1968. In brief, between 200 and 300 arrests were made and about 100 people injured.

It had started with a rally in Trafalgar Square, followed by a march to the embassy, where the battle began. It was an old-fashioned sort of tussle. The police were in traditional uniform; the riot gear seen later in the 1984 miners' strike or the inner-city riots was not yet standard issue, and they had just a dozen mounted officers with them. The demonstrators were in ordinary clothes and their most danger-ous, though still unpleasant, weapons turned out to be sticks from their banners and mud balls made from torn-up turf.

The march had come to a halt as it reached the square and pressure built up as more people pushed from behind. Some women were in tears. Then, 'A shout went up. "They've broken in", and there was a surge over the trampled wire fence into the garden.'

I was just behind the front line as they broke through and ran towards the embassy, which was shielded by a line of police. I repor-ted in *The Guardian*:

> They started to tear up the plastic fence inside the hedge and uproot part of the hedge. As they flooded on with smoke bombs being thrown, a cordon of police held them back from the part of the square closest to the embassy, but with a surge the crowd broke through. Isolated policemen continued to hurl a few back.
>
> After the crowd had reached the (far) hedge, some mem-bers started to tear up turf and make mud balls which they tossed towards the glass-fronted building with pieces of stick from their banners and occasional police helmets. A detach-ment of mounted police jumped their horses over the shattered fence and managed to drive back some of the milling crowd for

a minute or two ... as they were pushed back, one officer had his hat knocked off and was struck continuously on the back of his head with a stick from a banner as he clung, head down, to his horse's neck.

For about ten minutes the men were pinned against the fence under a barrage of insults, sticks and mud until, with the help of a cordon of police on foot, they managed to clear the corner. In an attempt another officer, his nose already cut, had his hat knocked flying and his reins seized before his companions could rescue him.

Most of the marchers were pushed back towards the north side of Grosvenor Square – the side they had entered from. One demonstrator stole a mounted policemen's baton. Several officers chased the man who waved the white baton over his head. Shortly after this truncheons were drawn.

The marchers were gradually edged back. At this point a battle of words – and pennies – developed with people at the windows of the Europa Hotel and some demonstrators tried to break in; the doors were barred but one man smashed panes of glass with a banner stick.

Incidents occurred with regularity in the 20 minutes or so it took police to clear the road. In one a girl was grabbed by a policeman who was then knocked to the ground as he clung to her foot and a tug of war developed. Another officer attempting to help him was also knocked down. Then another constable rushed from the back and cracked a truncheon on a demonstrator's head. The girl and an Asian man, with blood running from his forehead, were led away.

What is striking about this account is how unorganised and curiously innocent it now seems compared with later demonstrations.

The police were badly organised, easily routed and were clearly frightened. The demonstrators had little idea of their ultimate goal except protesting and making their feelings known to the embassy.

But this was small beer compared with what was happening in France. There student riots, starting with complaints about the teaching conditions at the Sorbonne, had, with political support from the left, turned into a challenge which even seemed to threaten the leadership of President de Gaulle. Whole areas of central Paris were under the apparent control of the demonstrators.

The Guardian's Paris staff were covering the crisis but I took a few days off to travel to Paris to see for myself. As I waited on a major boulevard on the Right Bank behind police lines waiting for a demonstrators' march advancing from its stronghold on the Left Bank, I found myself with reporters with whom I had covered the London disturbances. They were wearing protective helmets. 'Be careful,' said the man from the *Daily Telegraph*. 'This is quite different.'

The march arrived. Confrontation and a street battle ensued; smoke bombs, tear gas. It was at a distance. We were held back. The police succeeded in blocking the march. There was stalemate. I decided to return to the Left Bank. But, as I emerged from the Metro station, there was a sudden flurry of sirens and the corrugated Renault vans of the CRS (*Compagnies Républicaines de Sécurité*) riot police swept into the square, with helmeted officers, truncheons raised, spilling from them. We rapidly sought refuge back on the Metro platforms.

I disembarked farther down the line, near the Luxembourg Gardens where I was staying. Close by, in what was still 'liberated' territory, was the Odeon. Inside the old theatre, the corridors were still thick with the smarting swirls of tear gas. In the auditorium itself a running existential debate about the uprising continued endlessly. As I listened, one middle-aged speaker was challenging the students and their supporters on what their expectations and intentions were. All revolutions, he claimed, started with good intentions and high ideals, but then got taken over as greedy and ambitious human nature asserted itself. How would they prevent that? As it happened, the question did not require an answer as days later de Gaulle recovered his nerve and security forces reasserted control.

Being in Paris felt like the first stages of a revolution, a twinge of 1917. One of the striking things, adding dramatically to the atmosphere, was the way that art and design had been enlisted in the service of the uprising, as indeed it was in the Bolshevik Revolution. These were the days before ever-present logos and endless talk of image. But the protesters' simple graphic images and use of shock photographs in their newspapers and magazines, and particularly on posters pasted to walls, had a dramatic potency. To that extent, they won the communications battle.

I wrote in *The Guardian*:

> Not for nothing has it been called a cultural revolution. This side of Peking the technique of news by wall-poster – the symbol for the students of instant popular information – can rarely have been so spectacularly and enthusiastically demonstrated.
>
> The massive walls of the Sorbonne itself, until the police moved in, were gripped by a spreading speckled fungus of paper running in a head-high streak along it, some roughly scrawled with the latest news of factory strikes or student resolutions, other parts stamped with bold, arresting and often savage silhouettes, with brief pithy slogans.
>
> On dark silhouette posters found all over the city a clenched fist emerges from a factory chimney with the words, 'the struggle goes on'; a midget homburged man stands waist high to two workers, one black and one white, trying to push them apart,

'all workers – French and immigrant – stand together'; a derisive outline of de Gaulle is labelled, *'Le chienlit, c'est lui'*.

Some of the most numerous and devastating were reserved for the communications media, seen as peddling the government line. 'All the press and television are not exactly objective,' a student handing out posters told me when I asked why they had chosen this way of communication. It was the most immediate way to reach people and was cheap, fast and simple. The press had deliberately minimised the extent of the strikes and they had to give the real information.

A black medicine bottle made its appearance on one poster. The instructions: 'Press – not to be swallowed'. As for broadcasting, the sinister face of a riot policeman with a huge helmet over dehumanising goggles leered out on another; its caption, 'The police speak to you every night at 8' – the time of the main news bulletin.

On issue number seven of the news-sheet *Action*, the whole front page is given over to a simple headline: 'De Gaulle: Assassin Assassin Assassin'. Below, a disembodied and bloodied head fills the page. On an inside page, a comic cartoon poking fun at the security services shows a charging CRS operative carrying a shield but wielding a spanner to illustrate an article about a strike at the Flins car factory.

In search of their creators, I made my way to the grubby baroque environs of the École des Beaux-Arts, a venerable Parisian institution, where, I wrote:

> [a] huge white studio, perhaps thirty feet high, has been turned from a painting studio into a 'People's Workshop'.
>
> Every night at about nine a mixed group of artists, designers, workers, students and enrages, the generic term for anyone in sympathy with the militants, gathers to discuss the themes, the design and the slogans for the next day's posters. Eventually

a vote is taken. The posters are then printed during the night and distributed by volunteers.

The best time for this, says a notice on the wall, is 4.30 a.m. and goes on, 'Ignore provocations'. Another message advises that to keep the workshop clean is to take part in the struggle of the people, the struggle in which, as a slogan on the stairs reminds everyone, the artists are but the rearguard for the vanguard in the factories.

One of the students, distributing posters to vetted bill-stickers, explained to me that special visits were made to factories to find out what workers wanted on posters. He asked me about the attitudes of students in England and listened increasingly restively while I explained some of the demands they had made on universities. In France, he said, they had moved on beyond that; the real question was struggle alongside the workers, not university organisation. He handed me a typewritten sheet. 'We are against everything which rules today. What rules? Bourgeois art and bourgeois culture.'

Back in London, by bizarre contrast, I had a student encounter of a different kind. In retrospect, it foreshadowed a parallel but contrasting development: the tremendous gravitational pull that consumerism and the promoters of consumer brands were beginning to exert on students as their numbers and spending power grew. It barely featured in the anguished and contorted discussions of where 'student power' would lead, on which much of our attention was concentrated, but it arguably had a far greater effect than some of the idealistic discussions about the future shape of politics.

I had come into the office one Friday to find the news desk had made arrangements for me to interview a seventeen-year-old who was planning to launch a magazine, appropriately, if unimaginatively, called *Student*, which he claimed was the first pan-university magazine.

I went off grumpily, feeling that the news desk had been taken for a ride, and that I would be lucky to get anything into the paper. I made my way to a private basement flat in Connaught Square; an intriguingly expensive address. My own view, from my time as a student journalist, was that there was little market for a pan-university magazine. Students were interested in what was happening in their own institutions, or in the big national questions, not in some unfocused generality.

Among the basement piping I found a confident but rather cagey young man who told me that he would like the magazine to be regarded as a voice of British youth. Enterprisingly, he had secured illustrations by John Piper and Gerald Scarfe and a (very) short story by John le Carré. But his sights were set elsewhere. 'Young people's views', he explained, 'are almost wholly confined to low-level music publications and to minority media such as NUS conferences, school magazines and university newspapers.' His ambition was to fill the 'gaping hole' and to provide a platform for young people to go deeply into the issues that interested them. 'We want to get thousands of contributions on a subject, almost like a survey.'

I pressed him about where the money was coming from. He gave little away but explained that he had used reward money from a necklace found by his mother and claimed advertising was paying other costs. Actually, his mother had taken out an overdraft.

He was, of course, Richard Branson. The interview was the only piece of my reporting to make a *Guardian* commemorative supplement fifty years later. It is tempting to say that Branson had been swift to spot that trend to consumerism that would make the ever-enlarging student body a marketeers' playground during the later years of the century, but, in fact, it was little more than a first schoolboy attempt to be an entrepreneur, soon to be eclipsed by his musical ventures.

Student did not survive long. Later interviewers talked of having to push past bundles of unsold copies in the basement passages. In the long list of Virgin-branded businesses, publishing has not featured.

While the universities bubbled, race relations and, more particularly, the questions about immigration that always overshadowed the discussion were coming to the boil. The conundrums that would continue to bedevil the debate and defy convincing resolution for years were becoming familiar.

There was the National Health Service – did immigrants put more strain on it or was it only them who enabled it to keep going? What about housing? Did they put undue pressure on our crowded stock and irrevocably change communities or was it their labour and skills that supported our builders? Did their entrepreneurial activity revive declining areas? And schools – high achieving as Asians in particular might be, how could schools provide a good education when coping with a host of different language speakers?

Then there was the question of integration, a much-used word at the time. While activists struggled to focus attention on the importance of equal rights and treatment for the sizable communities already in the country, it was immigration and the numbers game that occupied the political foreground, and the government's energies.

In early 1968, there was one of the recurring panics that switched attention decisively back to the entry question. In Kenya, the African-run government was making life difficult for the Asians, who ran many of their shops and businesses under slogans like 'Africa for the Africans', and passed laws that penalised people who had declined to take Kenyan citizenship. Work permits and licences for non-citizens were refused, forcing many to close their shops and businesses. Nairobi airport was soon to be crowded out by Asians attempting to leave, mostly for Britain.

In the UK, it focused attention, and newspaper headlines, on the

large numbers of people throughout the Commonwealth who technically had a right of entry into Britain, whether or not they chose
to use it.

While we penned articles retailing views that the East African
Asians were exactly the kind of immigrants who would benefit the ail-
ing British economy; entrepreneurial, educated, skilled (an argument
largely borne out by their subsequent achievements), in February 1968
the government rushed through emergency legislation in just three
days. It limited immigration to those who could demonstrate a 'substantial connection' to Britain.

Then, in April, came Enoch Powell's 'Rivers of Blood' speech,
which enshrined immigration as a political issue. It was a strange
and explosive mixture of apparent intellectual argument from the
one-time Minister of Health and Classics professor – 'I see the River
Tiber foaming with blood' – and crude populist demonology. Powell
recounted the story of a woman who had lived in a street taken over
by immigrants who had had excrement pushed through her letter-
box and was shouted at as a 'racialist' when she went shopping by
children he described as 'charming, wide-grinning piccaninnies'.
He explained later that he had never met the person and endless
newspaper enquiries failed to find her.

It was horribly reminiscent of my experience in Bristol three years
before when misinformation, and willing misinformation, could exist
in a single street. ('Do you know that there are seventy people living in some houses at the end of the street?') But Powell's speech
had an enormous effect. Its clearest manifestation came the following month when some London dockers, traditionally leaders of
the Labour left, downed tools and marched in support of Powell's
demands for tougher immigration controls.

In this atmosphere it was difficult to find interest in what was actually being done to engage and involve immigrants in the community.

With the idea that immigration might be stopped or at least be a transient phenomenon, community relations still tended to have a strong flavour of 'noblesse oblige'.

In May, *The Guardian* ran a week-long series entitled 'How Human is the Health Service?' (An interesting linguistic sideline: there was hardly a reference to the 'National Health Service' or, in days before initials became obligatory for everything, just one to 'NHS doctors'.)

My contribution was a page-long article, which was given the title 'Who Carries the Bedpan?' The introduction began:

> If the striking dockers had their way and stopped all further immigration, Britain would lose by one act more doctors than her combined medical schools produce in twelve months. How great is the contribution – skilled and unskilled – which immigrants make to the Health Service and what sort of careers do they make for themselves? As consumers do they use the service more than other people?

The crossheadings rather signalled the drift: 'indispensable', 'bottle washers' and 'and promotion?'

To research the article, I went back to Birmingham. A few hundred yards up the road from where I had lodged seven years previously were two hospitals side by side. One was the local general hospital, Dudley Road, where I had once visited a sick parishioner. Beside it was Summerfield Hospital, with 950 beds one of the largest geriatric hospitals in the country, the final destination for what were then the, overwhelmingly white, aged residents of north Birmingham, including Handsworth and Smethwick. At Summerfield, 85 per cent of nurses were already from Commonwealth countries, a near synonym for black.

I wrote:

Of course Summerfield hospital is not typical of all hospitals although it may be of what are known in the clinical phrase as 'long-stay hospitals', the geriatric and psychiatric establishments where the Ministry of Health admit that in spite of 'the largest total number of nursing staff there have ever been' in Britain there are shortages.

As in foundries or cleansing departments, Commonwealth immigrants do the jobs the British would rather not.

I went on to quote a Matron who told me, 'English girls can get into other hospitals and quite a number of English people can't stand the pace here; there's a lot of lifting people in and out of bed.'

Next door in Dudley Road, just 6 per cent of nursing staff came from the Commonwealth. And in the prestigious London teaching hospitals, I found it different again. I wrote:

> In teaching hospitals, the proportion of Commonwealth nurses and doctors is very low. They reserve their junior doctor posts for their own graduates and have more than enough applicants. With competition for nursing places too (St Thomas's has four applications for each place) they can afford to be choosy about social background as well as academic qualifications. They require, for example, five O levels, instead of the official two. University College Hospital has 'a few' coloured girls among its thousand nurses; the main Commonwealth contribution is among portering and catering staff. At St Thomas's, about 60 per cent of the domestic staff (described to me as 'fairly light, clean work') is immigrant.

By contrast, I quoted figures that showed that, nationwide, between 43 and 46 per cent of junior hospital doctors already came from outside Britain and Ireland, although, extraordinarily, negotiations between the Ministry of Health and doctors had produced a report, which, in a triumph of wishful thinking over realistic assessment, characteristic of the debate, stated, 'We should not expect to retain more than a few overseas-born doctors in permanent career posts because the developing countries badly need trained doctors.'

Fifty years on, many of the same arguments continue to run.

On the broader scene, the battle to extend the Race Relations Act to cover employment and housing was won in 1968, with the help of a report commissioned by the government from the research organisation Political and Economic Planning (PEP). As well as extensive interview material, it used tools developed by the American civil rights movement, which we in voluntary organisations had also employed – sending people of different ethnicities, basically white and black, to apply for jobs or make enquiries about renting or buying a property and comparing the responses. PEP's use of a non-British European as one of the testers demonstrated even more clearly the racial bias of the respondents.

The report, published in 1967, had found extensive discrimination in employment, but the trade union movement and the employers' body, the Confederation of British Industry (CBI), stood out for a long time against legislation, insisting that voluntarism was the best way to manage workplace relations. From the union point of view, this overlapped with their opposition to the threat of legislation on union activity more generally, which would lead to the head-on confrontation in early 1969 with the government over Barbara Castle's White Paper, *In Place of Strife*.

But there was also an unwillingness to face the issue. Although, for example, Jack Jones, then an acting assistant General Secretary of his union, had told the Fabian Society in a speech in 1966 that 'even in the trade unions restrictions have been operated against the immigrant worker', members of the Trades Union Congress (TUC) General Council, such as the leader of a prominent union, the National Union of Agricultural Workers (NUAW), Lord Collison, were being quoted as saying he was 'not bothered a great deal with it as I have never met it as a real problem'. As late as April, the TUC and CBI were saying publicly that they saw no reason to change their stand against legislation and only in June, when it was clear legislation was on the way, did the TUC note that 'they did not altogether rule out the possibility that legislation might ultimately play some residual part in the process'.

The legislation came into force in October. But, by then, my attention was elsewhere. I was given the opportunity to inspect the baggage of empire on the ground, across a swathe of territories in south and Southeast Asia.

A *Times* journalist, Jack Cooper, had moved to what was then the Ministry of Overseas Development to advise on communications. One of their concerns was the general ignorance of what was called 'The Colombo Plan' and the contribution it was making to development in south and Southeast Asia. Established as a Commonwealth initiative, with an emphasis on technical cooperation (experts, training and scholarships), the Colombo Plan was enthusiastically supported by the old dominions of Australia, New Zealand and Canada, where it was relatively well-known, and had since been joined by the US and Japan.

Cooper's solution was a six-month secondment for a young journalist to travel around the region and file articles about projects and people supported by the plan, which he would then syndicate. He had a journalist in mind from *The Times* but at the last moment he could not go. Jack turned to *The Guardian* and asked John Cole, then news editor, if he could supply someone suitable. John asked me if I was interested, and there could only be one answer.

Chapter Seven

Asian perspectives

Twenty years on from independence, the baggage of empire was still liberally strewn around when I arrived in Ceylon, now Sri Lanka, in the autumn of 1968. Along Colombo streets ran familiar red buses, second-hand double-deckers, sold off by London Transport. If you hailed a taxi, like as not, it would be a battered Morris Minor.

At 'The Club' in Colombo, with its inviting swimming pool, where the expats disported themselves, Ceylonese were not usually admitted to membership, apart from one or two distinguished special cases. The menus in the old colonial hotels stirred visceral public school memories with steam puddings and soups and (badly cooked) trout. Up in the 'tea country', the lounge shelves of the (now Ceylonese) estate managers still received the familiar monthly selections of the Readers Book Club, posted from Britain, and they played rugby.

My hotel went by the name of Seaview. Although it was close to the coastal strip, it followed English seaside tradition and had no sea view. It was actually an old RAF mess, its prefab huts built around a garden courtyard and linked by a covered walk. The ceiling fans were busy but there was no air-conditioning. There was bacon and egg for breakfast and on Christmas Day they served us sausages. I became rather attached to it.

The guests were various and would probably have made a decent novel, or at least some short stories. They were mostly aid workers or advisors of some sort. Many of them were Eastern Europeans, Poles and East Germans from what was then 'behind the Iron Curtain'. The attempt by the Russian-led Eastern bloc to win influence in Asia and fill the gap left by the British retreat from empire was transparent. It would be apparent also when I worked in India with large numbers of students – including, I discovered in one encounter, the son of the King of Nepal's astrologer – taking their degrees in Moscow and elsewhere.

Other guests included an entertaining New Zealand scientist, a pre-war refugee also from Eastern Europe, who kept a mongoose. And for a few months we were joined by an elderly cockney watchmaker, who had been captured by the Turks in the First World War and marched from the Egyptian border to prison camp in Turkey. 'That Sinai!' he would sigh.

The offices of the Colombo Plan, 'The Bureau', were in a suburban villa farther along the coastal strip. I frequently caught the bus there, ignoring the advice booklet on living in Ceylon issued by the High Commission, which stated flatly 'Europeans do not usually travel by bus'. I was never sure whether it was meant as a statement of fact or an admonition.

Once there, the Information Officer, L. P. Goonetilleke, universally known as LP, welcomed me with a warm chuckle and was soon regaling me with his own and others' English poems. 'From rocky roads and unfamiliar places…' No air-conditioning here either. The ceiling fans did their best but in the afternoon if you rested your elbows on the desk, pools of water would swiftly gather.

It was a cosmopolitan place. The director was Canadian. The head of information was an Indonesian civil servant, John Senduk. Back home he still had a chicken farm because, as I was to learn, civil servant salaries there were not enough for a comfortable life. Most civil servants moonlighted. Fortunately, government offices in Jakarta closed for the day by one o'clock.

From time to time there would be a call from upstairs: 'Hello, I am Godfrey here.' Godfrey Jayatilleke was a Tamil, a gentle, bookish man who had found it difficult to get government employment because of discrimination in favour of the Sinhala language. He had been glad to find work in an international organisation. Soon after, a London imprint published his diligent history, *Ceylon: Between Orient and Occident*. He used a pen name and stated in his introduction, 'British domination has appeared on the whole to be a fruitful stage in the reform and reconstruction of an ancient society.'

They welcomed me as someone who was going to put the Colombo Plan on the map. But what exactly was the plan?

It had been founded in 1951, following a high-level Commonwealth conference on foreign affairs held in Colombo and attended by such luminaries as Ernest Bevin, Jawaharlal Nehru and Lester B. Pearson, later an influential Canadian Prime Minister. Its aim was to encourage 'cooperative economic and social development in Asia and the Pacific'. For the Western nations involved it was also seen as part of the effort to combat the spread of communism from China.

The old dominions – Australia, Canada and New Zealand – played a particular active role and were the principal donors alongside the UK. The plan was much better known in those countries. It made a particular speciality of technical cooperation. Scholarships to Commonwealth universities and the provision of expert advisors were a major focus. At the same time, bilateral project aid for, for example, farm or road or factory projects was also counted as Colombo Plan assistance.

But, by 1968, its clarity had been muddied by the accession of the United States, whose aid programmes far exceeded those of the other members and which rarely referred to the plan at all. It made it financially much bigger but more amorphous. The plan had also been widened by the addition of Asian countries outside the old British Empire like the Philippines, Cambodia or South Korea, and significantly Japan.

It was explained to me that one of the objects of my assignment was to get away from the usual Western notion of aid hand-outs to poor 'under-developed' countries and to emphasise as far as possible the way the region was helping itself with experts from different 'developing' countries providing expertise to each other.

I did my best, but there were some glaring contradictions, and realpolitik was never far away. At the time, India was the biggest recipient of aid in the world. But it was also, it was true, providing twenty technical experts and over 300 scholarships to countries in wider Asia. At the same time, the influence of its strategic priorities in the Himalayas was demonstrated by its decision to supply 700 experts to Nepal, where it was building major highways, and its underwriting of the development budget for tiny Bhutan.

And it took no great insight to notice how Japanese technical advice was usually associated with Japanese machinery, whether miniature tractors for farmers or outboard motors for fishermen. It was a deliberate policy, as was pointed out to me by an acknowledged expert in aid in Tokyo to whom the Japanese government introduced me. The Americans were consistent in linking aid with trade; the British more ambivalent.

Sensitivities were powerful. At that time, pictures of famine and starving children were usually associated with India in the way they are now largely seen as an African purgatory. After a visit to a Delhi milk sterilisation plant, supported by New Zealand, my guide from the Indian food ministry insisted on guiding me away from the families scavenging on a rubbish tip to a park where uniformed schoolgirls were playing cheerful games.

He explained that it was to give us 'a rest from machines' and pointed out how healthy the children looked compared with the pictures 'always put out of starving people' in the West. His explanation was a useful corrective but he was not with me ten days later when I was driven over the Hooghly Bridge into Calcutta, past pavements where whole families lived, ate and slept and their children played and washed in the gutters.

My explicit, and enviable, assignment was to visit as many countries as possible to write about success stories of the plan. The idea was to feed them back to Jack Cooper at the Ministry of Overseas Development in London. Then, with the help of the Gemini press agency, which specialised in Commonwealth stories, he would place them with newspapers around the world.

It was an approach, the good news story syndrome, that has become familiar to all of us. I have lost count of the number of times organisations have complained about their press coverage. 'What we need is to dig out the positive stories that are happening – there must be lots around the company – and publicise them.' It is an approach that is a staple of advertising campaigns, such as the 'World Class' series mounted by ICI just before I joined them. Its reverse is the sob story, favourite of news channels, where a selected individual's suffering apparently justifies a more general conclusion.

In this case, I think, on the whole, it worked. My pieces appeared, sometimes prominently, in publications as diverse as the *Sydney Morning Herald* and the *Los Angeles Times*, as well as, nearer home,

in *The Guardian* and *New Scientist*. I may still have a cheque for a handful of rupees sent by the venerable *Statesman* in Calcutta. What effect
they had was quite another matter.

My eight-month stint divided into two major progresses: one
through Southeast Asia from Malaysia and Thailand to South
Korea, where the plan was holding its annual meeting, and then
on to Japan, the Philippines and Singapore; the second from Pakistan
to India, Nepal and Bhutan. In between I travelled in Sri Lanka and
the Maldives.

They seem peaceful days in retrospect but they were heavily over-
hung by the shadow of the Vietnam War. There was a real fear of an
extensive communist takeover of Southeast Asian countries. Among
many, China's apparent economic progress spoke to its Marxist system. The shadow loomed largest in Thailand, where Bangkok was a
popular destination for R and R ('rest and recreation') for US troops.
My charming Thai government escort was alarmed and hushed me
when I ventured to make some criticisms of American policy at dinner. By contrast, back in Colombo, when I visited the university to
make some enquiries about student protests, I was followed by a
swelling group of students chanting 'CIA, CIA' after me.

In the north-east of Thailand, which jabs like a protruding fist
into the midriff of Indochina, I visited the government's accelerated
rural development programme. The reasons for it were obvious – the
part of Thailand most vulnerable to the communist activity over
the border, neglected in the past, with an income half the national
average, was already experiencing guerrilla activity. The United
States, with Australia, Canada and New Zealand, was helping finance
a crash programme, which was establishing roads for farmers to get
their produce to market, and an agricultural university, supported
by American land grant colleges with practical experience in raising
agricultural standards.

It was an uncomfortable place with a wariness about it. Villagers were pretty clear why the government was suddenly building new houses and community halls.

Then, in the north-west of the country, I joined Australian engineers alongside their plunging bulldozers and earth scrapers relentlessly carving a road through virgin jungle to the Burmese border. They brought their expertise from the Snowy Mountains Hydro-Electric company in building low-cost, all-weather roads across mountain terrain. It seemed an example of sensible technical cooperation, particularly as it involved extensive training of Thai staff.

Together with information officers from the Australian embassy and a Thai army cameraman, his presence never properly explained and his camera largely unused, our Land Rover lurched and bucketed along a forest track to the isolated village of Mae Sod, our progress disturbing elephants and their mahouts dragging teak from the forests. The village stood on the banks of a border river, a punt ride from Burma, where on the far bank golden pagodas glittered in the distance.

The Australians set up a screen and a projector on the village green, with a generator to supply electricity. When it grew dark villagers crowded round to watch a mixture of entertainment and propaganda from the Australian information services. 'Hearts and minds', to use the jargon of the time. But for me, it seemed for all the world like a church hall showing in England of the 1940s, a curious colonial hangover. It was mainly about the road but there was also footage of Australia. What the isolated villagers made of this curious place thousands of miles across the seas, whose engineers were burrowing their way towards them, one could only guess at.

At supper I sat with a local district officer whose view of the benefits of the road was simple. 'Trade,' he said. Later, I remarked how extraordinary it was to be sitting there when not much more than a month before I had been in London. 'Yes,' he said in a remark that chastened me. 'You are the good luck man.'

We stayed that night in a two-storey bamboo guest house, where an aging whore waited on a chair on the bedroom landing. In the middle of the night, with cockroaches walking across my back, I woke up to find the army cameraman in deep conversation with her in the adjoining bed. In the morning, he complained that she was pursuing him for payment although 'nothing had happened'.

Today, the road is part of the projected Asian Highway. The villagers have electricity and television and access to markets for their crops and timber while mining has been facilitated. I doubt if there are any more village green film-shows.

Highway construction was part of a consistent pattern across Asia; a deliberate development strategy to open up remote areas with the building of roads. In Sabah, in East Malaysia, I chronicled the work of other Snowy Mountains engineers as they staked out a route across the country from east to west through virgin forest. They enlisted local tribesmen, who showed an unexpected aptitude for bulldozer driving. It had a dreadful, but perhaps restorative, resonance for the Australians. In 1945, 1,400 prisoners of war of the Japanese, mainly Australian, had perished on a notorious death march along the same route.

You could argue that the road-building was a worthwhile, even inevitable development. I was not so sure about the cotton farm in Thailand, which the British embassy was keen to have me visit. Thai silk was world-famous but, although they had an internationally agreed export quota for cotton goods, they were not filling it. Now a mixture of old Africa hands and engineers were manning a demonstration farm and ginnery, equipped with British machinery, in an attempt to persuade farmers to switch from subsistence farming to cotton, a cash crop. French experts were struggling to adapt varieties and counteract the difficulties of pests and climate. The atmosphere was not optimistic.

It was in the heart of central rural Thailand, at a place called Takfa, but in the evening an event was held which would have surprised me less had it been in the tourist areas of the country. On a stage set up in a field, with an audience of men drinking beer at tables, young female dancers cavorted, with tickets on sale for onlookers to select a partner. Was this what opening up the country would bring?

Sadly, cotton production in Thailand has not been a success story. Levels now are far less than they were in 1968. The enterprise illustrated one of the problems I found in trying to identify interesting – and successful – schemes to write about in the face of officials' pet projects and those which were politically important – or, in some cases, politically sensitive. In Sri Lanka, I travelled to a major settlement and jungle clearance project in the east of the country and interviewed previously landless farmers. It seemed good news, but there was an underlying agenda – to increase the Sinhalese population in an area where Tamils were strong.

The other big challenge was to understand the context and the bigger aid picture. Here arguments about whether countries should concentrate on import substitution – like the cotton scheme – or on raising agricultural production or the real success of a green revolution, which relied on farmers being able to purchase newly developed seeds and fertiliser, were raging and were difficult to assess. It did not help that the numbers, though plentiful, were not very reliable and frequently baffled my interpretation.

It is a persistent problem for serious journalism. Years later, in television news I was made only too aware of the perils of using individual hard case stories to illustrate issues or reports, without serious factual underpinning. Too often researchers would simply find people to confirm what they expected to discover and provide the answer they wanted. Touching and heart-breaking they might be, but were they representative? The old legal adage 'hard cases make bad law' still seems appropriate. The only answer, I believe, is to try to be as rigorous as possible.

Arriving in a new country, often met by a British civil servant (I was, after all, technically one myself), I had to decide very quickly from a list of projects which were likely to be most interesting, or of any interest at all. A call would then be made on the relevant national government department and this was where difficulties came in. What projects or themes did they want to promote? Were particular projects accessible?

In Malaysia, the government were keen that I should write about agricultural development and their grand schemes for extending their oil palm plantations. I sat through interminable briefings and visited an agricultural university with British experts. The piece limped into being and may have found a home in the *Times Educational Supplement*.

But I felt that there was a much more interesting tale about the Orang Asli, the original Malaysians, sometimes styled aborigines, who still lived a partly nomadic life deep in the jungles. The story was about their Flying Doctor medical service and, crucially, how they were running the service themselves (apart from flying the helicopters) with a network of village medical orderlies and wireless operators. It was a classic cultural divide. As a Westerner, I was fascinated by the clash and conjunction of ancient and modern; how they bumped up against each other. My Malaysian hosts, their eyes on development, did not want reminders of their ancient indigenous peoples, whose customs and religion they did not share. I wrote that article too, although I don't know that it got much play.

In a demonstration of how fast development could progress, my next visit to Malaysia, in the 1990s, would be to film the success of ICI Malaysia in promoting the Dulux paint brand to the hundreds of thousands of newly prosperous Malaysian consumers anxious to decorate their recently constructed houses in the latest style.

Back in 1969, I wrote:

> I came East with no very clear impression of what I expected to find, but dirt, dust and starving children were included in it. I found them all at some stage although it was a while before in East Pakistan [now Bangladesh] I came across that appalling poverty which maintains its capacity to shock you with unexpected examples of degradation throughout the day.

It certainly was not the case in Colombo in fertile Ceylon. There were fewer beggars on the street than in present-day London, and they were sometimes well provided for. My friend Tissa Ranasinghe, whose monumental sculptures of Ceylonese politicians striking poses outside the Parliament building would not have been out of place at Westminster, told me of a local cooperative of beggars who lodged together and employed their own cook.

There were different stories, however, when I went to look at the progress of development on the mainland of the Indian sub-continent.

Chapter Eight

In the footsteps of the Raj

In January 1969, I travelled to the Indian sub-continent for the first time, with a mixture of anticipation and dread. My diaries at the time recorded my concern about confronting hardcore poverty. I flew first to Pakistan and what was then called West Pakistan. In Rawalpindi and Lahore it was cold and dry and I felt as if I was back in the Middle East. I soon had a reminder of how even the well-meaning baggage of empire could leave a permanent mark, but also a clue about how things might change for the better.

The valley of the river Indus, which runs from the Himalayas to the Arabian Sea, is potentially one of the most fertile in the region. I wrote:

> [T]he land which in winter blows about in clouds of powder-dry dust has soil so fertile that it leads geologists and soil scientists to reach for words like 'fantastic' and 'incredible' to describe it.

Under British rule at the turn of the century it was the
location for the largest irrigation scheme in the world. But as
the twentieth century has worn on, more and more farmers
have been driven from land which has puckered and become
overlaid with a white scurf of salt, carried up by underground
water which has risen to within a few feet of the surface and
waterlogged the ground.

The cause, it turned out, was seepage from the unlined channels
of the irrigation scheme. The potential answer had been produced
after a huge international study, supported by President Kennedy. Its
volumes stretched across eight feet of shelves and included detailed
information on such matters as land tenure and the working hours
of oxen – rarely more than five a day. The remedy was to sink tube
wells 100 feet down to pump up fresh water from the porous sand
to cleanse the soil and provide more water for irrigation. That is an
over-simplification but, as one of the British engineers explained,
'You are not writing for *New Scientist*.'

I visited the area close to Lahore, biblical, single-storey villages set
off by the tracery of small, whitewashed mosques and a scattering
of palm trees. At nearby Sheikharpur, an agricultural director sat at
a desk in gentle sunshine outside his office – so much of business in
Pakistan and India was conducted in the open air. Beside him a snake
charmer, his demonstration over, offered him some herbal powder,
licking it first as if to prove it was not poisonous. It was, he urged,
good for the backache.

The scheme, the director explained, was going wonderfully well
and cited figures for increasing yields and sales of fertiliser and tractors. In the nearby village of Bal, I met Mohamed Qasim, who farmed
six acres with his father and brothers. Yes, the scheme had done him
good; he could now plant all six acres year-round instead of only

four, and his rice was fetching a higher price. But, he said, there had been a rise in the damage from pests and disease, due, he ventured to suggest, to tampering with things, like the water supply, that were rightly the responsibility of God. The article duly appeared – in the *New Scientist*.

The scheme was a grudging success, but the pattern of increasing food yields – both in rice and wheat, based largely on the development of new varieties by research stations across the region with widespread American help – repeated itself wherever I went.

In the Punjab in India, I found experimental seed plots where the seedlings had to be given false labels to prevent their theft by eager farmers; in Maharashtra, I visited an experimental farm where Japanese experts were introducing new varieties and trying to get villagers to plant their rice in the straight rows that produce more successful results for their own small farmers; in Bhutan, farmers were assessing small Japanese hand-tractors.

I wrote:

> The name they have given it is the 'green revolution'. And if in some parts of Southern Asia that is still too optimistic a title, even in the more backward farming regions it can be said that some of the barricades are down and the forces of revolutionary scientific agriculture massing for the assault.
>
> In India, the target for the pessimism of too many armchair pundits, there is the same talk and evidence of an 'agricultural revolution'. If still premature over the country as a whole, it is undeniable in certain states.

The progress was one reason why I wrote that I finished my assignment more optimistic than when I started. 'There are obvious signs of success, particularly a marked jump in Asian food production which seems to be evidence of a change in kind, the result of a new attitude.'

Acknowledging the doubts, and the entrenched scepticism about the improvement that I was to encounter when I returned to England, I said:

> It is easy to over-estimate. Agricultural experts have suggested
> that the real test of the new high-yielding varieties on which a
> good deal of this increase has been based will not come for
> a year or two, when their resistance to pests will be challenged.
> Part of the improvement, it can be argued, is simply due to nor-
> mal good harvest years after a period of famine and drought.
> Much still depends on the establishment of viable credit and
> cooperative systems. In the end the area under irrigation will
> determine how much can be grown.

The green revolution did, of course, take hold, and in a few years the commonplace pictures of starving Indians shrank to a trickle, though poverty remained.

It was most devastatingly apparent on the streets of Calcutta, a city that I found the most fascinating in India. I wrote in my notebook:

> You don't have to go looking for poverty in Calcutta. It greets
> you half a step outside the hotel with the first beggar or thirty
> yards away with the boy covered in sores. It stops you as you drive
> as a crippled man, one leg outstretched, creeps painfully slowly
> across the road and cars change direction just slightly and keep
> going. Small children crap yellow into the gutter, sometimes
> full of water from an overflowing drain from the pump where
> people are always washing, necessarily, but it seems pointlessly,
> obsessed with cleanliness.

What one notices most about the streets is the never-ending filth: constant piles of refuse which the crows and small squatting groups of people compete to pick over, the black dampness of the gutters and the kerbs on which people cook and eat and live.

By the side of a stream or canal off the main Hooghly river patched tents cover the dust of the bank. Beside them there is an open space where whole families rest and live, their sole assets their brass cooking pots. A man stretches out a piece of grey material on two sticks as a kind of rudimentary windbreak to form his dwelling. It's cheaper than anything else but it makes the square-set rattan shacks a mile up the road look like semi-detached for the affluent in comparison. In other settings they would seem an image of poverty.

'Nobody here is idle,' says a name-dropping professor at the statistical institute. 'They are all looking for work.' But the sides of the streets are full of people washing and sleeping stretched out on filthy sheets of linen at midday.

I had been prepared for the street sleepers at night or brewing up on tiny stoves or a pile of sticks around 6.30 a.m. but to find people taking their rest, all covered up, during the day suggests a more completely weakening kind of poverty.

On my first day I saw a man walking naked through the crowds, a vest draped over his shoulders, penis projecting. He was quite sturdy in comparison with the rest of the crowd and the children whose bellies are distended with malnutrition.

In the evening I step outside the hotel to find a beggar waiting by the piles of books for sale on the pavement. As I look into a shop window, a thin, mottled girl in a brightly coloured shift asks me for the time. I explain that I am not wearing a watch. 'How about standing me a cup of tea?' she asks in a nasal voice which speaks English with almost perfect modulation.

The baggage of empire – the Victoria Memorial, the old Governor-General's palace, the Writers' Building where piles of dusty documents still crowded out the Georgian windows – was, and is, unmissable in the architecture of Calcutta. It was also, often bizarrely, present in the language, and pre-occupation with language, which marked out even chance conversations.

In the offices of the English language *Statesman* newspaper, over a bottle of whisky in an upstairs bedroom, journalists discussed syntax and the shape of sentences. Then, when I visited the Public Information Bureau, with an appointment to seek specific statistics for agricultural production, I found a small, grey-haired man berating journalists. 'You are all bastards or buggers, I don't know which.'

He turns to me, 'I imagine you are with the same profession.' I explain who I am. 'Well,' he says, 'as Lord Macaulay says, "He happens and by happy chance there it is,"' producing a piece of paper he just happens to be carrying in an envelope with *Guardian* written in red biro. 'Ah, yes, I had many verbal bouts with *The Guardian* and then exhausted my battery of abuse.' He departs, leaving me with the agricultural expert. He, in his turn, provides me with a book of statistics, none of them relevant.

On a train out of Bombay a few days later I meet a professor who attacks the shallowness of Indian newspapers and then turns on Mrs Gandhi. 'Indira has no depth. You ask her a question. She returns the same answer back – "What would you do?"' He then suggests that India is in danger of splitting into pieces. His companion suggests that India has come a long way since independence. But what, he replies, about the young people who can't get jobs or opportunities? On another train journey, I tune in to a vigorous discussion of whether India is right to persist with democracy, particularly when authoritarian communist China under Mao Tse Tung appears to be making so much progress. I note in my diary, '[W]hatever the political problems of India, one cannot accuse Indians of not discussing them.'

I would be involved in a similar discussion but in more bizarre circumstances when I reached Nepal a few weeks later.

In Kathmandu I visited mostly deserted palaces and temples which were mouldering away before the major international attempts to preserve them. It was the time of year when the city was full of villagers from remote areas of the countryside who had arrived, deep baskets on their backs, to make their seasonal purchases.

On the way back to the hotel, I came upon a man bowed down under a load of sticks, apparently leading a donkey. But, as I walked past, I was shocked to see that it was actually a woman, doubled up, head down, sacking spread over her shoulders, carrying the sticks. Others waited beside the crumbling steps of a temple where washing had been spread to dry.

There was a vegetable stall on the corner. A line of cabbage leaves had been scattered on the path. A middle-aged man walked extravagantly carefully along, stooping, and picked up every one.

From Kathmandu, I flew west to Pokhara. An important regional centre and starting point for many Himalayan expeditions, in those days it was cut off and had no access by road.

An old Tibetan lady, sitting next to me, told her beads compulsively as we flew. I dismissed her unnecessary superstition. Then the plane, an old, two-engined Dakota, swung to its left and descended into a clearing in the jungle. The pilot emerged from the cockpit and announced, 'Sorry, folks.' One of the engines had failed and he had brought us down onto an emergency landing strip, a field in a clearing. No fuss. Some hours later, another aircraft arrived and took us on to Pokhara.

The airstrip was another grassy field with a couple of huts for formalities and waiting. On a rise above it some more huts with a corrugated iron roof formed a hotel. Hot water for washing was brought in a galvanised bucket.

I had come to Pokhara to look at intra-regional aid. Here this meant Indian assistance. Nepal was of major strategic importance to India as its troops confronted the Chinese along the line of the Himalayas and the Indians were financing and building a major road system from the south. The Chinese were constructing a highway from east to west. For Pokhara and the surrounding countryside, it made sense. Communications were so bad that there were major shortages of salt and kerosene.

The road building I visited was a world away from what the Australians were doing in Thailand. Here there were just a couple of bulldozers and much of the highway had been hacked out through rocky valleys by the toil of human hands; men, women and children, up to 16,000 of them. Up on the side of the hill, work was continuing. Men carried heavy rocks up on their shoulders and women and children in traditional clothes hammered them into smaller pieces for the surface of the road. Other women carried gravel in animal skins to make cement. The vivid colours of their garments made it a picturesque but troubling scene.

Us and them indeed. The elderly Nepalese man who seems the only other guest in the hotel is dressed in impeccable English taste, down to his tweed overcoat and suede shoes and the brown loom dressing gown he wears for his morning ablutions. He is, he tells me, as he invites me to join him for supper at a local tavern, a landowner who has lost his land. I estimate that he must have got a decent price. He says in a slow, sad and self-conscious way that he now has nothing to do, although he explains that he had been an absentee landlord. But he resigns himself to it for the sake of progress.

He explains that his health, and his neurosis, had not allowed him to attend university but he had sat through many lectures since. Then he demands fiercely of me why Britain is not doing more to help his country. We could have built the east to west highway instead of the Chinese. I suggest that we might not have been approached and point to our Commonwealth commitments. We stroll past the airport and a wooden hut selling Chinese biros. My companion makes an enquiry first at one dwelling and then the next.

Here a woman looks intently at me and then leads us through a dim front room, where a fire flickers over ashes, into a pitch dark back room. A small saucer with a wick is placed on a bit of table and we sit on beds which occupy two sides of the room, glimpsing through flickers of light polished pink mud walls and stacks of tin trunks lining them, almost to the ceiling. It shows no sign of being a tavern.

My companion leans back and starts to praise Chairman Mao and make digs at 'so-called democratic India'. China, he says, is making advances as an Asian country without help from the West. He envisages China sweeping down through the Himalayas as they cannot afford to have India as a challenging comparison.

Then abruptly he talks of his love of English authors and of Russian. Just when I am imagining him as a Tolstoyan character, he says he likes Chekhov best. But after reading English, how can he get back to the magnificent slow progress of Chekhov? I ask him what he thinks of Levin in *Anna Karenina* and say he reminds me of him. He can't remember him and explains he has read an abridged edition. But he is right. He could have walked straight from the pages of Chekhov.

He explains that he has not been to Pokhara for eight years but he says it is good to be among the people. He talks of going to a mountain village for a few days and asking for hospitality. Then he says he is off to a UNESCO conference in New York. He clearly has connections.

Meanwhile, the mutton arrives to accompany the rice wine. The daughter of the family comes and watches for a while, listening.

The stew tastes strongly of sheep and is very tough. After a bit I suggest that with my tight schedule I need to be careful what I eat. He explains that he is usually careful too, and gives me leave to pass it up. As we leave, half a dozen of the family are crouched over the fire in the front room which is now burning brightly. As we bow Namaste our hostess smiles broadly. 'These people are used to it,' says my companion.

In Pakistan, the civil servants in Islamabad were insistent that I should fly the thousand miles or so across India to East Pakistan, the old East Bengal. In part it was because that is where they had come from themselves; in part because the strains of keeping together two wings of a country separated by 1,000 miles of someone else's territory, and with distinct climates and languages, were becoming all too apparent.

I passed from what felt like the Middle East to the borders of Indo-China. The delta of what is now marshy Bangladesh rarely rises more than a few feet above the waters brought down by the huge river systems from the Himalayas. Already half the population was under sixteen and I talked to teachers with no materials who had to scratch in the earth to teach children to write. They formed rudimentary abacuses out of bamboo.

In Dacca, shacks cobbled together from beaten oil drums and plaited wattle crowded like squalid henhouses along the railway line and in the market, barefoot men struggled to control handcarts, almost as big as bullock carts, loaded with piles of bricks. Two years later, I would watch the Pakistani Army systematically set the city ablaze.

I think it was Dacca that brought home to me most strongly the other major issue that impressed me during my stay in Asia. It has not had a happy outcome. It was what I called 'The thousand million question' – the population explosion. 'It is almost audible,' I wrote. 'The ticking up of the computer among the paddy fields and industrial

shanties of Asia, recording the increasing number of people born, and
mouths to feed and intelligencies to find jobs for.'

It is a subject since that has become almost taboo. Although it
seems to me the key factor in any discussion of scarcity of resources
and shortages of water or land or food, it has become the unmen-
tionable, an elephant in the room. Thanks, or no thanks, to the crude
application of the Indian sterilisation programme and the opposition of religious faiths, which unites both Catholics and born-again
American protestants.

In 1969, I could visit a training and research centre for family planning just outside Bombay, 'down a highway whose dusty flanks are
pock-marked by collections of sacking and beaten tin and old canvas
huddled together in a demonstration that population has already out-
run resources'. It had been supported by the United States. No longer.

I wrote approvingly of the programme's aims and mentioned a
shortage of fieldworkers. I had no inkling of the forced sterilisations
and crude incentives and what would became the notorious sterilisation programme, as India struggled to meet its targets, when I wrote:
'If they cannot make the programme more effective and get the birth
rate down to the target of 22 per 1,000, well, instead of the 540 million Indians in mid 1969, there will in twenty-five years' time – 1994
– be more than a thousand million.' And, indeed, the Indian population reached that figure, which we now, yielding to American usage,
call a billion, just a few years later, in 2000.

But that was still in the future. In 1969, my next destination was
the romantic mountain kingdom of Bhutan. I flew up from Calcutta
in the early hours of the morning on another Dakota. This time
the pilot stretched out for an hour or two's sleep in the cabin. From the
airport we followed the Terai, the strip of flat plain, across Bhutan's
southern border, where it continues for barely a mile before the serious mountains begin. The tarmac road was lined with sheds and

workshops; one a nuts and bolts factory, another a supply depot for spare parts for the ubiquitous jeeps.

It was a bizarre place, shot through with contradictions and the peculiar imprints of empire. First there was Jimmy Contractor. A warm, welcoming presence, with a friendly smile and a shiny dome of a head, Jimmy was a Parsee, a follower of the old Persian Zoroastrian religion. He had come from Bombay where his distillery had been closed when the local government went dry, banning alcohol – except for those, like us foreigners, who could apply for liquor permits.

As a result, Jimmy had moved operations to Bhutan, a few feet over the border, where he proceeded to turn almost every fruit known to man into alcohol, to the benefit of Bhutan's trade balance. We sat in a kind of magic cavern of coloured bottles – red, orange, green, black – displaying labels such as Bhutan Madeira or Sikkim XX Prize Rum. After dinner, aniseed, ginger and coffee liqueurs were brought out and we passed round, very carefully, an expensive sample of musk. Across the yard, recordings of bells and conch shells rang out from time to time from a circular shrine where Hindu deities flanked the Zoroastrian symbols.

The market for all this booze was India, where Jimmy explained that his big contracts were providing the Indian Army with gin and whisky.

The next night we watched them consumed at the neighbouring Indian army base, or cantonment. Saturday night was Corps night and festivities were beginning as we arrived to the sound of bagpipes played by the band of the Signals regiment. The guest of honour was the Queen Mother of Bhutan, who liked to drive her Mercedes along Bhutan's only flat tarmac road – all two miles of it – here in the Terai. She had a closely shaven head and wore the ample folds of traditional Bhutanese dress, as did two of the country's four Cabinet ministers – the Finance Minister and, my host, the Development Minister.

The evening started with games. There was betting on horse-racing and then a game of pass the pillow with a forfeit for the one left holding the pillow. The first to suffer was 'the Royal Mother', her face weathered below her razor cut. She was asked to sing a song. A long silence ensued after her first cackle of understanding. It became quite obvious that Her Majesty had no intention of sing-ing a song. Someone stood in. The Bhutan Finance Minister took charge, grasping the pillow firmly and making sure he held it until the music stopped. His forfeit: 'Shake hands with the prettiest and kiss the one you love the best.' He sensibly ended up with his wife.

Now the Colonel balanced a glass of whisky on his bald head and, flexing his right leg in a kind of pirouetting kick, began to dance on his haunches, with the look of a Turkish wrestler. He seized the Finance Minister by the hand and proceeded to a sort of minuet. A young Sikh officer and his friend joined in, and a few minutes later the Brigadier, another Sikh, his moustaches magnificently curled and twisted, was skipping languidly around the room, his arms outstretched.

The next day I was driven in a bone-shaking jeep up and across the mountains, through ravines and alongside rushing streams into Bhutan proper and its capital, Thimphu. I discovered later in the day that my driver was nicknamed 'helicopter'. On the sharpest bends he had a disconcerting habit of driving as wide and close to the edge as possible, peering down searching between his knees for the edge of the road.

It was another work in progress. Along the road we passed the lean-to wattle camps of Nepalese road workers, bright prayer flags fluttering, and women and children hammering at rocks. Eventually we caught up with a motley convoy of Royal Bodyguard jeeps, flying a variety of flags, and we passed into the inner valleys of Bhutan. It was a kind of Alpine world, although the two- and three-storeyed, half-timbered farmhouses would not have been out of place as manor houses in medieval Cheshire. They contrasted with the solid ramparts of the dzongs, part castle, part Buddhist monastery, part administrative centre, part food-store, which loomed over key points, red-timbered tile roofs rising above their forbidding stone walls.

By contrast, Thimpu, the capital, apart from the magnificent dzong which was the royal palace, was a drab place, a collection of prefabricated shacks running along the valley bottom, with a wooden cinema. I stayed in a single-storey guest house on the slopes. In the evening a great fire was built outside and a huge cauldron, perhaps three feet wide, was set. Above it hung long strips of pork being prepared for celebrations the following day, an important moment in the Bhutanese calendar. Lunch was hosted by the Home Minister resplendent in a gay Bhutanese gown, a ceremonial sword and a pair of silk patterned purple breeches above his boots. A military band wearing battledress and green berets arrived playing 'Land of Hope and Glory' and 'Over the Sea to Skye'. Baggage of empire in a land that the empire had never formally ruled.

Later we proceeded to the royal palace where archers of the King's bodyguard were having a competition. They set up targets at opposite ends of a field, perhaps 100 yards apart, and two teams then competed. As one fired, the others would stand for a while in front of the target, watching the flight, swaying out of the way of the arrows and taunting their opponents when they veered slightly off target.

In the following days, I visited various of the country's projects to earn foreign currency and advance its development. Japanese experts were advising on the growing of rice and the use of their hand tractors; Indians on a postal service and the publication of special stamps for the collectors' market. A Catholic mission (although conversion was forbidden) had established a technical training school; attempts were being made to spread the cultivation of temperate fruits like apricots and apples. But in the idyllic surroundings even the farmers in the manor houses were sometimes barefoot and ragged, and there was no sixth-form education.

Sri Lanka, by contrast, when I returned, was a green and still apparently peaceful refuge from the dry heat of India, its politics a tussle between two Sinhalese-run parties, the United National Party (UNP), led by the son of its first Prime Minister, Dudley Senanayake, and the Sri Lanka Freedom Party (SLFP), whose leader was the redoubtable Sirimavo Bandaranaike, widow of another Prime Minister, Solomon Bandaranaike. She had become the first woman Prime Minister in modern times after the assassination of her husband by a Buddhist monk.

In my last weeks there, as preparations for an election geared up, I was drawn to look at Ceylonese politics and particularly the divide between the Sinhala majority and the Tamils, who made up 20 per cent of the population. There was at that point little sign of the bloody conflict between the Tamils and the government that would erupt twenty years later.

Both Sinhalese and Tamils had crossed the narrow strait from southern India to settle in Ceylon in ancient times. The Tamils, arriving later, were still mainly concentrated in the north and east. The two groups had different languages and different religions. The Sinhalese were Buddhists, the Tamils Hindus, but with a sizable proportion of Christians. Tamil numbers were swelled in the nineteenth century by the importing from south India of what were known as Indian or Estate Tamils, as indentured labour to farm the tea estates and rubber plantations for colonial managers who wanted cheap labour and despaired of the Sinhalese work ethic. They made up roughly half of the Tamil population but had not been granted citizenship.

Under British colonial rule, the Tamils dominated civil service posts, for which English was the official language, and were regarded by administrators as more hard-working, brighter and frankly more congenial. It was a version of the British 'divide and rule', of which we were routinely accused across the old Empire.

In Ceylon, it fuelled Sinhalese resentment, and when independence came peacefully in 1948 it was followed in 1956 by the Sinhala Only Act, which made Sinhala the official language. Although moderated by the 'Sinhala only, Tamil also' agreement of 1958, the result was a huge exodus of Tamil civil servants because of their inadequate Sinhala. The civil service became almost entirely Sinhalese; many Tamils, like Godfrey in the Colombo Plan library, well-educated in English, struggled to find appropriate work. The Indian Tamils, meanwhile, had their right to citizenship restricted, and then in 1964 an agreement between the Ceylonese and Indian governments provided for a large-scale 'repatriation' of about 600,000 estate workers, while the remainder were to be granted citizenship – a scheme which was proceeding only slowly, with resistance from the estate workers themselves.

The SLFP, which had originally come to power promising the Sinhala Only legislation, remained aggressively Sinhalese and strongly influenced by Buddhist clergy. It also had a strong Marxist faction. The UNP was more conservative but no more accommodating on the question of the Tamil minority.

I interviewed the UNP's strong man, J. R. Jayawardene, a long-serving politician who had proposed in the colonial-era State Council as long ago as 1944 that Sinhala should replace English. In our discussions about development, I was surprised to find him obsessively returning to the subject of the Tamils. He was a shrewd politician, and later became President, but it seemed to me that either his history had blinded him to the importance of reaching an accommodation to relieve communal tensions, or else he felt he could not risk the displeasure of his Sinhalese constituency. But to be fair to 'J. R.', he did make a partial contribution to solving the problem of the estate Tamils when he was President by granting them citizenship.

My discussions with the Tamil parliamentary leaders were equally dispiriting. They had lost hope and drive and merited the description Gladstone once gave to the opposing front bench of 'extinct volcanoes'. Almost literally so. In the middle of one interview, their parliamentary leader erupted in an explosion of sneezes, explaining that it always happened when there were thunderstorms about. I came away with a feeling that both sides were sleepwalking into trouble, although no one could have imagined its terrible scale.

In the discussions, there echoed the same question I had been asked by Turks and Greeks in Cyprus or by the Israeli representative in Ceylon, supposedly to demonstrate that their situation was unique. 'Where else in the world will you find two communities divided by race and religion and language?' The answer returned by the twentieth century: 'in too many places'.

It was to be fewer than two years before I returned to Asia to find two of the countries where I had witnessed peaceful development engulfed in flame.

It started calmly enough. With advice from a friend in the Indian High Commission in London I put together a project to cover the 1971 Indian elections, the most populous expression of parliamentary democracy in the world. I started in New Delhi, where I attended election press conferences of the major parties and made the acquaintance of the emerging Hindu nationalist Bharatiya Janata Party (BJP), interviewing its leader and writing a piece about the mechanics of election from an interview with the election commissioner.

Then I spent a bizarre day with the former Nawab of Pataudi, the charming Oxford Blue who had captained the Indian cricket team, now known in supposedly egalitarian India as Mansoor Ali Khan. Tiger, as he was known, was trying to become an MP for the local regional party. Together with Richard Lindley of the BBC, we went from village to crumbling village of the Gujars, or thief caste, where he addressed gatherings of bemused villagers and his party workers held negotiations with village elders. I asked one prosperous farmer how he might vote. He replied that the village leaders had not yet decided. Noblesse obliged but did not win the seat.

In central northern India, Mrs Gandhi was campaigning around her constituency in towns redolent with imperial history. There was Kanpur, a gritty textile town that has a dark page in empire history as Cawnpore, where a British garrison including women and children were massacred in what is alternatively known as the Indian Mutiny, or the First War of Indian Independence.

Then on to Lucknow, close to Mrs Gandhi's constituency. Once it had been the capital of Oudh, famed in the eighteenth century for its poets and musicians and courtly manners. I found time to visit the ruins of the old residency. Here another British community held out for months under shot and shellfire before the troops who finally relieved them took brutal revenge.

It was an eerie experience. The redbrick walls of the residency and the dance hall where the wounded were tended still stood by the river, roofless and ragged, puckered by cannon shot and explosion, empty of visitors. One could almost imagine the unimaginable. Close by, a huge arched stucco building arose. I climbed unimpeded to its top floor, where birds fluttered about its equally empty vastnesses. It was the great Muslim Imambara, a monument of an earlier imperial past, now deserted as much of the Muslim community of Lucknow had left at partition. The treatment of those who remained in the avowedly secular Indian state was an issue in the election.

I looked out from the Imambara roof. Below me the bricks of the British residency were crumbling away. Across the river, bullock carts still rocked along dust roads past mud-hut villages as their ancestors must have done as they watched the empires come and go.

Mrs Gandhi's rally in Rae Bareli out in that countryside was a standard big politician affair. A stage, an over-amplified mic, lots of large men and introductions and then the set speech from the Prime Minister, shawl over her head. Interview request refused. A rapid exit. What we did not anticipate was that, following a tenacious campaign by her outgunned opponent, her use of public money in these villages would lead – four years later – to her disqualification from election for corruption and then her assumption of emergency powers.

My report that night was telexed by another of Lucknow's uncertain minorities, a sad Anglo-Indian, descendant of a mixed British and Indian marriage or liaison, now looked down as much by the Indians as they had been by the British.

My reporting had been severely hampered by a long strike in the UK by the Post Office, which at the time included the telephone service. The result was no phone connections and no guidance from the office and my reports were laboriously wired to London via Reuters or other intermediaries.

But I was aware that a potentially bigger story was unfolding only a few hundred miles away, where Pakistan had just held its own election although it remained under military rule. In the election, a majority of the seats had been won by the charismatic East Pakistan leader, Sheikh Mujibur Rahman. He had benefited from the outraged reaction to a terrible tidal surge that had left much of his country under water and led to accusations that the West Pakistan-based government had failed to provide proper assistance. Now Mujib, who could have become Prime Minister, was refusing to travel to the West. Instead, he was insisting on greater autonomy for the East, the old East Bengal, now being referred to as Bangladesh, and a campaign of general strikes was under way.

By now I had reached Calcutta in neighbouring West Bengal to report on how a Communist Party government under the resourceful and austere Jyoti Basu had been running the extraordinary city with some measure of success. I made repeated offers to cross over into Bangladesh but had had no response from the office. So I went to the airport to take my scheduled flight to Colombo only to find that an Indian Airways strike had grounded all planes. On my return to the hotel I received my first phone call from the office for three weeks, asking me to cross the border.

The crossing was not a problem. I took a taxi north-east to the border and the Indians, revelling in the discord of their Pakistani rivals, waved me through. The Pakistani customs officials were more diligent. There was no problem about entry; as Bangladeshis they were delighted to have a journalist to chronicle their grievances. But what about my books? I had various books about Indian and sub-continent politics. But were they, they asked, 'the received texts'? Baggage of empire? It felt like the Cambridge Tripos had come to the Bengali countryside.

My problems started beyond the customs post. Here I was in the middle of the countryside with suitcase and typewriter and a general strike paralysing the country. The capital, Dacca, lay hundreds of miles away. Fortunately the line of trishaw cyclists were in no hurry to see their livelihood disappear and I was conveyed to the nearby town of Jessore and a small concrete hotel. Here the puzzle for me, and other guests, became how to get to Dacca, with no public transport, general unrest and no certainty that the river crossings on the way would be open.

A day was wasted trying to find a taxi driver who would risk it. I linked up with a Scandinavian aid-worker who thought he had found someone and spent my time being addressed as 'gentleman' and being harangued by the few local English speakers about their grievances as crowds of small boys gathered. But it came to nothing.

The following day another guest, a West Pakistani businessman who was based in Chittagong, far to the east of Dacca, invited me to share his taxi. I accepted with relief but without fully appreciating the hazards. The West Pakistanis were increasingly being seen as the enemy and it was risky to be associated with one. His habit of shouting at people, which punctuated the journey, did not make things safer. He, on the other hand, may have seen me as a useful protection. Europeans were still treated as special, not, as later, as targets or potential bargaining chips.

The journey through the lush countryside would have been idyllic apart from the sense of uncertain menace. At one point we were halted by a river but the ferryman was attending to his raft and poled us across. Eventually we met the main stream of the Ganges, a small dock, and – wonder of wonders – a waiting steamer. More extraordinarily, sitting calmly and reassuringly in a cabin, writing his sales reports, was a British businessman. Later he would give me a series of letters to take back to England, all of which would be seized by the Pakistani authorities.

The ship soon sailed for Dacca. The taxi driver who had become increasingly nervous and tetchy with my West Pakistani companion took his money and departed in haste. When we reached Dacca, my companion set off for Chittagong and his family, where three weeks later I fear he was murdered when the revolt erupted and there was communal bloodshed.

In Dacca, I booked into the same Intercontinental Hotel where I had stayed peacefully two years before. Now it was a media hub, with correspondents from the wire services and other British newspapers and the BBC ensconced. Communications remained a problem. The mixture of Pakistani restrictions, local strikes and the Post Office's industrial action meant it was almost impossible to communicate with our offices and we fired off expensive telexes via Manila in the hope of getting through, which they mostly did. Our only news of our despatches came via the BBC World Service, carefully monitored by the local British government representative. He helpfully managed to pass a message to *The Guardian* that I had arrived in Dacca.

Communications about what was happening were, if anything, even more difficult. Negotiations of a sort were going on with Sheikh Mujib about increased autonomy and maybe a new constitution. There was little information from the military government. A rather ineffectual major was appointed as a spokesman and our minder. We had frequent fruitless meetings.

On the Bangladeshi side, Sheikh Mujib, avuncular but distant, held open house in the garden of his villa. But thronged with aides and well-wishers and endless comings and goings, there was little satisfactory to come out of that. We had informal briefings from a couple of his acolytes who attached themselves to us, but the key question – the attitude of the military government – remained unknown.

Progress of a sort seemed to have been made when aircraft started to ferry in the political figures from West Pakistan. They included the dapper and self-confident figure of Zulfiqar Ali Bhutto, the former Prime Minister whose People's Party had run second to Mujib, a collection of mullahs and our hope of sensible explanation, the Pathan leader Wali Khan. Wali, who showed some sympathy for Mujib, gave us the kind of political explanations that you might expect from a seasoned Western politician. But his reasonableness failed to convince.

As talks dragged on, we tried to find subjects to write about. We did the obligatory collapsing economy story and we went to see the self-defence preparations of the increasingly alarmed Bengalis. In practice, they were derisory; old men and students using sticks as rifles and learning to march. Unfortunately our reports were to be used by the Pakistani authorities as evidence of organised revolt to justify what came next.

Journalists drifted off, as other events like the South Vietnamese Army's dramatic defeat in Cambodia took precedence. One evening

I was discussing whether it was time to go home when a colleague came into the bar. 'I think your question has been answered,' he said. 'The troops guarding the hotel have turned their guns inwards.'

Next morning I wrote a despatch:

> The Pakistani army has put Dacca to fire and the sword. I saw the sword this morning raised in the hand of an army private as his truck drove behind a jeep fluttering an enormous Pakistani flag.
>
> The fire billowed from various sites around the town, most noticeably from a massive conflagration in the direction of the new university campus where rocket launchers opened up at 1.20 a.m. and from which smoke is still rising nine hours later.
>
> From my hotel it is not possible to get a clear view of all that has happened – and since 11 last night we have not been permitted to leave. But this is what we saw at about 2.15 a.m. more than an hour after firing by automatic weapons appeared to become general and an hour after the floor-shaking tremors of artillery were first felt.
>
> We overlook a crossroads opposite which is a two-storey multi-market with a number of small shops. Down one side is a broad alley across which two cars had been drawn. The area was quiet when two jeeps with machine guns came round the corner and opened fire down the deserted road. They then sent fire arcing up the alley and into the cars. There was some shouting from the roof of the market and the guns opened up on its first-storey corner window.
>
> A group of soldiers tried unsuccessfully to fire a bazooka at the building; then two infantry sections milled about the cars, shifted them and continued to fire occasional bursts down the road and into the waste ground. They broke down the entrance into a scrap yard and started a fire before moving on to the offices

of the *People* newspaper which has been outspoken about Bengal independence and army brutality. After calling on those inside to come out so their lives could be spared in Urdu (although the language here is Bengali), soldiers broke in and swiftly set fire to the entire range of one-storey buildings.

While this was going on, a group of about 15 youths emerged farther down the street and raised a slogan. When machine-gun fire was directed at them, they scattered. The soldiers retraced their steps with cheers of '*Pakisatn Zindabad*' (Victory to Pakistan) and '*Narai Tokbar*' (Victory for God).

If this is what happened on one street corner, once can only guess at what happened at places where barricades were being erected as early as 11 p.m. last night. The heaviest firing during the night came from the direction of the university halls of residence. There must have been at least a dozen widely spaced howitzer reports with their preceding flash in the area of Mohsin Hall, the girls' hostel, before at 2.30 a.m. the lights of Iqbal Hall, the central boys' hostel, were blotted out by a huge tongue of flame. Another fire was in the direction of the police headquarters from which a telephone call earlier had spoken of troops surrounding the building.

It is impossible to estimate casualties accurately but the figure must run into thousands. One fears what may be found at the university where students had trained militantly but like first-year schoolboy cadets, with drill rifles and bamboo sticks.

A military spokesman told us that the army had prior knowledge of arms dumps at the university halls and had targeted them, which explained the big explosions there.

The army believes that it now has the province firmly under control. As one Captain put this morning, 'Things will be better now. Now no one can come out and speak.' At first

we did not take this seriously but now we have taken it very
seriously.

Another captain physically propelling us from the hotel fore-
court towards the lobby said, 'If I kill my own people, I can also
kill you. I can deal with you in a second.'

Getting our stories out was impossible. The army, which had launched an obviously pre-planned operation following disturbances
earlier in the day at Chittagong, invoked censorship laws inherited
from the British Raj which even called for the handing in of typewriters. I led the group's demand that we should be allowed to fly
out. It was a long flight. Because of the closure of Indian airspace we
would have to travel around India via a refuelling stop in Sri Lanka
to West Pakistan. I calculated that in the Colombo stopover I could
get my story out via my cousin who was a businessman there, and
maybe even escape from the Pakistani grip.

In the meantime, we had an audience with Mr Bhutto, still in his
silk pyjamas and dressing gown. He refused to condemn the army's
actions. Finally, we were taken to the airport past burnt-out market
stalls that had lined the road. We were kept all night and our notebooks, film and documents were confiscated. I kept my report hidden
in my shoe. But, by the time we reached Colombo and I arranged for
my cousin to collect it, it was the weekend and the *Guardian* deadline
had passed. I was back in London before it was published.

It seemed urgent at the time to beat the news blackout and to get
the information about what was happening in Bangladesh out as fast
as possible. In the following days I found myself being interviewed
on the BBC and broadcasting commentary on the World Service.
I also spoke at a public meeting, making the argument that although
a journalist's job is to report objectively, there are times when you
witness something so shocking that you must speak out.

A few months later, as others covered the fighting on the ground in Bangladesh and the Indian invasion that would deliver independence from Pakistan, I found myself back in Sri Lanka to cover a rebellion, not by Tamils, but by dissatisfied Marxist Sinhalese.

In two years things had changed. In the election that had taken place just after my Colombo Plan assignment, the conservative government had been replaced by a coalition led by Mrs Bandaranaike's Sri Lanka Freedom Party together with the Communist Party and the Trotskyist Party.

But the government was taken by surprise when, at the beginning of April 1971, well-organised groups of young people with a philosophy even farther to the left overnight mounted an attempted revolution, raiding unsuspecting police stations for arms and occupying towns and villages.

When I reached Colombo in late April, the 'Ches', as the groups were nicknamed (after Che Guevara), were still in occupation of parts of the country, particularly in the south-west. The government, bewildered by the unexpected uprising, was struggling to respond. The army, like the police, whose weapons had been seized from their stations, were poorly armed. At one point, forces were attempting to bomb guerrillas with grenades dropped from helicopters. If it had not been so serious, one would have called it 'toytown'; certainly Heath Robinson.

The whole country had the jitters. As the taxi brought me from the airport we came up behind an army lorry, with soldiers poking their ancient .303 rifles out of the back. They started to point at me. I had what was sometimes called a Che Guevara moustache; it turned out to be one of the indicators of a terrorist that the security forces employed in their round-up of suspects.

We passed it off as a joke, but the round-up was much more sinister. The bewildered authorities were arresting young people wholesale and setting up what they called rehabilitation centres even, I wrote, 'if they are those against whom nothing can be proved'. I found growing concern about people taken away on suspicion and not heard of again.

As the army advanced, I went with a Reuters correspondent to the recently liberated areas. There were the remains of coconut palm barricades, felled telegraph poles and burnt-out shops. Bodies in rivers had become an everyday sight. At a recently established military headquarters, soldiers were bringing in suspects, checking the palms of their hands for traces of burns from bomb-making. One was led away. There was a night-time curfew and the police had just arrested twenty young people who had left the village just before curfew and returned just after it was lifted.

It was an uneasy situation. It brought home just how superficial foreign coverage can be when you don't have the language and are mostly dependent on the current authorities. In one village young men in blue shirts had been set to dig across the road from the police station. The taxi driver told us, *sotto voce*, that they were digging their own graves and would be shot after we had left. The police superintendent laughed at the suggestion when we asked him outright. We had to return to Colombo before the curfew, but I still ask myself: 'Could we, should we, have stayed? Would it have made any difference?'

Back in Colombo, the round-up was in progress too. I met one man who had two sons of nineteen and twenty-one. He thought they supported the conservative opposition United National Party. But they had been taken from his house. He had been told not to accompany them and his wife had been shooed away from the police station.

A government minister announced the takeover of a university as a rehabilitation centre for those arrested on suspicion. They would be held under the emergency regulations and live under a regime like a cadet camp. 'The whole purpose', he said grandly, 'is to impress on them the force of argument and to wean them away from the argument of force.'

Ceylon had the highest rate of literacy in Asia, no food scarcity but a huge unemployment rate among graduates. It had strong feelings about its international standing and expectations were stirred by an acute political consciousness.

I wrote:

> It is now becoming clear who the rebels were – largely the educated children of well-off peasants, disgruntled with the pace of change in a social framework which barred them from opportunities because of the excess of educated people. They were enticed by groups with a crude left-wing bias, backed up by local prejudices over caste or community and wrapped in secret organisation.

In an assessment written on my return from Colombo, where our reports had been subject to censorship, I linked the causes to the population explosion I had been only too aware of during my previous assignment: 'The population explosion is commonly thought of as making its havoc felt through starvation and food shortage. Watching Ceylon and West Bengal, where political consciousness could be said to be almost overdeveloped, another hypothesis suggests itself. The explosion may be fiercest from the frustration of ambitions aroused by education.'

We learnt to call it 'the revolution of rising expectations' and its effects would multiply across the globe for the rest of the century and into the next.

Chapter Nine

Changing faces, changing places

Returning to London in 1969 after nine months away, times had changed. The Wilson government, which had come in with such transformational hopes in 1964, was drawing to a disappointing close. It had been forced to devalue in 1967, its much-trumpeted National Plan had proved an empty wish list and it was clear that improving Britain's industrial performance was going to be a long and complex job. There was talk of rising unemployment although little obvious sign of it yet in the south of England. But, as redundancies increased and unemployment did rise, Downing Street tried to give it a positive spin, talking of a 'shake-out', as part of the restructuring of industry.

As the government struggled with industrial policy, it pressed the advantages of scale, encouraging the growth of bigger units. It forced a marriage between the shaky British Motor Corporation, a conglomeration of many of the famous names of the British car industry, with the Leyland company, which had built its success on trucks and buses and had significant export orders.

I had just come across a Leyland salesman in Jakarta, attempting to sell buses to the Indonesians with British government assistance. He was very persuasive. But his bosses failed to make the radical reorganisation needed and the troubles of British Leyland became a recurring nightmare for the rest of the century.

At the same time, the days lost through strikes were soaring, rising fourfold between 1967 and 1970, and the government had become involved in a momentous battle over regulating the powers of the trade unions that would define national politics for years to come, and which would draw me in.

At the time, I was more engaged with social policy and the new 'modernising' forces that were reshaping the landscapes of our cities, particularly at this stage London, threatening some of our cherished imperial heritage, a list that included, before long, what was popularly described as 'the heart of the Empire', the area of Piccadilly around Eros.

The student protest I had covered the year before had transmogrified, dissipating into more scattered and anarchic protests in which the reshaping of London was also entwined. I soon found myself reporting from No. 144 Piccadilly, the Queen's childhood home, a 100-room mansion close to Hyde Park Corner. It had been left derelict to await redevelopment by a property company, but then a rather inchoate group of hippy squatters and leftovers from a Hyde Park concert, led by a recent graduate nicknamed 'Dr John', moved in, highlighting the amount of property lying empty, 'liberating' their breakfasts from a nearby café, and tossing boules at the police from upstairs windows. On a September Sunday morning I watched the police suddenly charge across a makeshift drawbridge with no apparent opposition and clear the building. Today the site lies under the Four Seasons luxury hotel.

In a revealing coda, groups expelled from the building roamed central London looking for a new site. One attempted to occupy a house in Russell Square but was turned away; others had the gate slammed in their faces at an old school in Endell Street, already the scene of a rival occupation by squatters. Their spokesman said, 'We are turning away everyone from Piccadilly. They are an undisciplined mob.' The Endell Street squat, cleared a few days later, was in sight of what would be yet another subject of targeted protest, the recently completed Centrepoint office tower. For years it lay emblematically empty, as its value, and the potential leasehold price its owner, Harry Hyams, could charge for letting the building whole, kept rising.

I moved flats to share with friends in an 1890s brick mansion block in Victoria, close to Westminster Cathedral. On Victoria Street itself the old brownstone façades on our side were already under notice; those opposite had been replaced by brutalist concrete.

At *The Guardian*, I slotted back into reporting duties, after a few articles about Asian developments. I kept a particular eye on community relations. Here things had moved on too, but not a lot. In race relations, the new powers for which we had lobbied had come in with a new Race Relations Act. There was also a new Community Relations Commission, a slightly beefed up version of the old National Committee for Commonwealth Immigrants. It was headed by an ex-Cabinet minister and veteran trade union leader, Frank Cousins. But much of the staff were the same and Cousins's press briefings were so embarrassingly patronising about immigrants, I found myself not reporting his comments. In today's media world, we would probably have highlighted them to his embarrassment.

The extension of the Race Relations Act was far more significant. But the Race Relations Board moved cautiously on the cases referred to it. I established good relations with its chief officer, John Lyttle, and found myself being offered interviews by the board to explain itself in the face of critics from two persuasions – those who thought it was not doing enough, and those who were already complaining of interference and the growing size of 'the race relations industry'.

In essence, however, the problems that we had highlighted remained the same. Immigration was what grabbed the headlines and took politicians' attention. The work of encouraging the integration of the new communities, usually in already deprived areas with limited local facilities, received far less attention, except perhaps in education, where the challenges of language were plain to see.

Looking back it is striking how many of the issues of the time are still the substance of political controversy in the early twenty-first century, almost half a century later. I recently reread what I had written for a party news-sheet in advance of the 1970 Labour conference.

There was the health service: 'How can we expand a service in the face of rising costs and the needs that have been neglected – for example those of the mentally handicapped and the very old?' There was employment: 'There will possibly be yet more unemployment, particularly among the middle-aged with a change in the pattern of jobs and automation.' There was education: 'The problems of down-town schools, of the relation between school and community and what we are educating people for in the context of a rising unemployment rate.' There was housing shortage, and, perhaps most interestingly, there were questions even then about legitimacy. I warned of 'increasing complaints about the way people are unable to influence big companies which grow bigger, and government and local authority bodies'.

In London, I became familiar with the complex community politics of Notting Hill, or North Kensington, close to where I had first lived in London. The area had been notorious for the 1958 race riots and later for the brutal landlordism of Peter Rachman, who had bought up tenanted properties and systematically driven out the protected tenants by intimidation of various sorts, selling on the properties for gentrification. Some of the same was still continuing. It was a multi-ethnic area, known for its drug-dealing as well as its second-hand markets, and the problems of race and poverty were intertwined.

Community-based organisations, led by increasingly experienced activists, were trying to deal with the situation by campaigning, taking up individual cases and attempting to get new housing and new facilities for the area. A key focus was Westway, the elevated M40 motorway which was under process of construction, cutting the area in half. The neighbourhood remained very racially mixed, tensions remained between the black community and the police, and relations with the local Kensington and Chelsea council, which was dominated by Conservatives from the south of the borough, were difficult.

I helped produce a local news-sheet and tracked developments, later analysing them among four case studies in a pamphlet on community action for the Runnymede Trust. It brought together my experiences in different parts of Britain. I introduced it as being about confidence – 'the confidence that people of different races living in deprived and overcrowded circumstances can work together. And by doing so can bring changes in the environment in which they live and help determine its future shape.'

I described it as a study of four neighbourhoods where local people – housewives, schoolteachers, dustmen, social workers – had taken action. They had not, I pointed out, received great support from local authorities, but the local authorities needed the efforts of the voluntary groups as much as the groups needed official assistance.

The plan had been to look at three groups of which I had experience – the interlocking Notting Hill associations, the Campaign for

Racial Equality in Leeds and the historically important Sparkbrook Association in Birmingham, all with different objectives. But, when I returned to Birmingham, I found another encouraging example of local initiative on the borders of Handsworth, one of the first areas of heavy West Indian settlement, where I had found Mosley active in 1960.

The group was called the Westminster Endeavour for Liaison and Development (WELD), and had been established by teachers in a local junior school, called Westminster. Eighty per cent of its pupils were black. They believed that the problems experienced by their pupils, common to many in deprived areas, could only be dealt with in a wider context.

They had started by establishing a summer activity centre for the children (rare in those days); keeping the school open for three weeks in the summer holidays with the help of volunteers and parents. A network of street representatives and tote agents in many of the surrounding streets raised money for the scheme and their activities spread wider into the community with a newsletter and community advice. At the same time many of the committee were involved in a locally run housing association, which was successfully creating low-cost accommodation for local people.

The group impressed because of the way it had developed from limited but clear aims and seemed genuinely anchored in the community. It was a warming demonstration of the voluntary efforts communities all over the country were making to deal with the pressures that the changes in the imperial order were both causing and highlighting.

WELD later expanded into educational, literacy and art projects but in an increasingly fractious Handsworth its premises were fire-bombed in 1978.

In North Kensington, the issues were different. The community was much more fractured and poorer than what I typed as the

more middle- or upper-working-class environment where WELD at
that stage operated. The most visible problem was the effect of the
new motorway.

Properties had already been demolished in the road's immediate
path but for people still living in Acklam Road, which ran parallel to
the new highway, the prospect was dreadful. One side of the road had
disappeared under the construction but residents in the houses on the
remaining side looked directly into the new highway, their windows
only a few feet away. It was a classic case of disregard for poor people.

A total of thirty-three houses still stood in the terrace, plus a block
of relatively new flats. Of the houses, twenty-four had never been
fitted with a bathroom or hot-water supply and one still retained gas
lighting. Most of the four-storey houses were occupied by three or
four families. They were a mixture of old London residents, half of
whom had lived there for an average of eighteen years, and immigrants from the West Indies, Ireland and Gibraltar, with an average
stay of more than five years.

A local group had been established with the encouragement of an
individualistic community worker, George Clark, an old CND stal-
wart, to campaign for re-housing, but were not making progress. The
official opening of the motorway, though – press conference and all
– provided them with a marvellous opportunity.

As the celebrations began and the cameras whirred, the residents
appeared on the motorway with banners demanding re-housing and
gate-crashed the press conference, completely taking over the story.
The council caved in and, as I wrote in a leader-page article for *The
Guardian*, 'If they had retained the best PR firm in the business, they
could not have bettered the publicity they have achieved these past
few weeks for the victims of inner city development.'

But, as I also wrote in words that would not be out of place in
21st-century London:

Once again we have seen the general problems of the inner city, present and future, dramatized and turned into appalling paradigm in one small area of London.

When the residents of Acklam Road move out they will leave behind them in the 60-odd acres of the Golborne ward, and in the areas beyond, thousands of people whose problems of high rents, cramped and fetid accommodation, lack of playspace and lack of opportunity can only be solved by extensive redevelopment which would almost inevitably mean their moving to areas where increasing transport costs would prohibit them travelling to their present jobs.

Today this area of Notting Hill has changed dramatically. The detached houses in the adjoining streets of Cambridge and Oxford Gardens have housed the Bransons and the Ossie Clarks and change hands for multi-millions. Social housing and some tree planting have replaced the old slum houses in Acklam Road, though some buildings remain. There are community gardens. The empty bays under the motorway which local groups demanded as community spaces have been filled with activities like restaurants and a gym. But among them is the headquarters of the Westway Trust, which administers twenty-three acres of land, including that beneath the motorway. It sponsors sports and art and learning activities in the local community. It is the landlord for businesses employing 1,000 people.

And it was not just the deprived. In 1971, I had first-hand experience of the new property market when my fiancée, Ann, and I tried to find a house to accommodate us and her son Sam on their move down from Manchester. It was the time of gazumping and as fast as houses came up for sale, they were snapped up. We only found ours because it had come suddenly on the market after a contractor had punched a council inspector coming to inspect unauthorised work. It had a sink in every room.

Over in affluent St John's Wood, people were actually camping out to buy new flats at prices which today would equate to a couple of million pounds. It was a new experience; half a century later horribly familiar. But, at the time, it seemed a development sufficiently significant to feature in *The Guardian*'s annual 'Bedside Guardian' selection. We treated it rather lightly under the headline 'A very nice class of queue'.

The neighbours, said the lady camping in the building rubble with her sun lounger and vacuum flask, were very nice. The sightseers were the trouble.

As well they might be, for even in the Bentley and Jensen belt of fashionable St John's Wood you can't get too snooty and unpleasant about the well-heeled and the well-off who want a three-bedroom flat for £24,000 or thereabouts, going up £500 per floor. And yesterday and on Saturday those very people whom your average sightseer and man on the bus likes to tag as rich were themselves suffering the indignity common to many young-marrieds in the new housing estates of the south-east – queueing for days to get somewhere to live.

They were waiting for Tuesday morning when the building firm of Wates will take deposits and sell the 50 or so one-, two- and three-bedroom flats on the eleven floors of Buttermere Court, off Boundary Road.

They reclined mostly on sun loungers with their flasks and plastic cups propped handily on the low wall behind them. The only Nescafé on view was strictly Continental Blend. One woman, who reckoned she was number five in the queue, had brought her friend along to share the vigil so that she could go to the loo or pop around the corner to visit friends. She had her car with her and some neighbours were kindly allowing her to park it in their driveway. Other neighbours had brought them out tea.

Most of her companions in the vigil had similarly arranged things very nicely with friends and relations taking their places in the line of chairs. 'I have been here 20 minutes and I have been told not to tell you anything,' said one substitute. When photographers arrived they turned their backs and put up umbrellas.

There were of course compensations, the major being getting a flat in a nice position at all. Number Five said she had sold her house and been looking for flats for nine months. Conversions would cost as much, she claimed, while the only other flat she had liked and agreed a price for had been sold when her solicitor telephoned the next morning.

Number One, trilby tipped over his upturned nose and chocolate biscuits resting on his tobacco tin, remarked when asked if it was not really rather an expensive price to pay, 'Try buying in Germany or New York.'

And there were always the worse off, even among those who can think in terms of £14,000 for a single-bedroom flat or up to £28,000 with three bedrooms. 'How many single flats are going?' asked a passer-by eyeing the queue. Had he got a card, they asked. He had not. Then, the queue advised him with a slight swelling of the chest, he had no hope at all. They had all got cards months ago, cards to view, then cards to be able to buy. It was a case of first come, first served.

It was only about two miles but it could have been a world away from the Golborne ward of Notting Hill.

I spent most of 1970 away from front-line reporting, instead organising coverage as assistant news editor of *The Guardian*. With a settled pattern of working and my evenings free, I had time to become involved in local Labour Party politics in Westminster. I was elected a councillor in the Millbank ward in May 1971 together with

Richard May. Richard, a barrister, would later preside over the opening of the trial of the former Serbian leader Slobodan Milošević, at the UN's International Criminal Tribunal for the former Yugoslavia.

As the Labour leader on the Town Planning Committee, I soon found that it was not only the deprived and rundown areas that were threatened by development. The regular meetings of the planning committees and their subgroups were fed a regular diet of office conversions of old Mayfair houses, with the council attempting to preserve some living accommodation usually in the form of caretakers' flats. But bigger projects steadily arrived for consideration.

One was for a major office development amid the old Georgian terrace of Queen Anne's Gate, next to St James's Park. Pictures published in an architectural journal sounded the alarm about its height and mocked up its overshadowing effect on the historic street where generations of famous politicians had lodged. We signalled our intention to oppose the scheme in a full council debate. A few hours before it, I was invited to the offices of the town clerk, ironically in the council's own concrete tower.

He explained that the council's own officers were concerned about the height of the new tower but, under regulations allowing an automatic increase for development of a certain percentage, they could not forbid it. But why not suggest in my speech to the council that the development be refused and the council then pay compensation to the developers? I did so, but to no avail. The government rapidly moved to lease the new building. It became the Home Office.

No proposals came bigger, however, than those for the redevelopment of Piccadilly Circus, where the area around the statue of Eros was popularly known as 'the heart of Empire'. The plans were exhibited to us in the foyer of New Zealand House, a bleak, concrete tower built a few years before, just down the hill from Piccadilly on the Haymarket. The incongruous tower was a fitting setting for the plan – three enormous concrete towers on three sides of Piccadilly, which would sweep away a network of small streets around it. The paperwork described their existing buildings as having little of architectural interest.

When we first saw the model, it was difficult to think how to oppose it. What was being proposed was so much of a piece with what was going up elsewhere, as New Zealand House itself demonstrated. But we sensed the outrage and a small group formed to fight the plans. We met in the threatened Rupert Street premises of Pizza Express, which had just been founded by Peter Boizot, who saw the proposals as threatening his fledgling business. The Labour group called a special meeting of the council to oppose the plans and I seconded our motion, attacking what I called the imposition of 'giant tomb-stones' over Piccadilly.

A long battle ensued into which the GLC was drawn as a result of its overlapping planning responsibilities. In the event, a joint working party was established and we argued street by street and building by building against the scheme and associated demolition.

At almost the same time, I was reporting on the public inquiry against proposals by the very same GLC to demolish the historic Covent Garden market. Again, it was being opposed by local groups including celebrated local clergy. I do not remember much of the inquiry in detail except that the GLC's challenging barrister seemed significantly less effective in the afternoon after his lunch. But I do recollect the argument being made repeatedly that, without the fruit market, which was moving south of the Thames to Nine Elms, the area would be left derelict. Today that seems unbelievable.

But we were standing, did we but know it, on the cusp of a major change in public and political attitudes. Our working party on Piccadilly came out against the major redevelopment. The buildings around it, some which had lain derelict for years awaiting redevelopment, were refurbished and brought back into more imaginative use.

The Covent Garden inquiry ended up backing the GLC redevelopment plans, but these were then thwarted by the decision of the Conservative Environment Minister, Geoffrey Rippon, to list over 200 potentially affected buildings. So Covent Garden market survived and the buildings around it became a magnet for all kinds of different retail and other activities. It was a lesson in the values of perseverance, and a signal warning of how sharply political attitudes can change.

At almost the same moment, my friends, Horst and Margret, German architects who shared my flat, were working on a competition for a new development in Paris where the city was tearing down the picturesque market of Les Halles, its equivalent of Covent Garden. How many Parisians contemplating Covent Garden since have wished that they had retained their market buildings.

Chapter Ten

Reporting the unions

In the autumn of 1972, I began my serious engagement with another mighty empire – the world of the trade unions and the Labour movement. It was the moment when its influence began to reach a peak. I became the assistant labour correspondent of *The Guardian*, working with Keith Harper.

I was following a distinguished line. Among previous labour correspondents were numbered John Cole, now news editor, who would become a household voice when he joined me at the BBC as political editor, and the respected columnist Peter Jenkins.

Then there had been Bernard Ingham. Bluff, engaging and helpful when I had regularly run across him in my Manchester days, he was a workaholic who had ensured that the job that I now took was known as one of the most hard-worked on the paper because of his thoroughness in covering so many disputes. Bernard had left the paper because he felt his detailed reporting was not sufficiently appreciated and he had been passed over for the top job. But he was now a key part of the government's communications machine as director of information at the Department of Employment.

It was a fascinating but challenging opportunity. Industrial relations and the power of the unions would be central to British politics for most of the next two decades, seen as central to the government's attempts to manage the faltering economy. How to control inflation and the influence that wages had on the economy, together with the role of the unions in assisting the remaking of worn-out British industries, were to be battlegrounds for all governments.

It was a critical moment for the attempts to regulate wage settlements and industrial relations by statute. This was currently being pursued by the Heath government but had been the culmination of a continuing and bitter argument that had begun four years before with the publication of the Labour government's *In Place of Strife* proposals.

As the hopes of Harold Wilson's new Labour government had faded and it had become clear the British economy was in serious structural trouble, with inflation now persistent, unemployment rising for the first time since the war and traditional industries failing, political focus had become concentrated on rising wages and growing industrial unrest. The decline of deference had affected the unions too and there was a rising number of locally originated disputes that could remain stubbornly intractable even when union leaderships called for a return to work.

The objective of both the Wilson and Heath governments had been clear: to curb the growth of this anarchic strike action, the so-called 'wildcat strikes', often linked with the phrase 'shop steward power', which had seen the days lost through strikes escalate. As many of the disputes were in important industries, such as car manufacturing and the docks, they were seen as hindering, some said crippling, the country's economic recovery.

The argument – and the position of trade unions – had become central to British politics. That was clear. In a phrase popular in trade union speeches at the time, you didn't have to look in the crystal ball when you could read the book.

However, below the surface turbulence, there were other currents running that shaped the '70s, and my engagement with the Labour movement. One was the culmination of the argument developed by TUC General Secretaries, from George Woodcock onwards, that unions should be engaged in the decision-making processes of government and that would be their price for cooperation over wages and industrial relations.

It continued to meet fierce resistance on the left. Its protagonists argued that if you signed up to a pay policy, you would be drawn into policing it against workers' interests, and unions should instead rely on industrial pressure. At its most extreme, it argued that industrial action was the key to defeating governments. The battle was joined every year with a string of rival resolutions passed at union conferences through the summer, leading up to challenge and often confrontation at the annual TUC Congress at the start of September.

But the proposition and its consequences – the creation of a string of tripartite bodies regulating subjects like health and safety and day-to-day industrial relations, as well as a mass of consultations and enquiries – made inexorable progress throughout the decade.

It was assisted by another trend – an unparalleled growth in trade union membership. In the whole of the '60s, it had grown by little more than half a million, but in the 1970s almost 3 million more people joined trade unions. Membership rose from 10,472,000 in 1969 to its peak – 13,212,000 – in 1979.

Much of this was growth in white-collar membership. For salaried and professional workers, trade unionism became both more respectable and more appealing as wage-bargaining at a time of inflation became critical. The decline of deference and appetite for change encouraged it. For the many in my generation who had looked for the Labour victory in 1964 to modernise Britain, there was general goodwill towards the unions and a willingness to sign up. Over the '70s, the unions benefited not only from these individual decisions, but from a mopping-up operation in areas like banking or scientific research where existing staff associations were absorbed into formal union structures. The mouthy Clive Jenkins of ASTMS was particularly successful in stitching together a significant-sized union out of a patchwork of associations; almost a private enterprise operation. Meanwhile, the big industrial unions scrambled to bolt on or develop white-collar sections.

It led to what came to be called 'white-collar militancy'. It was not just the big, industrial, largely working-class battalions who were prepared to take industrial action; the middle classes could be involved too and would be increasingly articulate about it.

Our challenge was to report this many-layered scene with understanding and due attention to the views of different sides. As usual, the difficulty was to dig behind the rhetoric to find out what was really going on.

The argument had now reached the tipping point. The new Conservative government had brought in the 1971 Industrial Relations Act, which introduced statutory regulation, and it was being tested by the unions who had refused to cooperate with it. To no one's surprise the biggest confrontation had come in the London docks, traditionally militant and now in mortal decline, as bigger ships and new methods of cargo handling were introduced to its competitor ports on the Continent but management and unions repeatedly failed to cut a deal for their measured introduction to Britain.

That summer, dockers had been picketing a refrigeration store that was part of the great meat-importing empire of the titled Vestey family in defiance of the Act. It was duly invoked and five shop stewards who became known as the 'Pentonville Five' were jailed. Such uproar followed that a previously scarcely known functionary, the Official Solicitor, was brought out to represent the men and play the 'Get Out of Jail Free' card on the government's behalf. They were duly released, but the battle lines had been drawn for a confrontation that would end only with the Heath government's defeat in the first of two 1974 elections.

Attending the TUC Congress that September, while I was still a general reporter, I found the union leadership in bitter but determined mood. I watched as a long roll-call of thirty-two unions who had agreed to comply with the Act and register was intoned at the rostrum and they were suspended from the Congress. It was an indication of the strength of the feeling of solidarity that underpins the Labour movement and the force with which that solidarity can be asserted.

I also had my first close encounter with the labour and industrial correspondents, positioned uncomfortably on press tables immediately under the rostrum from which speakers would routinely denounce the misdoings and misinterpretations of the press. It was a sobering introduction. The love/hate relationship between unions and the media would feature increasingly strongly.

My decision to apply for the Labour job followed a thread that had started with my experiences in Birmingham and had run through encounters with unions in the mines and mills and docks in Yorkshire and Lancashire. There I found thoughtful and responsible regional officials working through complex issues but had difficult passages with entrenched officials over issues of race.

I held a generally beneficent attitude towards the unions. For those of us working in journalism it was distinctly personal because we depended on the National Union of Journalists for our wage negotiations. That goodwill could, however, be tempered for those involved in the nightly production of papers by the face-to-face intransigence, and sometimes corruption, of the print unions.

I had already covered an historic industrial dispute – the 1972 miners' strike – the first national dispute the National Union of Mineworkers (NUM) had called since the General Strike of 1926. I had been sent as a general reporter back to Birmingham, to the Saltley coke works. There miners had mounted a large and growing picket and were trying to prevent coke being distributed with the aim of choking off supplies to dependent industry, though in fact much was destined for hospitals and schools.

The police allowed the miners to mount cabs to speak to drivers arriving at the plant, but if they still decided to drive in, the police had to link arms to try to hold back the surging lines of pickets as they fought to bar the gates. It was generally peaceable but there were some ugly incidents. Aggressive push and shove sometimes led to confrontation, arrests were made and some miners were bound over to keep the peace. It was rapidly building into a symbolic trial of strength – close Saltley, and the miners might be on their way to an unexpected victory.

There was a wary respect between the hundreds of miners – the so-called 'Flying Squad' from Yorkshire, but the bulk from south Wales and the Midlands – and the police. It was in the days before riot gear and shields and the police were in traditional uniform, while the miners shoved and swore but there was no throwing of missiles. More generally, the miners, at that time a largely forgotten constituency, were already winning public sympathy as the paucity of their wage rates – seventeenth in the national league table – and the demanding conditions of their jobs were becoming apparent.

I looked for a leader among the pickets. A small, balding, rather unsmiling man in a donkey jacket was clambering onto the running boards of arriving lorries to remonstrate with the drivers. In a quieter moment I approached him and identified myself as from *The Guardian*. Normally this brought a friendly response from trade unionists and activists, who saw the paper as being on their side. Not so this time. 'What do you want?' he challenged. It was my first encounter with Arthur Scargill. We would continue our wary relationship for the next seventeen years.

The following morning, we witnessed what might have been a scene staged for an Eisenstein movie. As miners and police continued their ritual shoving match, over the hill appeared columns of engineering workers, many of them women in overalls with headscarves, who had taken time off to support the miners. As they passed they sprayed packets of Park Drive – the cigarette of choice in Midlands factories – over the heads of the police cordon into the reaching hands of the picketing miners.

As 6,000 demonstrators pressed 700 policemen, in a decision which would have consequences for more than a decade, the local chief constable ordered the gates of the coke depot to be closed.

Scargill scrambled up on a wall and declared it a marvellous victory that would go down in trade union history. Later, his reserve thawed, he gave me a lift back to the city centre in a large bronze Ford Zephyr. In the car he told me that when he saw the trade union banners sweeping up the hill, 'everything I have always believed in and idolised crystallised'. I wrote at the time, 'It has been something of a personal triumph for Mr Scargill, a member of the NUM Yorkshire executive committee.' It was one of the first introductions to the public of Arthur Scargill.

It proved a psychological turning point in the strike. The dispute ended with a huge pay increase and other benefits for the miners, while Arthur rose rapidly to become president of the Yorkshire NUM, as older men retired. Saltley remained etched on his memory and his attempts to close British Steel's Orgreave Cokeworks in the 1984 strike in order to shut down steel production was an attempt to repeat the psychological blow he had struck twelve years before. By the same token, the Thatcher government's use of the police was animated by a determination not to repeat what it saw as their retreat at Saltley.

In the years that followed, other trade unionists would sometimes remonstrate with me, arguing that too much credit had been given to Arthur and the picketing and not enough to others who behind the scenes had worked with the Birmingham Trades Council – the local collective of unions – to bring out the other workers in support.

It was a timely reminder of the strains and jealousies, and some-times outright hatreds, that lurked below the brotherly surface of the trade union movement which we industrial correspondents had to navigate at our peril.

The industrial landscape spread wide at the time; Britain was still making her own passenger airliners and launching ships from more than a dozen yards; motor factories were turning out a record num-ber of cars (nearly 2 million, although imports were rising rapidly); the steel industry had big plans for expansion while coal, hacked and blasted out of more than 250 pits, made up the overwhelming source of fuel for the power stations.

To huge political outcry unemployment had just topped 1 million for the first time since the 1930s (by contrast, in 2015 the figures for those claiming benefit was regarded as not too bad at around 2 mil-lion). Trade union membership was increasing.

For industrial correspondents, the challenge was to chart the ups and downs of this huge range of industrial activity, while following two powerful themes. There was the progress of the annual wage round, where government wages policies – norms, ceilings, infla-tion markers, call them what you will – would be challenged by one group or another and with it the government itself. Secondly there was the reaction to the government's legislation on the conduct of industrial relations and how far union resistance would explode into mass action.

By now the Heath government was embroiled in the most complex and casuistic attempt to regulate wage-bargaining with a gallimaufry of supervisory boards and a tangle of red tape that could mean a worker's right to a special London allowance was determined by the numbers of changes he made on the journey to work, or a miner's pay adjusted to take account of the time he had to wait for the lift to take him down the pit.

In retrospect, this almost insanely detailed edifice, taking in prices as well as incomes, seems inevitably doomed, but it came surprisingly close to success. Tripartite discussions, as they were labelled, between government, trade unions and industry represented by the CBI, continued even as the unions were refusing to register under the new industrial relations legislation.

The fallout from all of this made up our daily routine. A mass of meetings and negotiations, often going on for days or late into the night while an agreement was patched up or nothing very much was decided; further talks scheduled or not; then a final crunch close to the anniversary of the last agreement.

The wage-bargaining calendar set out a roadmap. A mix of lower-paid local authority workers to start the autumn off, often delaying to see how the wind blew and what more powerful groups could achieve. The first skirmishes of the private-sector pay champions, the Ford workers, in October, then the newly rediscovered muscle of the miners flexed in the public sector in November. Others watched and waited. By Christmas it was usually obvious how far a policy, or a norm, or a guideline and ultimately a 'social contract', had stuck.

Our role could most accurately be described as 'hanging about'.

As a newspaper reporter, the key skill was to know when a negotiation was going to come to a head. No point in going down to the Ford garage in Bayswater or the Coal Board headquarters in Victoria too early. There was plenty to do in the office, and calls to make. Perhaps a visit at lunchtime with a drink in the pub with some delegates, often also hanging around while their leaders negotiated, and an indication of when the crunch might come. Perhaps a sighting of a management press spokesman, with news of an opening pay offer, inevitably bound for rejection.

For a broadcasting reporter, there would be a different step to the quadrille. Arrive before the meeting, try to record a few, though usually meaningless, words from the negotiators and then hang on, gleaning what you could from delegates slipping out from the meeting for a drink or lunch or hints and briefings from management staff. The best of these would come from Ford, a thoroughly responsive press office who would disclose a pay offer once the unions had had time to digest it.

In the '70s, before the use of video cameras was approved by BBC News and its unions, the key negotiations saw deployments of almost military proportions. Great olive-painted BBC pantechnicons, one towing a generator, the other equipped with its own transmission suite, would rumble into position, cables would be played out, power connected and two heavyweight cameras on thick tripods would be hauled out and heaved into position. It meant a shelter from the elements and some brewing up in the support truck. And, in Scotland, a particularly forceful local hamburger.

I shudder to think how many broadcasts I was to make with little or no information at hand, but, as I told the BBC in my interview for the job, what they most needed was accurate information fast. For daily newspaper reporters it was no different except that in those days before the internet's digital news pages they had a precious hour or two more to garner information before the final deadline of the following day's paper.

It was all a matter of contacts, and here I was quickly confronted, and shocked, by the depth of division within the Labour movement itself.

On Tuesdays, as a newspaper reporter, I would travel regularly to Peckham in south London for the weekly executive of the Amalgamated Union of Engineering Workers (AUEW). It was the country's second largest union at the time and represented skilled workers in all the most important manufacturing industries. It policed and negotiated a network of agreements so complex that every month the Confederation of Shipbuilding and Engineering Unions (CSEU) would shut themselves away for two days in the long drab corridors of the Station Hotel at York to negotiate with the employers in fine detail.

The union was soon at the epicentre of the battle over the Industrial Relations Act and would see its assets seized because of its refusal to recognise the special Industrial Relations Court set up under the legislation.

We charted the remorseless drift into confrontation week by week. But, in those days, as was common throughout the movement apart from some of the ambitious expanding white-collar unions, there would be little help from official union sources. There was a spokesman who could tell us nothing and we waited in the entrance hall while a request was sent to the union's leading officials for briefing. We rarely received one but week by week the Press Association's endlessly patient correspondent, Nobby Clark, waited it out for us.

The union was precariously balanced between the left and the right of the Labour movement, and illustrated the gulf between the two, with which I was becoming rapidly familiar. The president, Hugh Scanlon, was caricatured as one of the 'terrible twins', together with the Transport Union leader Jack Jones, because of the way they had bullied the preceding Labour government into emasculating its plans for industrial relations legislation.

Scanlon was the more inflexible. He had moved that unions who registered under the Industrial Relations Act should be suspended from the TUC, arguing that 'a single scratch can lead to gangrene'. He was firmly on the left but the General Secretary, a Salvationist, John Boyd, was uncompromisingly of the right. The executive was roughly evenly divided. But, with all officials regularly up for re-election, the union seemed to live on the brink.

Starved of briefing, we retired to the pub at lunchtime to rub shoulders with, and buy drinks for, the individual members of the executive in their lunch break. Except that it was never one pub, but two. Left and right drank and schemed separately. And the fault line ran throughout the union movement; it was the same with the miners or the railwaymen: separate factions, separate pubs. It was a surprise and quite shocking to me; a graphic demonstration of the bitterness and rivalries stored up over years.

The shorthand used to describe trade union positioning was often crude. Given that Labour is usually seen as on the left and the Conservatives on the right, it could be confusing to describe, as we did, trade union leaders as being on the right or the left. In the broad sweep of things, they were all on the left, and almost every union was affiliated to the Labour Party. Those who were not members of the Labour Party were, with few exceptions, farther to the left, members of the orthodox Communist Party of Great Britain or fissiparous Trotskyist groups like the Socialist Workers Party or the Workers Revolutionary Party. The Communist Party was well represented among union executives and office bearers; the small Trotskyist groups had few adherents.

But they, and sympathisers in the mainstream, represented a

powerful strand in the Labour movement of a Marxist or Marxist-influenced belief in the importance of struggle and the use of industrial action to achieve their goal of a socialist state.

It was complicated by international politics. The Cold War was at its height. The Communist Party of Great Britain (CPGB) had its links with Moscow and the international trade union movement was divided into two federations, one Western-leaning, to which the TUC was affiliated, and the other supported by the eastern bloc. Old loyalties died hard. In spite of the impact of the Russian invasion of Hungary in 1956 which had split the CPGB, there were many trade unionists who clung to the memory of Russian support for the anti-Franco forces in the '30s and the international brigade in which some of them had fought.

At Congresses, the Labour attachés of major embassies, including the American and German, rubbed shoulders with their eastern counterparts. And, of course, the Special Branch retained an interest.

Left-leaning trade unionists were often typed as 'militants' by comparison with the supposedly more mainstream 'moderates'. It was another unsatisfactory labelling. It was more difficult for the moderates to take the high ground in debate because they lacked the clear ideological thrust as the social democracy which they, and most trade union members, espoused had less clarity and excitement. But there was often nothing moderate in the way they behaved, battling against the left, and using every stratagem to maintain their positions, including close relations with the tabloid press. In some cases they were supported by an organised, anti-communist Catholic network.

Our job, of course, was to get to both sides, but it was also important to discount the spin from selective briefing. This was most transparent on the left, where the Communist Party of Great Britain usually had a number of members on executive committees, the most prominent perhaps Mick McGahey, who became vice-president of the NUM. To my chagrin, I could only watch across the bar as the industrial reporters of the party's newspaper, the *Morning Star*, simply opened their notebooks for a briefing from the party members on a union executive. We others had to elicit what information we could by more widespread questioning, while trying to keep a clear head while the rounds piled up.

The importance the party attached to this channel of information for CPGB and other activists was made clear when the paper's labour correspondent, Mick Costello, was promoted to its industrial organiser. Mick was a shrewd and dedicated operative who would check out new reporters on the beat and did his cause no harm by forming a strong bond with *The Times*'s industrial correspondent, Paul Routledge. It made for interesting competition.

But these sessions with officials and delegates, although overly protracted, could be time well spent, particularly with those from outside London, when they talked with understanding and engagement about what was happening in their industries and neighbourhoods, and could be frank about their attitudes. I remember in particular miners' leaders making it quite clear that they did not wish their sons to follow them down the pit but to get a better education; a nuanced contrast to the insistence by Arthur Scargill, who had no sons, of the right of miners to have jobs down the pits for their sons. Or steelworkers who lobbied me to visit their works to see the changes in productivity they had achieved.

This back-door, or back-bar, approach to information extended to the TUC itself. These were the last days of Vic Feather's term, and although Vic made a virtue of his affability, his press officer, the crusty Bob Hartwell, belonged to the school of 'tell them as little as possible' but would occasionally share useful nuggets with selected journalists.

As a result, the Bloomsbury hotels close to the TUC's Great Russell Street headquarters, bizarrely named after Walter Scott's novels,

Ivanhoe, Kenilworth etc., became the venues for pumping the members of the General Council who wished to make their point of view known – although almost always off the record.

We generally went along with it, keener to winkle out information than to expose our sources. It was a different approach from much of 21st-century journalism, where anyone's private comment appears fair game and ripe for exposure.

There were no formal rules of engagement, except when our caucus, the Industrial Correspondents Group, which had an official and regulated membership, held occasional briefing lunches with union leaders and politicians. Here, Chatham House rules, which prevented direct attribution or identification, generally applied. It was similar to the parliamentary lobby.

I recall once appearing on a BBC programme that examined relations between trade unions and the press and being asked what could be done to make unions better understood. My answer was 'to say publicly what you tell us in private'.

Another source of information, also much used with politicians, was lunching. Most union leaders would agree to be taken to lunch, usually at a good Soho restaurant, during which they would speak frankly about their concerns, once they had established a basis of trust with you and often, again, anonymity. It provided a good opportunity to understand their thinking and assess them. Today, when journalists rarely leave their offices at lunchtime, and entertainment is frowned on as a self-indulgent and possibly corrupt perk, my personal view is that this lack of human contact is an opportunity missed.

The other division was the one that applied to ourselves, between labour and industrial reporters. Broadly the trade unions and the Labour movement were covered by different reporters from those, mostly working for the financial pages, who wrote about the industries they worked in.

The divisions were not absolute. The tabloid papers tended to run the two roles together, but on the main broadsheets – *The Times*, *The Guardian*, the *Daily Telegraph* and even the *Financial Times* – there was separation. You could argue reasonably that the pressure of events meant it was a sensible division of effort, but it coloured the way issues were perceived. It encouraged management and labour to be seen in separate camps. This was heightened by the way that labour correspondents, because of the unions' crucial influence, were inevitably sucked into reporting Labour Party politics as much as business success and investment.

It was a relief and pleasure when I joined BBC TV in 1978 to be expected to cover both sides.

Initially, I had little to do with the CBI. That was the province of the industrial correspondents and they reported things through a different, and sometimes more respectful, prism. A key difference on the broadsheet papers was that they reported not to the paper's news editor but to the financial or City editor, who was not only in a separate department but sometimes physically removed in a separate office housed in closer proximity to the City of London and its financial institutions.

Although we shared information, and had particularly good personal relations with an old Manchester colleague, Vic Keegan, the *Guardian* industrial correspondent at the time, the different focus was apparent in the stories we wrote about some of the same issues.

On a broader spectrum, it made it difficult to bring together the debate about investment in industry. It was regarded by both sides as important – from the unions' view preserving jobs and industry and from management's side as a key to future profitability – but both sides blamed the other for obstructing it: the unions claimed that management were putting immediate profitability first; the management that industrial unrest and the unions' unwillingness to change their practices were ruining the climate for investment. After the monthly meeting of the tripartite National Economic Development Council (NEDC), the three sides – government, management and unions – would brief separately.

The other handicap to reporting was that we rarely visited the workplaces about whose conditions we were writing. Once again I found a benefit of working for television was the requirement to film at the places where the action was taking place and talk to the people there. In the 1970s, with film that still had to be laboriously processed and spliced, it could be a complicated business, but the advent of video (known as Electronic News Gathering, ENG, at the time) opened up the possibilities. I would find myself discussing the provisions of a Budget live as they were announced, on a car-factory assembly line or in a small-scale East End engineering works.

Too much of the reporting, however, was done at one remove. There were always meetings and policy developments to cover. In the summer there was a round of seaside conferences at which one union after another formed its own policies and fleshed out what it wanted from the TUC and Labour Party conferences in the autumn. We could, and perhaps should, have written a handbook on resorts, from the boarding houses of Bridlington, where each nylon sheet and pillow slip was a different colour, to the idiosyncratic delights of Blackpool, from the historic but quaint Imperial Hotel to the barrack we simply called Colditz. It was another bygone empire.

It would be fair to say that many of us benefited from our previous experience or upbringing outside London – an indication perhaps that there was sense in the NUJ's pressure for trainees to start in the provinces – but too often we were covering disputes and issues with limited understanding of life on the ground.

I remember a briefing on a dispute from the leader of the National Union of Blastfurnacemen, Ore Miners, Coke Workers and Kindred

Tradesmen (NUB) – the skilled workers who have the job of heating iron ore to unimaginable temperatures and then controlling it as it runs liquid from the furnaces. As he waxed verbose about the heat and discomfort of the job, the man from the *Daily Mirror* broke in: 'Stripped to the waist?' A gale of laughter followed – 'They would be burnt to a crisp!'

It must be said that there was little encouragement to visit places of work from business and industry. The National Coal Board was an exception. When I was chairman of the Industrial Correspondents Group I was met with some astonishment when I suggested to a very defensive British Steel that we could all benefit from a visit to one of their increasingly successful plants. In the end the visit went ahead and produced good coverage for them.

The CBI was the equivalent, only roughly speaking, to the TUC. In 1965, on my first day in journalism I went to an early-evening reception in Manchester to mark its founding by the merger of the old FBI, the Federation of British Industry, and two other employer bodies, the British Employers' Confederation and the National Association of British Manufacturers.

The obvious aim was to speak with one voice to the government, if not to the public. But deference was slow to die in British industry (dining rooms in company headquarters and factories were still segregated by rank) and over the years business leaders found the transition to public debate difficult. They remained uncomfortable about speaking in public where they were not protected from impertinent questions and given the respect to which they were accustomed.

But their inadequacy in public debate was being starkly laid bare in the tripartite discussions with the Heath government and the TUC that were taking place at the moment when I joined the Labour beat. While the TUC side, led by Vic Feather and including the determined and clear-minded Jack Jones, pressed their points hard, I was privately briefed by Bernard Ingham about the government's dismay to find the CBI leadership fighting their corner much less determinedly.

The CBI's weaknesses were recognised and eventually addressed by its Directors-General, first by John Methven and later by Terry (Sir Terence) Beckett, with the assistance of battle-hardened information directors like Keith McDowall, a former *Daily Mail* industrial correspondent, and John Dunkley, who had done a similar job for *The Guardian*. But the discomfort displayed by leading business people at the public interface was recurrent and remained palpable. I believe it was a major contributor to Britain's industrial decline.

Looking back, it is difficult to recreate the atmosphere of almost continual crisis of the 1970s, crises which seemed bound up with the fortunes and behaviour of the Labour movement. Whether it was the three-day week, with blackouts and power cuts, or the difficulty of dealing with household finances during an extraordinary rise in the inflation rate. This reached a now unimaginable 25 per cent before the intervention of the International Monetary Fund (IMF) and the signing of the social contract between the unions and the Labour government.

As labour and industrial correspondents, our reporting became a key part of the national drama. For a while, some said, we became more important than the political correspondents, such was the power of the unions in economic affairs and the Labour government's crucial relations with them. I think it was an exaggerated view but as each dispute or disagreement was flagged up as a challenge to this government policy or that, we found ourselves at the heart of Labour politics and rarely off the front page or the *Nine O'Clock News*.

In fact, I was so frequently in the cold and wet reporting outside winter negotiations that, to my huge amusement, the great Terry Wogan announced a new campaign on his morning radio show called SMASH – Send Martin Adeney Somewhere Hotter. Sadly it made little difference.

The Conservatives had an ambivalent relationship with us. While some, like the emollient Jim Prior, saw us as an important constituency to be brought on side or at least to have an understanding of his party's case, for others, such as Nigel Lawson, we were decidedly left-leaning and important to bypass.

While I would resist Lawson's view as far as it related to my own coverage, he had a point. At the time when I joined the industrial beat, I was myself a Labour councillor in Westminster, something *The Guardian* thought would do me no harm in terms of access. When I first went for a briefing with Len Murray, then about to become TUC General Secretary, he groaned out loud, 'Not another prospective Labour candidate!' Over the course of time, a number of the labour and industrial correspondents stood for Labour seats and at least one, John Tilley, was elected. The general presumption was that we were left of centre, and apparent Conservatives who joined our ranks, such as Roland Rudd, later the founder of a highly successful financial PR agency, risked ridicule until they proved themselves.

But the most concentrated and detailed attacks on our coverage and the assumptions behind it tended to come from the left, the most celebrated being from the Glasgow Media Group, which targeted television news coverage in three studies: Bad News, More Bad News and Really Bad News.

The drift of their criticism was that we accepted the establishment formulations that it was workers and strikes that caused the problems of the British economy, that strike action was automatically bad and that representatives of the workers and the unions were given less time and sympathetic treatment than management employees.

Their original critique predated my time at the BBC and we understood the drift of some of the criticism, but our general experience was that management was so reluctant to step up to the plate that we heard far less from them than from trade unions spokespeople.

A telling flavour of this approach was the criticism directed at me personally after a debate with Arthur Scargill about coverage of the 1984–85 Coal Strike at the Edinburgh Television Festival. I had shown video clips, including one of trucks transporting coal into a steelworks being picketed by miners. I described it as 'a successful run', meaning that the drivers had succeeded in their objective, but my comment was taken to mean that I supported the operation.

So, with that as background, what did we have to report?

The 1971 Industrial Relations Act overshadowed everything. Both government and the unions had had a big fright over the Pentonville Five in the summer of 1972 and there had been immense relief at the successful advent of the official solicitor to get the men out of jail, not just among the government but also among the TUC, which had committed itself to a one-day general strike.

Now both sides were drawing breath and looking for some accommodation. As the government brought forward approaches that would draw the unions into tripartite talks on economic policy (something welcomed by even such a committed left-winger as Jack Jones), there was concern that some unlooked-for incident, most likely unofficial action, might drag both sides back to the cliff edge.

The government were at pains to emphasise how remote the chances were of further imprisonment of individuals for flouting the statutory pay policy. With a briefing from Bernard Ingham at the Department of Employment, I wrote a lengthy piece – 'Obstacle Course to Martyrdom' – setting out the many different legal proceedings and consents, eight or so 'gates' that would have to be passed through before individual trade unionists would confront 'the studded doors of one of HM prisons'.

The government had set up a new Industrial Relations Court headed by Sir John Donaldson, who later became Master of the Rolls, one of the most senior judicial appointments. He set out to make it a model of clarity. It was housed in one of the more modern parts of the gothic law courts on the Strand. There was no flummery. Donaldson wore a suit and no wig. His judgments were made in clear language and transcripts – manna to the time-pressed journalist – were promptly available. He must have suspected that it would not last, but if there was to be judicial regulation of industrial relations, his court did his best to make it seem fair and contemporary.

Not that that cut any ice with those determined to have no truck with the law. The AUEW's refusal in principle to have anything to do with the Act saw it inexorably passing through one after another of the government's 'gates' so that a comparatively small local dispute processed stage by stage to the point where the union's refusal to rec- ognise the court and comply with its demands led to the seizing, or, to give it the proper word, 'sequestration' of its financial assets. The union maintained its unyielding position to the end. Only when the fine imposed was paid by an anonymous donor after the 1974 elec- tion were the union's resources eventually freed.

The issue that precipitated the demise of the Heath government, however, was wages. At the end of 1972, with the failure of the tri- partite talks, the government announced a ninety-day freeze on wages, prices, dividends and rents and a statutory incomes policy from January 1973.

This marked the beginning of years when pay policies, whether it was statutory norms, government guidelines or agreed percentages under the social contract, became the currency and taskmasters of our reporting. Every year there would be a debate about whether there should be a norm, what the figures should be and how it should be policed. Battle would be joined at the TUC Congress debates in the first week in September, after which the ritual progress of the wage round would test the durability of the proposed figure.

It was a commonplace among industrial correspondents, and an article of belief on the left, that wages were the key persuader to bring people out on strike. Working conditions and redundancies might influence the atmosphere but when the chips were down, it was wages that mattered.

As the national impact of those decisions was raised, the question of how they were reached became a matter of growing interest and political debate. Wage negotiations would take place at a national or local level. Whatever agreement was reached or was not would then be reported back to union branches in factories or other places of work and decisions made accordingly.

Different unions and sometimes different branches used different ways of reporting and coming to a decision. Sometimes it was just branch members, with the vote of each branch, arrived at in a variety of ways, being totted up. The most democratic procedure was the mineworkers', with a secret ballot held at the pithead and counting supervised by the Electoral Reform Society. There were jokes that in the past there had sometimes been two ballot boxes for the secret vote – one for yeses and one for noes – but there was no challenge to current arrangements.

The big bone of contention was mass meetings, a particular favourite of the motor factories. Here the form was for workers to assemble in a big, usually outdoor area, a field or a sports ground; for shop stewards on a platform with a microphone to spell out their interpretation of an offer and propose a motion, sometimes with a speech from a national official and then voting by show of hands, judged by the officials on the platform.

Press were often excluded. I recall being hustled away from the walls of the open-air swimming pool where Ford Dagenham workers were holding their meeting. There was no independent check on the numbers involved or the way the vote was judged.

As for negotiations, I must have spent years of my life waiting outside what were still then smoke-filled rooms. When I moved on after seventeen years I found myself writing, not entirely tongue in cheek:

> I am still left with unsolved questions – what actually does go on
> in these sessions? Why does it take so long before it is announced
> that not even full and frank discussions, just plain old boring
> talks, have taken place and that the trains or the water or the
> car production lines will or won't run?

I was once in a group sitting round a TV set in the press office of the TUC at Congress House. It was near midnight and the railway unions had been battering away all day above us. Suddenly the tousled head of a union president poked round the door, exclaiming with delight at the sight of the telly.

Starved of information, we pounced on him with delight. 'Oh, we are not involved,' he said. 'The General Secretary has occasionally been called out to meet the conciliators with a proposal or counter-proposal. But I am fed up. We have read all the papers. We have finished yarning about old times, and we've nothing to do.' He settled with relief in front of the television.

After the 1984–85 miners' strike, which included a prolonged series of talks in the autumn of 1984, I asked one senior TUC official how they had managed to have so many meetings without making a decision. 'Don't you understand?' he replied. 'That was the whole point; we had to *avoid* making a decision.'

I enjoyed a story from Ireland about a minister who had called in unions and reached a settlement within a few minutes, but then held them back for hours with his hospitality with the remark, 'You can't go yet; they will think we haven't considered it properly.'

Small wonder that negotiators developed their own devices to pass the time. One steel industry manager tracked malapropisms during talks. There was the man who insisted, 'I have only got two pairs of hands'; the negotiator who said 'never mind the long-term, what will we get in the intimate period?'; or the shop steward who complained that the walls of a messroom were 'dripping with condescension'. Perhaps they were.

And it was not just the management who sought means of enlivening enervating proceedings. In the middle of nitty-gritty Ford negotiations about allowances, a sudden rapping was heard from under the table and a quavering voice cried out: 'What about death benefit?' It was Reg Birch, a mischievous Maoist, who led the motor negotiations for the Engineering Union and was a shrewd observer of his fellow negotiators' foibles.

I had my own brief experience of the stately pace of talks while I was at the BBC. The dispute was about pay differentials and how much correspondents might be paid because of their expertise. Amazingly, the BBC had its own pay relativities unit – a sign of the bureaucratic importance industrial relations had achieved – and we had pleaded our case unsuccessfully to them at a hearing in Cavendish Square. Now we had arrived at ACAS, the government-appointed conciliation service in St James's Square in central London.

They followed an established pattern. Both sides in separate rooms, with officials shuttling from one to the other with proposals or responses from each side. But the first question that confronted us, at about eleven o'clock, was whether we would be staying long enough to require sandwiches for lunch.

In big industrial negotiations, as, for example, in the car industry, the delegates or shop stewards might wait for hours in a room while their negotiators met management separately. This shuttle could be manipulated to produce unexpected results. Moss Evans, who was the Transport Union's lead negotiator for the motor industry before becoming General Secretary, liked to tell a tale of pay talks for a group of engineering workers in a smaller enterprise.

He persuaded the employers to offer an extra sixpence and then went into the room where his members were. They received it with delight but he advised them not to accept it immediately and then went back to the employers with the news that his members had found it quite unacceptable, so securing a larger rise.

With deadlines approaching, and little information, it was bad enough trying to decide what to tell the reader or viewer. Long sessions could either mean that things were very difficult or be interpreted as a sign of hope that the two sides were still together. Often the long wait came down to a dispute over wording.

Then the statements that followed were usually deliberately obscure and often misleading. You had to know the shorthand. A recommendation to accept was what it said. So, apparently, was a recommendation to reject. But it probably meant 'go back and try for a better offer'. Opening offers were not usually accepted.

A recommendation to 'reject and consider industrial action' was a stronger steer but on some occasions was intended to do no more than test the water and sometimes even to scare people into acceptance. 'No recommendation' usually meant that the negotiators did not want the opprobrium of making a deal but expected the membership to do so. And when it came to strike action it was the proposed timing that was important. The farther away the date, the greater the indication that a settlement was being looked for

Industrial correspondents had to become adept at knowing to which pubs the participants had adjourned and finding out what had really happened. Over the years the miners' executive must have kept a string of breweries afloat, and they produced some splendid information before much later a canny Arthur Scargill prolonged executive meetings beyond lunchtime opening hours.

One of the catchphrases of the times was 'smoke-filled rooms'. Cigarette smoking was ubiquitous and after a negotiation had taken place and a door opened it was common to see a cloud of blue smoke billowing out. We even filmed the ashtrays full of cigarette butts. It was the source of jokes but at the time there was little comment on its effect on health.

What was much more obvious was the effect of drink in public life, which I believe has been routinely underplayed. It was not, of course, confined to trade union negotiators; Parliament was notorious for the use MPs made of its bars and *Private Eye*'s nickname for a journalist, Lunchtime O'Booze, was based on many examples. But the waiting around, and the need for lengthy rounds of negotiations, encouraged heavy drinking which could turn to incoherence and alcoholism.

We all knew who it affected. While workers in heavy industry like miners or shipyard workers were accustomed to hard drinking – the Scottish miners' leaders would chase their pints down with drams of Scotch and the invitation to their conference dinner would be 5.30 for 8.00 p.m. – there were casualties along the way. The saddest was the eloquent and well-read Lawrence Daly, an articulate and charming man with a powerful grasp of Labour history, who was one of the very few who could and did demolish Arthur Scargill in public debate. After being a respected secretary of the Scottish Miners, he became a briefly effective General Secretary of the NUM and delivered a masterful performance in presenting the NUM's evidence to the Wilberforce Committee, which resolved the 1972 miners' strike. But drink took its toll in spite of attempts to dry out. He ended pathetically ineffective and disregarded by those around him.

By contrast, Arthur Scargill rarely took a public drink, and rode the jokes about his meanness in buying a round. If he did take a drink, and I think he only accepted one from me once, it was only a half-pint. He valued a clear head.

The availability of drink could even be a tactic. On the one hand you heard complaints about long meetings where you could not even get a drink. The Department of Employment had a policy of deliberately waiting before they sent in refreshments and then always preceding drink with food. On the other, there was an occasion when the financier Jimmy Goldsmith, bidding to buy the Express Group, arranged a meeting with the printing unions. He left them for two hours with a full trolley of drinks, after which few of them were in a condition to negotiate anything.

In many ways, their conduct of relations with labour and industrial correspondents was a luxurious situation for the unions. They complained regularly and bitterly about how they were reported, but they could make public statements that said one thing and then, off the record, explain what they really thought without fear of being directly recorded or quoted. In Mrs Thatcher's first term, the lack of public candour to which union leaders had grown used prevented them working out the implications of a Tory victory, with disastrous consequences, as they maintained it was simply a temporary blip.

But, in 1972, this was some way ahead. The Heath government's great enterprise came to grief, although not by much, when its attempt to regulate down to the finest detail came unstuck with the 1974 miners' strike. My colleague Keith Harper was abroad for much of it on a *Guardian* cricket tour to India, so I bore the burden of the coverage.

Looking back, the most striking thing about it was that success was achieved without the mass picketing that was such a feature of the dispute ten years later. Under the leadership of the wily but personable Joe Gormley, the NUM struck deals with the very unions it would fail to bring on side in 1984, particularly the power station workers. Trains stopped and lorries turned back at token pickets with the agreement of their unions.

The dispute also demonstrated the power of the accidental. The miners had voted to seek a huge increase, with little expectation that they would get close to it, and certainly not with the intention of bringing down the government. In the event, a few even received more than they had asked for.

In an article for *The Guardian*, entitled 'How the miners led Heath on a road to ruin', I detailed the mistakes and misjudgements as government rigidity consistently plucked defeat from obvious compromise and the Labour Party and the TUC went to unprecedented lengths to secure a deal.

At one extraordinary and never-to-be-repeated juncture, the TUC, much to the displeasure of the left, even offered to make the miners an exception to what was now Stage Three of the pay policy, proposing that their settlement should not set a precedent for any other group of workers. At another, a possible deal allowing miners payment over the odds for the time they spent waiting for the lift and then being wound down the shaft was blown apart when the Labour leader, Harold Wilson, got wind of it and blurted it out in the House of Commons as if it was his own idea. No political opponent could accept that.

Finally, the much-trumpeted Relativities Board, specifically designed as a safety valve to relieve the pressure of a rigid scheme, emerged late, and when it did so, produced a painstakingly argued but derisory pay award.

The fascination of covering the twists and turns, with the edge of suspense that only the best unfolding news stories have, of genuinely not knowing what will happen next, was heightened by the dramatic surroundings.

The three-day week, when factories had to close to conserve electricity supplies still so dependent on diminishing coal stocks. The darkness in streets and shops, let alone your own home, when power was cut off unexpectedly. In politics, the endless to and fro-ing. The Energy Secretary, who exhorted us all to brush our teeth in the dark and then kept all the lights in his house on, two streets away from us, inevitably to be photographed for the front pages of the Sunday papers.

Then the sudden recall of Willie Whitelaw, the supposedly emollient fixer, from his apparent success in improving the situation in Northern Ireland, to the key post of Employment Secretary, racked up the melodrama. Particularly when at his much-heralded first meeting with the miners at his department, the lights did indeed go out. The meeting, to our delight, transferred to an Italian restaurant across the road, where the two sides talked under candlelight, and we pressed against the windows.

And so to the first of the 1974 elections, called unexpectedly on a 'who governs Britain?' argument. A turning point, it seems now, but its result nail-bitingly narrow and not easily predictable.

I spent part of it, shared with the now-returned Keith, with the task of following Harold Wilson, the Labour leader, as he travelled, or more often, it seemed, trailed, around the country. He would make two or three speeches a night to big gatherings in different public halls, always slightly different but containing a common central passage which would have been fed earlier to political journalists in London for the following day's story. To accommodate his schedule, he would usually arrive part-way through an election rally already in progress which would then pause for his speech.

Truth to tell, he did not look like a winner, more like a dead man walking, as he trudged into yet another town hall. The old Wilson zest and sharp humour was not much in evidence as he delivered his lengthy lines with little sign of what later generations would christen a sound bite.

With him came an entourage. It was led by a man seconded from the *Daily Mirror*, which traditionally put resources at the Labour

Party's disposal. His name was Alf Richmond and his job was to make sure that Harold got to the rostrum and all attention was turned on him. I still remember a night at Preston Town Hall when, with Harold a few paces behind, Alf marched up to the rostrum and switched off the mic, cutting off the long-forgotten warm-up speaker in full flow. It did not put the audience in the best frame of mind for the leader's speech.

Sleepwalking or not, Wilson won the most seats at the election, although without an outright majority. He became Prime Minister with tacit support from the Liberals. Heath had clung to office for a while, but it was clear his great experiment with its complex regulatory structures and a logic that appealed to civil servants like the head of the service, Sir William Armstrong, had been rejected. Now Labour would have to find something different to deal with galloping inflation. It would do so in cooperation with the trade unions. The time to test a social contract had arrived. Trade unions would be at the centre of the political stage.

Chapter Eleven

The rise and fall of the social contract

One of Harold Wilson's first actions on assuming office in 1974 was to appoint Michael Foot, the guardian of the left-wing conscience in Parliament and a man who had never held ministerial office, as the Secretary of State for Employment. His first job was to settle the mineworkers' dispute.

We were introduced to him at a briefing at the department. In answer to questions, he set out his ideas for a settlement. When I asked him, 'Doesn't that mean effectively meeting all the miners' demands?', he smiled, 'Would that be such a bad thing?'

It was a clear enough signal of how times had changed. Over the next five years, until Jim Callaghan was forced by the electoral calendar to call an election, the trade unions reached an unparalleled peak of influence, increasingly involved in almost every aspect of government. As annual inflation surged to almost 25 per cent, their yearly pact with the government, which came to be called the social contract, determined the country's economic fortunes almost as much as the escalating price of oil.

I started the period on *The Guardian*, before moving in 1977 for a more senior job as the industrial correspondent of the *Sunday Telegraph*. It was an eventful year in which my stories made the front-page lead for about half of the fifty-two weeks: a graphic indication of how labour and industry dominated the news. Then, in 1978, in the wake of criticism of the BBC's coverage of industry, I became the labour correspondent of BBC Television News, an extra post created after the Annan Committee on broadcasting had complained that 'broadcasters do not represent adequately the industrial and commercial life of the country'.

With no overall majority in Parliament, Labour had to govern with the consent of smaller parties. It led to another election later in the year, in October, in which it obtained a slender overall majority.

The new administration faced growing difficulty as the economy struggled under the impact of the 1973 oil shock. Following the Arab–Israeli Yom Kippur War, oil prices tripled as the Arab-dominated Organization of the Petroleum Exporting Countries (OPEC) finally started to work together and forced price increases. Serious unemployment was still a relatively recent phenomenon, but was rising remorselessly. Key industries were collapsing and repeal of the Industrial Relations Act and calming of industrial unrest were priorities for the first days of the new government.

In opposition, Labour had formed a liaison committee with the trade unions to agree policies. The unions, with the assertive Jack Jones to the fore, were pressing for a social contract. A series of agreed measures were pushed through, setting the tone for an administration in which unions came to expect that their influence would steadily be extended.

In the few short months before the autumn election, a tripartite Health and Safety Executive was established as part of a new Health and Safety at Work Act, a long-time union priority. With the help of the smaller parties, the Industrial Relations Act was scrapped, and a new Conciliation and Advisory Service to help resolve industrial disputes, a long-term Jones ambition, and another union priority, was created. Both the new institutions have survived as an accepted and embedded part of the industrial landscape.

There remained the question of incomes policy. Harold Wilson put it bluntly to the TUC that, even after the election, there remained a majority in the House of Commons for statutory restraint on prices and incomes. Inflation almost doubled in 1974, to 16 per cent, reaching nearly 25 per cent in 1975. Prices went up by 17 per cent; wages by 25 per cent. With the help of the social contract and later a fiercely argued initiative by Jones for a universal flat rate increase, it fell to as relatively little as 8.3 per cent by 1978, Labour's last year. But by then union opinion had swung against agreed wage restraint and the Winter of Discontent followed. Significantly, Jack Jones had retired. It opened the way for Margaret Thatcher.

Knife-edge negotiations and individual union votes over pay became the stuff of our reporting and the government's concerns. It reached its most dramatic moment with Chancellor Denis Healey's belligerent appearance at the 1976 Labour Party conference justifying his decision to seek a loan from the IMF.

But, increasingly, our attention was being drawn to the gloomy background music from crises in the workplace; the remorseless rise in unemployment and the troubles of British industry, as industrial empires started to follow the path of imperial decline.

Like the rest of my generation, of all classes, I had been brought up to believe the persistent imperial mantra that British was best. We handled articles stamped 'Made in England' with confidence: a sign, we knew, of quality. Ships from British shipyards were a particular source of pride, especially if you lived in Southampton, while the different marques of British motor cars were endlessly fascinating – and admired. The problem was that after the immediate post-war years when British manufacturing capability had overshadowed countries far more devastated by war, other countries started to catch up. It was not just that their modern machinery had surpassed ours. There was also their outlook.

As became excruciatingly clear to me when I came to write a history of the British motor car industry, the 'British is best' feeling prevented management from realising the extent and sophistication of their foreign competitors until it was too late for most of them. 1976 would be the year in which, for the first time in half a century, the numbers of cars imported into Britain would exceed those we exported abroad.

The troubles of the famous names of British industry had already shown up graphically during the Heath government. The Rolls-Royce company, the symbol of excellence, now overwhelmingly concerned with building aero-engines, had run out of money in developing what would become the hugely successful RB-211 family of engines. Faced in 1971 with the collapse of what really was a world-beater, although badly managed, the government, much against its will, had nationalised the company. Its recovery was slow and painful but became one of the few success stories when it was privatised in 1987.

There would be no such happy ending with the shipbuilding industry, which in imperial days, when Britain really did rule the waves, and immediately after the war, had built far more ships than anyone else. Here the reality of Britain's decaying position had been highlighted under the Heath government by dramatic events on the Clyde. Upper Clyde Shipbuilders, a grouping of four yards patched together by the previous Labour government in an earlier attempt to modernise, had run out of money, although it had a full order-book.

The government refused it more capital. But workers, inspired by a charismatic group of left-wing shop stewards, had staged an imaginative response; an effective political coup. They mounted a work-in, continuing to build the ships in the yards.

The Heath government made a famous U-turn and implemented another restructuring. Today just a little survives. One yard, Govan, has continued to operate, through a series of different ownerships. But the others are long gone. They include the most celebrated. The John Brown yard at Clydebank, which had built the Queens, was sold to an American oil-rig constructor and later closed.

Restructuring had been a short-term fix and the problems of the shipyards still remained. A gallimaufry of unions representing different trades made everything more complex and led to demarcation disputes. The yards, which relied on the traditional method of working in the open and sliding half-completed vessels down the bank into the river, were increasingly outdated in comparison with the new facilities being built particularly in Japan and Korea. There ships were mostly constructed under cover in dry docks with a high degree of prefabrication. British firms had not invested sufficiently.

The government's favoured solution to the problems of shipbuilding would be nationalisation, but time was against it.

The plight of what had been christened 'lame duck' industries would come to preoccupy the government and its Conservative successor under Mrs Thatcher. Now, with Tony Benn as Industry Minister, a White Paper on 'The Regeneration of British Industry' was quickly followed by an Industry Act, which established a new body, the National Enterprise Board (NEB). It was supposed to be forward-looking, to provide funds for industrial investment and to promote rationalisation to make particular industries more effective. It would establish a company, Inmos, as a UK producer of the silicon chips that were driving the computer revolution, a reasonable, if laggardly, success. But its energies were increasingly drained by the demands of the lame ducks which it sheltered. They included Alfred Herbert, the maker of the machine tools fundamental to the engineering industry, and the electronics company Ferranti.

But the lamest of all the lame ducks were to be found in the fabled British motor industry. As one chief executive, John Egan of Jaguar, put it to me, 'By the '70s, the standard performance for a British car company was to do badly and go out of business.'

The industry, for which I had turned out the first pressings in the Birmingham factory, was heavily centred on the Midlands. Because of its spread and complexity, we tended to leave much of its coverage to local specialists – the BBC had a Midlands industrial correspondent and *The Guardian* looked to its northern industrial correspondent, the diligent Geoff Whiteley, who was based in Manchester.

Our involvement with the industry, except when things got so bad they precipitated a national crisis, tended to centre on Ford. Its largest plant was at Dagenham in the East End of London and its national bargaining procedures brought together representatives of its plants all over Britain to offices above a garage in Bayswater. Because of their industrial strength, and early settlement date, the Ford unions' negotiations became a key benchmark and an annual trial of strength in the wage round. With the company's international spread, it could also serve as an uncomfortable marker of the difference between British and continental plants, with Ford's comparable mainland European plants consistently turning out more cars per day.

Even so, where Leyland floundered, Ford, assisted by its international focus, was increasingly successful. By 1988 I found myself writing in my motor history, 'Thank God for Ford, but God save the Rover Group', Leyland's latest manifestation.

Leyland forced itself on our attention. I was at one of those union seaside conferences when news was brought by Mick Costello of

the *Morning Star*. He had heard through one of his shop floor contacts that British Leyland was in trouble. Managers were supposedly
scouring the plants to reduce costs and cutting back their stocks
of materials. The biggest British motor manufacturer, the product of
that shotgun, poorly consummated marriage between British Motor
Holdings and the truck and bus maker Leyland Motors under a previous Labour government, was in trouble. It needed new capital.

The government panicked and sent in the NEB chairman, the former chairman of the Mirror newspaper group, Lord Ryder, to plan
its future. The Ryder Report proposed major rationalisation, colos-
sal government investment and layers of committees. It was poorly
thought through, badly implemented and its ensuing failure would
occupy us for years.

A plan was certainly needed. The company was an agglomera-
tion of many of the most famous names in the British industry. The
two biggest empires, Austin, founded by Herbert Austin and based
in Birmingham, and Morris, founded by William Morris, later Lord
Nuffield, in Oxford, had joined together in 1952. As they had failed
or faltered, names like Riley and Wolseley had disappeared into the
larger companies. Jaguar was absorbed in 1966 and Leyland brought
in the Rover, Standard and Triumph marques in 1968. Meanwhile,
the smaller Rootes group, founded by Lord Rootes, marketed its cars
under the names of Hillman, Humber, Singer and Sunbeam-Talbot.

The failures to rationalise as one faltering firm after another was
taken under the Leyland wing had come home to roost. The old
Austin and Morris empires were still producing rival and increasingly unsuccessful cars to satisfy separate dealer networks. The
Midlands tradition of piecework, where each job had its price and
wages depended on the quantity turned out, contrasted with the
more predictable Ford system of measured daywork. At a time of
hyper-inflation, it was a disaster, leading to endless renegotiations

while its complexity discouraged moves to modernise or introduce new models.

In addition, labour relations in the plants were dreadful and highly politicised. One of the sanest observers and a key participant was David Buckle, the District Secretary of the Transport Union in Oxford, himself a former worker at Cowley. Buckle had no time for the old management, criticising working conditions, denial of employee rights and failure to invest sufficiently. But he was critical of the militant extremes.

His verdict on the serial unrest was that the vast majority of car workers had nothing to do with it. They were caught between 'bad management and politically motivated extremists as shop stewards'.[3] Buckle would relate how he asked one left-wing shop steward how it could make sense to put in for massive wage increases which they knew they could not win. He was told 'the working classes have to go down to one defeat after another until they learn the only way to change is by revolution'.[4]

The Ryder plan was a rushed job, poorly thought through, neither good management nor realistic industrial relations. It paid lip-service to current management and trade union fashions, lumping different forms of car manufacture together so that, for instance, the Jaguar assembly plant in Coventry became 'Large/Specialist Vehicle Operations' and setting up an elaborate system of councils and committees to bring workers and managers together in endless discussions on the running of the company.

But, to the despair of its personnel managers, it laid no requirements on the labour force. Instead it did worse, enshrining the

---

3   David Buckle, *Turbulent Times in the Car Industry* (2011), p. 47

4   Martin Adeney, *The Motor Makers: The Turbulent History of Britain's Car Industry* (Collins, 1989), p. 265

government in its management with the stipulation that payment of each stage of what would eventually turn out to be government support of £1.4 billion would be dependent on evidence 'that some tangible contribution is being made both by BL's workforce and its management to the reduction of disputes and the improvement of productivity'.

Perhaps worst of all, its projections were based on an optimistic view of market prospects when the company's market share was visibly shrinking.

One reason was the increase in imports, particularly of Japanese cars, often more reliable and equipped as standard with extras like radios, which motorists wanted but British manufacturers charged for. In 1977, there was the humiliating sight of a delegation of British manufacturers arriving in Tokyo to ask the Japanese for a voluntary ceiling on their imports into Britain. It was called 'prudent marketing' and worked out at about 11 per cent of cars sold in Britain.

The Japanese were also showing up the deficiencies of other industries. The television tube industry, making the prime component of TV sets, had collapsed with thousands of redundancies. Another voluntary agreement was reached with the Japanese, this time restricting the import of black-and-white televisions. But Japanese companies were setting up to manufacture in Britain and I found myself being lobbied by the British industry against the application by Hitachi to build a factory.

We were taken to an efficient British factory on a new industrial estate at Washington in the north-east. My impressions there were balanced by an experience a couple of years later in Plymouth where the unstoppable Japanese, in this case Toshiba, had effectively taken over the Rank factory in a joint venture. As I spoke to workers on the line, they provided some clues to the Japanese success. An attention to detail and consistency that meant, for example, the end of the old practice of speeding up at the end of the day to meet targets. Instead, the flow remained steady. And, one employee explained, senior managers would no longer take people off the line to help them recover their escaped horses. Recent international studies have demonstrated that it is the regular operation of a production line that is more important than its speed.

Ironically, by resisting the arrival of Japanese factories, the British companies were discouraging what would turn out to be the salvation of British manufacturing: efficient and well run, if foreign-owned, plants. A few years later, the first Japanese car plant, Nissan, would be built close to the television factory we had been invited to visit.

The report of the Ryder committee, whose deputy chairman was Jack Jones's deputy, proposing its wealth of joint committees, showed just how far union, or shop-floor, influence was becoming embedded in the institutions of industry and beyond.

To coincide with the 1976 TUC Congress, I wrote a series of articles querying how well-equipped the union movement was for the new responsibilities. It serves as a handy summary of the extent, real and potential, of the drive for union involvement at that moment.

Under a blunt headline, 'The unions have the brawn but where are the brains?', I wrote:

> It has become a commonplace of British politics that the trades unions have assumed over the last two years more responsibilities than ever before. Not only do they negotiate with government over wage levels and now tax levels but they also argue across the whole field of economic and social management.
>
> At the workplace, a torrent of new and still not completely digested legislation – the Trade Union and Labour Relations Act, the Employment Act, the new Health and Safety legislation – has enormously expanded the duties and the scope of involvement

of union representatives in industry. By the end of this year a quarter of a million trade unionists are expected to be formally appointed as safety representatives throughout industry.

In the melting pot at this minute is a new code for industry suggesting far wider disclosures of information to unions; the prospect of the first planning agreements which require union agreement with management, and of course the whole range of proposals for widening industrial democracy, from giving workers half the places on companies' top-tier boards (which the TUC wants) to employers' more favoured proposals for consultative machinery.

The growing question is whether trades unionists are going to have the necessary back-up in terms of training, information and analysis to carry out the huge responsibilities they have persuaded the government to thrust upon them.

Among the examples I gave was of the Transport Union, Britain's biggest, with just seven research officers – one for every 180,000 of its members. But I also pointed out how trade unions were beginning to pull in help from academia. Jack Jones had approached John Hughes, the head of Ruskin College, the Oxford trade union college, to prepare detailed materials to back up wage claims for the important Ford and ICI negotiations, a development duly noted by the Sunday business pages.

The high watermark of successful union aspiration came with the publication of the Bullock Report into industrial democracy. A mixed bag of government-appointed businessmen and trade unionists under the chairmanship of the academic Lord Bullock had pondered the introduction of employee representatives onto company boards. They rejected TUC proposals for the two-tier board system common in Europe where employee representatives had half the seats on a

Supervisory Board but proposed that a third of the seats on existing boards should go to employees.

The proposals were stillborn. There was a dissenting report by the business representatives who made up three of the ten members and it was too close to the general election for controversial legislation. Significantly, there was also fierce opposition from the left of the trade union movement to anything less than a fifty / fifty split, while others went further, attacking the whole concept as 'giving capitalism a blood transfusion'. At the other end of the spectrum, in a private briefing with the International Crisis Group (ICG), the Chancellor, Denis Healey, by coincidence a former schoolmate of Lord Bullock, described the report by the Latin word for 'bollocks'.

Healey's brutal disdain may have had something to do with the fact that it was by now becoming obvious that the social contract would not hold. As the bruising experience of prices and incomes policies over the previous decade had shown, even when accepted, they could not be maintained for more than two or three years, and when, in the phrase of the time, 'the dam burst', pent-up demand resulted in a huge spike in wages.

The ensuing flood engulfed the Labour government, and the country with it, in the turmoil of the Winter of Discontent. By 1977, the TUC was not only unable to deliver another year of an agreed formula for wage increases, it was struggling to agree on its fall-back proposition that unions should not pour in an immediate torrent of claims but instead wait for twelve months before making fresh demands; a convention previously unchallenged.

As the leaders of the movement gathered for the 1977 TUC Congress, I wrote:

> The certainties of a decade are being challenged. The question is
> whether the break with the government over agreed pay policies

plus the evident dislike of many trades unionists for governmental links which are seen as too smothering, will further loosen the cosy TUC–government embrace.

Will this mark a halt to the steady post-war advance of the trades unions into the heart of the country's economic management – an end in fact to all that has followed from their participation in the National Economic Development Council in the days when Selwyn Lloyd was Chancellor?

Generally the answer from senior trades unionists is that 'no one retreats voluntarily from the corridors of power'; and yet at the same time there are striking signs of discontent with a too-close involvement in decision-making and signs of a hankering for a return to the traditional defensive 'adversary' role.

That role would become only too apparent over the remainder of Labour's term. The government imposed its own wage guidelines – a limit of what now seems an extraordinarily generous 10 per cent annual increase. It was soon tested. A few days after the TUC Congress, I was searching for a story to write. I picked the forthcoming Ford negotiations, where the unions were seeking 15 per cent plus and looking to set down a marker for the private sector. I got little help from my Ford contacts but deduced that the company's first offer would be just a little less than the 10 per cent guideline.

To my surprise, the paper chose to lead on the story, which turned out to be accurate. On the Monday morning, a group of workers at Dagenham walked out in protest because they believed that I had been briefed by the company in advance of the talks. I think it was the only time in my career that I can point to any tangible, if short-lived, consequence of my reporting.

In the event the company settled for about 12 per cent and the government backed away from the sanction of cancelling its orders for government vehicles. It was against this background that, in the spring of 1978, I joined BBC Television News as its labour correspondent, working almost interchangeably with Ian Ross, its respected industrial correspondent.

The stresses of pay demands on the government were now the stuff of politics. I won some early brownie points when I explained at an internal meeting, to general amazement, that the miners had no appetite for strike action because of the increases they had already received as well as the large sums they were earning because of new productivity agreements, shrewdly negotiated by the resourceful Joe Gormley.

The decision of the Prime Minister, Jim Callaghan, not to call an election later that year was a turning point. Before his speech to the TUC there was huge speculation about whether he would do so. But, in spite of clear signals of trouble ahead, with the TUC demanding a return to free collective bargaining, he decided to soldier on. The government tried to impose a disastrous 5 per cent norm for the public sector workers whom it effectively employed, which it hoped would act as a guideline for the private sector.

This time Ford workers came out on a sustained strike and at the start of 1979 lorry drivers, followed by local authority and health workers, started to take action in what became known as the Winter of Discontent. A million workers were put on short time as a result of the drivers' dispute even though the most graphic warnings of business people about bringing plants to standstill were not borne out by events. Businesses had warned of factories being closed within a week or two. We went back to test their predictions and found them largely still operating, if on a reduced basis.

But the shortages and difficulties resulting from lack of deliveries were then compounded by the erratic consequences of the public sector workers on strike. A key decision of the principal union involved, the National Union of Public Employees (NUPE), was to devolve decisions on action to its local branches. In various places, gravediggers went on strike, caretakers refused to open schools, admissions to half the country's hospitals were affected and everywhere uncollected rubbish piled up. The misery was compounded by particularly cold and icy winter weather.

The decision to leave matters to local decision had another consequence. National union leaders could often explain to industrial correspondents what they really thought without fear of being directly recorded or quoted. But in these disputes, when they passed responsibility for action to local officials who had little experience in dealing with the media, the unions were shocked and embarrassed when their words were recorded and taken down at face value.

As Jack Jones wrote ruefully in his autobiography about polls that had shown public distrust of the unions, 'Maybe it was our own fault in not explaining our role to the public over the years. All too often trade union officials, when asked questions about strikes or difficult industrial situations, have said "No comment" or even worse, "It's none of your business."'[5] I could recognise that.

In this case, words and actions at local level coloured people's impressions of the strikes in spite of a very active media campaign by NUPE nationally. After a lunchtime report of one demonstration outside a school by frustrated parents demanding its reopening by caretakers, the union head office telephoned the BBC TV news desk to complain about bias.

The TUC Congress that year was full of bitterness about media coverage with Alan Fisher, the insouciant NUPE General Secretary, making a particularly aggressive attack on journalists allegedly creeping round graveyards to find stories with which to attack his low-paid members. The usual industrial correspondent reply to the traditional

5   Jack Jones, *Union Man* (Collins, 1986), p. 229

vote of thanks to the press at the end of the Congress with a few decent jokes and self-deprecatory remarks about press coverage seemed distinctly inadequate.

But, by then, the game had moved on. There was a new government, elected in part as a consequence of the Winter of Discontent, with a manifesto commitment to rewrite the terms of union involvement.

On the morning of the announcement, the great and good of the TUC were gathered at Tenby in south Wales where the Wales TUC was holding its Congress. The BBC had a helicopter standing by to fly me back to Cardiff to edit the piece, so important did their reaction seem.

My task was to interview them and to ask what seemed to all of us the essential question. Would they do business with the newly elected Conservative government? The answer, with a few expected qualifications, was yes.

But it was the wrong question. It should have been: 'What will you do if Mrs Thatcher decides not to do business with *you*?'

Chapter Twelve

Thatcher and all that

I was sitting in 10 Downing Street in an armchair in Bernard Ingham's office. An antique clock ticked on the mantelpiece. Opposite sat the Prime Minister, Margaret Thatcher. Courtesy itself. When I explained that we would be going live into the BBC2 News, she ventured that she often watched it and said how much she liked it. 'It is at twenty-past seven, isn't it.' 'No, Prime Minister, tonight it is at ten-past, and we are on air now.'

No one would have guessed that this assured and relaxed woman had just spent more than an hour with the leaders of the very trade unions who had campaigned so vigorously against her, and whose powers she had sworn to curtail. When I put to her points made by Len Murray, the TUC General Secretary, in a rapid briefing after the meeting, she smiled, spoke well of him and said she understood why he had made those remarks. Then she took her leave politely. It was the iron hand in the velvet glove.

That would be the only time that Mrs Thatcher formally met the TUC. The message in terms from the new government was that the days of 'beer and sandwiches' at No. 10, let alone the full-blown meal that Denis Healey provided at No. 11, were over.

The Conservatives had signalled their intention to legislate to restrict union powers. But Mrs Thatcher's clear message to the union leaders was that neither could they any longer take for granted the access to government decision-making to which they had grown accustomed, not just with the Labour government, but also with Edward Heath. For all the confrontation over the Industrial Relations Act, Heath had impressed union leaders. Even the tough-minded Jack Jones wrote, 'Amazingly he gained more personal respect from union leaders than they seemed to have for Harold Wilson or even James Callaghan ... No Prime Minister, either before or since, could compare with Ted Heath in the efforts he made to establish a spirit of camaraderie with trades union leaders and to offer an attractive package which might satisfy large numbers of work-people.'[6]

Now, times had changed. The battered Heath baton had been passed to Jim Prior, whose rubicund and friendly exterior hid a sharp mind and a determination to fight his corner, even when the consensual approach was out of fashion. Prior had learnt from the bruising encounters of the Heath government, of which he had been a combative member. In opposition he had patiently set about building bridges as employment spokesman. One link he was keen to construct was with the industrial correspondents; a strategy to make sure his proposed reforms were understood and to temper accusations of being anti-union, reinforcing messages he was giving directly to some union leaders. At a series of lunches in his flat in the shadow

6   Jones, op. cit., p. 259, 262

of Westminster Cathedral, he welcomed us, explained his views and listened, with a small team of supporting MPs.

The Conservatives' objectives were clear enough; the debate was over how fast to implement them. They came in two parts: the rolling back of union powers and prerogatives and the imposition of new requirements, most particularly encouraging secret ballots before industrial action. As always, particular elements of legislation would be driven by the specific pressures of the moment, a perceived outrage, or a particular dispute.

Prior fought successfully for a step-by-step approach. His Employment Bill concentrated on five elements: encouraging the move to secret ballots for union elections and strike votes by offering government cash but not yet making them compulsory; limiting picketing to a person's own place of work; weakening the closed-shop system in which new employees were obliged to join a union by requiring an 80 per cent vote to introduce new closed shops; giving a right to compensation for people dismissed for refusing to join a union through personal conviction; and outlawing coercive union recruitment tactics.

At the end of 1978, when Labour was still in power, I had addressed the question of compulsory secret ballots in a feature for the television programme *Assignment*, backing it up with an article in the BBC magazine, *The Listener*.

Controversy had been sparked that November when a vote had been held on a return to work by the striking Ford workers at Dagenham after their lengthy stoppage. In line with tradition it had been held at an open-air meeting. Shop stewards declared the result after a show of hands. They called it as an overwhelming vote to stay on strike, which it clearly was not, although it was probably narrowly in favour. Some union members objected, repeating well-worn allegations of people holding up two hands, of groups deliberately

positioned close to the platform all voting one way to set the tone
and, undeniably, of only one side of the argument being put. Three
weeks later, a similar meeting voted for a return to work. This time,
union activists noted, there were no media complaints.

Our programme looked at both sides. The unions were divided.
By now there was a new leader of the Engineering Union, the second biggest. With the retirement of Hugh Scanlon, union members
had voted for a shift away from the left and the confrontation policy which had seen union assets seized by the courts. Instead it had
elected a little-known Midlands official, Terry Duffy. Duffy was less
articulate but had an instinctive grasp of where his supporters were
coming from. His view was:

> It is incumbent on shop stewards to ensure that everyone has got
> the message. It is very difficult to do that at a mass meeting by
> speeches. I have found that there are quite a lot of people pre-
> sent at the meeting who haven't heard the message which has
> come from the platform.

He argued for the written message with the company and the union
view both set out, together with the claim, as was the practice at
Leyland Cars.

The opposite view came from Ron Todd, himself a former Ford
worker, who had taken over supervision of the motor industry
from Moss Evans and who would succeed him as General Secretary.
He defended the status quo:

> These mass meetings took place when people were not at work.
> What would be the mechanics of a secret ballot then – contact-
> ing 57,000 individuals? The other thing I am opposed to is when
> people talk about intimidation at meetings. With a ballot, with

a document going into a man's house, he is also vulnerable to
editorial comment and various leaflets which could be issued
to him by the companies themselves.

This concern that companies must not communicate directly with
employees at their homes but leave it to the union negotiators was a
leitmotif that ran through many industries. Management attempts
to do so could sometimes spark a new dispute. In the coal industry,
they made sure that the industry newspaper, *Coal News*, was made
available at pitheads, not sent to homes.

Our programme argued that, historically, there was nothing intrin-
sically anti-trade union about a ballot. 'The ancestors of today's union
leaders put the secret ballot among their top priorities in national and
local politics.' We pointed to the miners' commitment to pithead ballots with their union rules stipulating the requirement for a ballot
before industrial action. We also gave space to a warning from British
Rail's thoughtful industrial relations chief, Cliff Rose:

> What we should be careful about is imagining that the sim-
> ple imposition of a ballot will solve all our problems: it won't.
> I think the secret ballot has to grow from within. We have got
> to persuade the membership to change union rules so that they
> can be properly consulted when they think they ought to be.

Rose spoke from experience: a ballot forced under the Heath Industrial Relations Act had led to an overwhelming vote for a strike on
the railways.

It was a measure of the central place unions had come to occupy
in politics that arguments should now rage about their own workings. There was room for genuine concern. When the Transport
Union had elected its new General Secretary in the previous year,

I reported in the *Sunday Telegraph* that the union had printed enough election addresses for only 10 per cent of its members and did not reproduce them in the union newspaper. It simply reminded members to vote. Ballot boxes sat in union offices for a month.

For now the Conservatives stopped short of insisting on compulsory secret ballots. But it seemed only a matter of time.

In parallel with its moves on trade union legislation, the new government was turning its attention to the problems of the loss-making nationalised industries.

The most pressing concern was British Steel, responsible for the majority of the country's steel production and losing about £1 million a day. The new Secretary of State for Trade and Industry was the deep-thinking but perpetually anguished Thatcher confidante, Sir Keith Joseph. At one of his first press briefings he was asked a question about the management of British Steel. He tipped his head back, seizing it between his hands, and groaned, 'I don't see how anyone can run a nationalised industry.'

The travails of these industries consumed much of our time. They were vital parts of the industrial scene – the old 'commanding heights' phrase from Labour's nationalisation manifesto still mostly applied. They employed a large number of people, heavily or completely unionised, had a tradition of more union consultation in their management than private firms, and could cause major public disruption, to railways, power supplies and so on.

The people who ran them shared their concerns and frustrations in a Nationalised Industries Chairman's Group, which came together to compare notes and consider how to deal with their governmental masters. They sometimes gave press briefings about their deliberations, where unsurprisingly their key concern was how to get more money out of the Treasury for investment rather than day-to-day operations. The eternal stumbling block was the public sector borrowing requirement (PSBR). This meant that any assistance showed up as government borrowing.

It was not until the '90s, when many of the industries had been privatised, that with the advent of the Private Finance Initiative, quantities of money, borrowed through public–private partnerships, were able to flow into government enterprises without affecting the borrowing figures. It meant greater cost long-term; a stratagem with questionable consequences, though investment went in. But would it have been better to bite the bullet and relax the PSBR?

The National Coal Board was the most prominent of these industries. We came to know it well, not just in London but out in the various coalfields as well. Apart from the regular cliff-hangers over strikes and ballots, the unions were bound into all kinds of discussion about its financing, whether it was new investment or closure of old capacity; a regular feature as old seams became exhausted or geological conditions worsened.

Following the oil price shock of 1973, the need to increase coal production was a priority. But one effort after another failed and increasingly a productivity agreement appeared the answer. Voted down in 1977 in a national ballot, Gormley managed to introduce it piecemeal through a series of local NUM decisions. Production increased but the NCB was still a money-loser, and everyone in the industry was aware of the tail of uneconomic pits, although the precise list would vary slightly from year to year.

Throughout the '70s, the 'Derek and Joe show', the duo of Coal Board chairman Derek (later Lord) Ezra and Joe (later Lord) Gormley, routinely toured the coalfields in their attempts to boost production, while in annual negotiations miners steadily accrued more and more fringe benefits, such as better bath facilities and company-supplied working clothes, alongside wage increases.

The effects of this largely unsuccessful cheerleading, and what

Nigel Lawson dubbed the 'paternalist, corporatist mentality'[7] of the board, as Derek Ezra targeted what he called the 'maximum area of agreement', were duly noted by the Conservatives. By the time they came to power, a new worldwide recession was dramatically slashing coal demand and the fruits of the productivity drive were piling up as unused stocks.

The Coal Board's inclusivism extended to its treatment of the media. In a continuation of the Robens policy, patiently driven by Geoff Kirk, its long-serving director of public relations, it made a point of explaining the issues to journalists, reacting quickly and helpfully to queries and encouraging an understanding of the industry. The London staff worked hand in glove with colleagues in the major mining areas from which they had mostly originated. They shared a personal commitment and affection for the industry. It was a model.

The NCB organised regular visits to pits and when the first shafts and drifts were driven for the new complex of mines in the east of Yorkshire, near Selby, we were invited to travel to a recently renovated German mine to make comparisons and understand the importance given elsewhere to coal. It proved a false dawn.

I wrote in The Listener: 'The Board is clearly enjoying the first opportunity it has had of planning a coalfield from scratch. By 1988 a tenth of the entire British deep-mined production will come from the five pits linked here at levels of productivity over double that of today's show pits.' Anecdotally, I noted that 'underground, the strongest impression is of damp. Water streams from the rock and is noisily pumped away.' Sadly, Selby never lived up to its potential. A succession of problems, much of them linked to water, meant that its streamlined pits were closed while older collieries still continued.

---

7   Nigel Lawson, The View from No. 11 (Bantam, 1997), p. 155

Apart from formal visits, our understanding of life underground was enhanced by the anecdotes from our regular pub sessions with the union executives and invitations to speak at their weekend education conferences, where we would meet a variety of working pitmen.

But if the Coal Board was recognised as a model of good public relations, then British Railways was an example of how thoughtful spin combined with a striking openness from the top could produce an invigorating change in perception.

From the time when post-war British Railways had imposed a standard drab livery on all its trains, a perpetual disappointment to us as children, the sprawling monolith had been seen as a drain on government finances. There had been endless attempts, most notably the historic Beeching cuts, to keep the subsidy down. Now, after the unsuccessful chairmanship of a former Labour Transport Minister, Richard Marsh, the government had appointed Sir Peter Parker. He was that rare animal, an overt Labour Party supporter who had genuine experience as an effective businessman. For some years he had been marked out as a potential chairman for government boards and industries.

The engaging Parker brought with him his own PR advisor – an early example of something that would become more common practice among industrialists taking on big jobs. His *compañero* was Will Camp, another Labour supporter who had advised the party and worked for British Steel. Parker and Camp set about trying to change the image of the railways. Their first act was to eliminate the subsidy, then running at about a billion a year. They did it simply by renaming it. For Parker, it became 'the contract', the payment the government made every year for the railways to run essential loss-making services for it. The distinction was carried through into the presentation of the accounts, and railway performance looked quite different.

It was of course a sleight of hand, but it allowed Parker to talk in a much more upbeat way about railway performance and to energise people in the industry as he set about making changes with new investment and a vigorous attempt to change working practices. For a time, BR figures improved year on year, and the company ceased to be a byword for inefficiency.

He was assisted by modernisation already under way, particularly the advent of the new InterCity 125 diesel trains, the world's fastest. It enabled him to mount a marketing effort with genuine appeal, with slogans like 'this is the age of the train' and advertisements fronted, alas, by the then popular Jimmy Savile, who boasted of the thousands of miles he travelled by train. We became used to invitations for the record-breaking runs which flagged up the message of success.

That was the shiny side of the industry but much of the system was still antiquated, as we could see for ourselves when we filmed in the traditional engineering shops, housed in the brick Victorian sheds in great railway centres like Doncaster. In one clip of film our library cherished, a long line of men were painting carriages by hand with brushes and cans of paint.

And there was failure too. The much-touted Advanced Passenger Train (APT) with a tilting mechanism that allowed it to reach high speeds on old track was introduced too early and soon scrapped, perhaps too hurriedly as well. Today's tilting trains rely on Italian technology. The demise of the APT was hastened by breakdowns but it never recovered from its maiden voyage, where the press corps on board were made to feel extremely queasy as it tilted. Someone suggested unkindly that they had been too well entertained the night before, but the damage was done; a sad reverse for the policy of openness.

A belief in the power of sweet reasonableness let Parker down in the end. He put too much trust in unions' willingness to change. Although he wooed them with some considerable success, at last his flexible rostering proposals, which proposed changes in established shift patterns for drivers, represented by the small but powerful ASLEF

(Associated Society of Locomotive Engineers and Firemen) trade union, were fiercely resisted.

The long dispute, which ended in uneasy compromise, soured relationships and poisoned Parker's reputation with the government. But his long chairmanship, of seven years, in which he headed off proposals for drastic cuts in the network, began a transformation of the railways.

It was a different story at steel. The industry had only been renationalised in 1967. It still maintained much of the organisation and attitudes of private industry and the individual companies. There was a huge investment programme, largely centred on establishing a few huge plants usually close to the sea. But this meant the closure of smaller inland plants often with historic traditions in Labour heartlands, such as Ebbw Vale in south Wales. Much of the rationalisation had been ducked under the Labour government.

Things were made difficult by the obvious antipathy between the Labour-appointed chairman, Sir Charles Villiers, a banker and believer in consensus, and his abrasive chief executive, Robert 'Black Bob' Scholey, whose grumpy exterior hid a huge commitment to the industry and determination to force through changes. Villiers, a brave wartime soldier, was not helped by his quiet-spoken, patrician manner. A drooping moustache brought him the nickname 'Mr Pastry' from the industrial correspondents because of his resemblance to a bumbling comic in a popular television series.

My early days at the BBC were studded with visits to closing steel plants, meeting reasonable men often baffled by the decisions to shut down, and officials from the Iron and Steel Trades Confederation (ISTC), the principal trade union for the industry. Ironically, it was one of the most cooperative unions and well-grounded in the communities around the plants.

In fact, some called it a 'sweetheart union'. The first time I entered the office of its then General Secretary Dai (later Sir David) Davies and ventured to ask how pay talks were progressing, he told me that it was none of my business and he was not interested in telling me. But now, under his successor Bill Sirs, it was provoked into the first big industrial confrontation of the Thatcher government.

The trigger, ironically, was not closures, but pay. Though the background of closures had much to do with it. Just three days before meeting the unions for annual pay talks, the British Steel Corporation (BSC) had announced that it wanted to cut its labour force by a third – 50,000 people. Then, in response to the unions' 20 per cent pay demand, it offered just 2 per cent. The union took it as an insult, and a tape made available to me recorded the surprise and pandemonium in the room.

After that, it was a sleepwalk into disaster. I sat with the strike coordinator, Sandy Feather, Vic Feather's son, on the morning of the strike that began on 2 January 1980. He told me then that they had never believed it would happen; that there would be an eleventh-hour approach.

But by then there had been too many mistakes: an opening offer that was too low but eventually greatly increased; premature reaction and over-optimism from the union; the government's professed neutrality belied by its public statements; an ill-timed TUC intervention.

Picketing became a major issue. The government saw images of pickets struggling to block entry into still-working private steel mills and stockyards as helpful to the passage of its new Employment Bill. But it was then attacked by its own supporters for not being firm enough. The union struggled with communication. In the days before mobile phones, it took days even to get a second fixed line into the strike coordinator's office. It took three weeks for pickets to set up at south coast ports. Although the railway unions blocked transport of steel, lorry drivers, in spite of calls from their union, continued to carry it to such an extent that the railway unions complained that they were stealing their contracts. It was almost a blueprint for events in the miners' strike four years later.

In the event, the steelworkers stayed remarkably solid for thirteen weeks, with no strike pay and minimal assistance. The dispute was settled for 14 per cent, close to the rate of inflation, after a face-saving inquiry, and an exhausted workforce accepted the redundancies. I wrote at the time, 'the myth of trade union power is being shown up as the tattered garment that it is'.

It was a sad story, but there turned out to be a happier sequel due both to the way that the workforce set about reshaping the industry and the arrival of a new chairman, the Scottish American Ian MacGregor, the very man who would later preside over disaster in the coal industry.

In the aftermath of the strike, it was obvious there would have to be a change of leadership. Villiers went and the obvious successor, Scholey, was too divisive a figure to replace him. Instead, the government hit on MacGregor, a successful industrialist in the United States where his company AMAX had made a mint by mining supplies of molybdenum, a key component in the manufacture of quality steel. He was known to have an interest in addressing the problems of British manufacture and was already on the board of British Leyland, where his advice was valued by a new chairman, Michael Edwardes. Jim Prior's son worked for him.

His expertise seemed to fit. He brought no apparent baggage with him. His transatlantic turn of phrase – 'I am a hoary old bastard who only wants to win' – was slightly endearing. A potential showstopper about the size of his salary and compensation to the merchant bank where he was a partner subsided surprisingly quickly. It was assisted by his rather awkward comparison, suggested by Prior, to a recent large (and ultimately less successful) football transfer.

MacGregor set about implementing the rationalisation already planned but, crucially, he managed to invigorate a disillusioned management and persuaded Scholey to stay, recognising his understanding of the industry. It was a sharply different approach to what happened at British Coal, where MacGregor made clear he had little confidence in management. At steel he was no indiscriminate axeman. He recognised that there must be a limit to cutbacks and that British Steel needed to retain sufficient capability to compete. With his penchant for a phrase, he called it the 'Alamein line', behind which he would not retreat.

I had an ambivalent relationship with MacGregor. The public relations battle during the strike had gone the way of the union. It had been accessible; in Bill Sirs, its General Secretary, it had a quietly spoken and reasonable protagonist, and at a time of rising unemployment steelworkers faced with redundancy received public sympathy. After the strike, British Steel's public relations got, if anything, even worse. Doors to interviews were firmly shut.

A year or so later I made a long feature on the industry for a new programme, *Newsnight*, which had brought together the resources of two different, and often competing, BBC empires – news and current affairs. The programme looked at changes in the industry as a whole, including the growth of foreign imports as a result of the strike. It carried positive news of improving productivity and labour relations at some of the corporation's problem plants.

But the genesis of the piece was nothing to do with the Corporation's centralised press operations. It came from my conversations with union officials and shop stewards from the plants concerned, in particular in Llanwern, near Newport in south Wales. The plant was regularly mentioned as a candidate for closure but my contacts told me that major changes were occurring and pressed me to come down and see them. BSC rather grudgingly agreed, but once there both management and unions were eager to show how practices had changed by agreement and suggestions from the workforce, and the success they were having. An interview with MacGregor or anyone from head office was refused.

The plant was soon being seen as an exemplar, and came off the threatened list. Similar improvements followed elsewhere and eventually, after three years, I was able to lead the *Nine O'Clock News*, unusually, with the good news that British Steel was in profit. Before that I had made another film for *Newsnight*, a profile of MacGregor himself. I followed him, by arrangement, on a visit to Scottish plants. But, even though we chatted and shared transport, and I recorded his public words, he permitted no interview.

Meanwhile, coal was somewhere between a problem to be sorted and an accident waiting to happen. Early in 1981, as coal stocks piled up and demand fell, unions became concerned about the pace of closures being negotiated in the regions. At the subsequent national meeting, the chairman, Ezra, broke with the convention that closures were handled at local level and gave a figure of between twenty and fifty pits to be closed over five years. In truth, it was little different from what was already happening. But there was uproar; some local areas started immediate industrial action and Gormley proposed a national strike ballot.

On the morning of 18 February, and through most of the day, the firm guidance given to us from the Department of Energy was that there was unswerving government support for the board. That evening, at a meeting with miners, to our amazement, the news came that the government had backed down. It was a spectacular U-turn, and it came from the top. Mrs Thatcher had decided that now was not the time to take on the miners; stocks still had to be built up. The closure programme was withdrawn. Characteristically, Gormley kept the government on the hook until he had agreed a series of new investments and extra benefits for his members.

It was a strategic retreat, but it increased the determination of the government to prepare in every way possible for a showdown with the miners. It was Gormley's last stand. The following year he reached retirement age and Arthur Scargill was elected as his successor.

The troubles of the publicly owned industries spread wide. The government dismantled the shelter for lame ducks, the National Enterprise Board, with the objective of releasing its aviary into the private sector as soon as possible. But it found ostensibly more solid businesses also draining Exchequer funds. In came a succession of private businessmen to help turn things round. We interviewed them and monitored their progress, or lack of it.

The aggressively Thatcherite John King was appointed to British Airways and soon assembled a frightening tally of paper losses, which, to no one's surprise, he managed to reduce in the following year. At British Shipbuilders, its yards increasingly left behind by modernisation in other countries and union rivalries rife, an ineffective Admiral was replaced by another naval veteran, this time from the private steel industry. Robert Atkinson proved little more successful in turning things around. His campaign to have the replacement for the *Atlantic Conveyor*, sunk in the battle for the Falklands, constructed in a British yard, did succeed. But it diverted attention from dealing with the underlying problems and marked a last hurrah for an industry earmarked for effective closure.

The biggest headache remained British Leyland. If Mary Tudor had Calais engraved on her heart, Leyland would be the word that obsessed Mrs Thatcher.

After Lord Ryder's disastrous chairmanship, the Labour government had appointed Michael Edwardes as chairman. Energetic and aggressive, he had had a ringside seat of BL's troubles as a member of the National Enterprise Board. Approached in 1987 to be chief executive, with Ian MacGregor as chairman, he insisted on becoming both chairman and chief executive. An understanding MacGregor became a board member and one of his key supporters.

Confronted by a strike on his first day, Edwardes had moved quickly to produce a plan involving the cutbacks and closures shirked by Ryder. His approach followed a pattern. Rapid assessment, a clear and public challenge to the trade unions to accept plans or see the company founder, and communication over union heads to workers using leafleting and the media: the techniques which we had high-lighted in our examination of balloting and union decision-making.

Edwardes had arrived with few staff. He brought his personal assistant and, significantly, like Parker at British Rail, his own PR advisor, John McKay. With it came a rationing of personal access to the media to allow only a brief, clear message to be delivered – often through the open window of his car as he halted briefly on a car-park ramp, before accelerating away. It was a powerful and early demonstration of the art of spin. Edwardes never had any doubt he was playing on the national stage. 'Every minor dispute is carried out in full pub-lic glare,' he said. 'BL is the anvil on which every one of society's ills is beaten out.'

For us, committed to interviews where we could interrogate the interviewee, it posed a problem. Once he had delivered his mes-sage, Edwardes could simply wind up his window or speed down the ramp. When the phone calls came that he would be available in his car at a particular time and place, we decided on occasion that we would not play his game and declined to turn up to be manipu-lated. In today's world of saturated news and comment, that would no longer be an option.

Edwardes had moved swiftly to halve the size of the board, decen-tralise, and return power to line management. He wrote to managers: 'Act firmly and you will be backed. Repercussions? Yes, of course there will be, but I give you my word you will not be let down.'

Individual brand loyalties were resurrected – 'Large / Specialist Vehicle Operations' became Jaguar once again. He was worried by the lack of new models and amazed at the absence of profit and loss figures on individual marques.

By the time the Conservatives came to power, his regime was showing results. But it was a rollercoaster ride and Margaret Thatcher became exasperated by the repeated demands for extra subsidy as new crises broke. As the government hesitated to approve a new corporate plan, the management took the provocative step of dismissing the company's left-wing convenor, Derek Robinson, popularly nicknamed Red Robbo. We found ourselves staking out the Stafford private hotel beside Green Park as Edwardes thrashed out the wording of a deal with national union officials allowing Robinson's eventual departure.

The government meanwhile, sceptical of success, had calculated the huge cost of closure both to the Exchequer and the 300,000 or so people employed or dependent on the company. They reluctantly backed the plan. But from now on, the pressure was on to sell off parts of the widely spread empire.

The government decision was made against the background of remorselessly rising unemployment. It was my task every month to attend the press briefing on the latest unemployment figures, given by the Department of Employment. We would request a follow-up interview with a minister, and often they obliged. I particularly enjoyed sparring with Norman Tebbit, who had taken over from Jim Prior as Employment Secretary in 1981. He was always alert and combative and you had to stand your ground when you challenged him to admit that things were as grim as we knew they were. He would play variations on a number of themes – things were not as bad as we made out; changes were necessary and bring inevitable short-term pain; this was a global phenomenon as recession bit, and, by the way, look at the figures for new jobs. But he enjoyed the tussle and spoke his mind.

Later, with his successor, the equable Norman Fowler, a former *Times* journalist beside whom I had once sat at community relations press conferences, the bland effect of television interview training was apparent. A first question was replied to (answered would be too strong a word) with a rehearsed statement; further questions were brushed aside or just not answered. The spin doctors had triumphed.

Along with reporting the cold figures, we sought context by travelling to areas particularly affected by unemployment. It doubled in the first three years of the new government to reach 3 million for the first time since the 1930s. Tebbit's response was to talk of 'gradually fighting back in competitive terms against our rivals'.

I marked the dreadful milestone in Abingdon where the MG factory had closed the previous year making 700 people redundant. With the help of the unions I traced some of them and talked about the difficulties of finding work. One man I interviewed, Eddie McAvinue, who had been at MG for twenty-one years, told me he had now stopped looking for work and was instead looking after his grandchildren. He was no longer bitter: 'When I look around and there's young people with A and O levels and they can't get jobs, I just accept it now. I can't do anything else.' After my report was aired on the *Nine O'Clock News*, I was contacted by an employer who wanted to offer him a job.

I also made two visits, a couple of years apart, to see how things were faring in the historic industrial heartland of south Wales – to Ebbw Vale, the constituency of the leader of the Labour opposition, Michael Foot. The steelworks was already closed and efforts continued to attract new industry onto spreading industrial estates on the fringes of the town. But it was a dispiriting story.

At the job centre I met a 45-year-old ex-steelworker, searching for vacancies, who told me he feared that he would never work again. His was not an uncommon reaction. After years of taking full employment for granted, the loss of familiar industries and your own job was a paralysing experience.

In a row of terraced houses I talked to two next-door neighbours who had each been made redundant twice after finding jobs when the steelworks closed. The wife of one explained how they had regularly complained about the way the discharges from the works had stained the washing that they had hung out to dry – 'Now we would gladly have those days back'.

Up in the industrial estates, there were signs of new employment: a tile depot, a Japanese battery plant, and other initiatives, but some were already struggling and when I returned, some more had closed.

As the debates raged about the price of oil, the need for import controls, excessive public cutbacks, the need to rationalise old-fashioned industries, roughly a third of British manufacturing industry went to the wall. Through the '80s, a generation of British industrial managers was brought up on the belief that their key skill was how to cut back.

The TUC and the trade union movement was bewildered by the firestorm. It took a long time to adjust to the realisation of just how thoroughly it was being excluded from the corridors of power. Its predicament was not helped by the changing of the guard. Both Jones and Scanlon, whose unions' size and voting power outstripped the other unions, had very clear ideas about where they stood.

Jones, disciplined and determined, was intent on giving the working man more say at every level, from shop-floor to boardroom, as a point of principle. Scanlon, from the time when he had been an isolated left-winger on a hostile rightist union executive council, championed a conventional left-wing agenda. Both were prepared to use their industrial muscle where it mattered, as Harold Wilson's much-quoted remark to Scanlon in the midst of the argument over *In Place of Strife*, 'Get your tanks off my lawn, Hughie', had made clear.

But their successors, Moss Evans and Terry Duffy, were less sharply defined. I described them in *The Listener*:

> Moss Evans has a temperament and a philosophy which led him more to react to members and to trawl for consensus than to press new initiatives in the Jones manner; Terry Duffy is more interested in his internal engineering union battles with what he persists in calling 'the Coms' than in taking any significant TUC role, while David Basnett (leader of the third biggest union, the General and Municipal) has failed to leave a distinctive mark.

The big gap had been left by Jack Jones. His successor, Moss Evans, though nominally of the left, had difficulty in setting out a vision. It was no secret that Jack Jones would have preferred his old colleague and deputy, Harry Urwin, to have run instead. Finally, any hopes that Moss might have set a clear direction were swept away when he was diagnosed with aggressive cancer and spent months out of action.

The vacuum might have provided an opportunity for Len Murray, the TUC General Secretary, to have taken a strong lead. He had been visibly constrained by the 'terrible twins' but now seemed reluctant to step forward. Crucially, the TUC has no votes of its own. It can only seek a consensus or a majority for its policies by persuasion and the support of powerful allies. And Murray, too, had his health problems. A heart incident took him away from his desk for weeks, and when he returned I found him notably more tentative and risk-averse.

A year after the Conservatives were elected, I wrote in *The Listener* of confusion and a lack of confidence among trade unions as they met for the 1980 TUC conference.

For those who talked so much of union power under a Labour government, the events of the past year must seem almost unbelievable.

Union power could not halt even such vulnerable services as transport on an official TUC day of protest on 14 May. Union power could not prevent a steady run-down of the steel industry as workers opted for redundancy money in spite of the solidarity of the thirteen-week strike. And union power has simply been an onlooker as, with the minimum of Parliamentary opposition from the unions' allies, the government has passed not only its Employment Act but also measures that deliberately reduce benefits for strikers' families.

It is a catalogue of impotence that senior trade union leaders acknowledge, without being clear how to respond. For the first time for years they have seen membership actually falling, workers agreeing to forgo pay increases and in some cases even taking cuts while union financial resources are being eaten away by a combination of inflation, their members' difficulties and expensive campaigns like the steel strike. Above all, there is unemployment. It is now reaching levels that many union officials – and managements – have not experienced in their lives.

Old industries, accustomed to decline, are crumbling at an accelerating rate while parts of the country which have escaped some previous recessions are tasting serious unemployment for the first time.

Like prudent captains, union leaders seem at present simply to be taking precautions to deal with a passing, if savage, storm. They are battening down the hatches to hold onto as many members as possible, thinking about rescuing some of the unemployed over the side, while intoning the old litany of reflation, import controls and opposition to pay policies and industrial relations changes.

The great strength and the great weakness of the position is that it is so rock-solid. Announcing a recent addition to the corpus of union demands, Len Murray emphasised how TUC objectives, once put on the agenda, remained and were not withdrawn awaiting a favourable moment; the immovable object approach to bargaining. This is the TUC attitude – no changes in industrial relations law and a wait for the conversion of the government on economics.

The TUC may not yet appreciate that it could be facing not a passing storm, so much as a permanent change in the weather.

At the Congress that year, our media coverage came under particularly heavy attack. Repeatedly delegates blamed the lukewarm response to the Day of Action on hostile reporting. This time, it was my turn to make the reply to the rather ironic vote of thanks to the press. After the barrage of criticism, I decided that it was time for more than the routine knockabout. I began:

> The tradition of this speech is that it should be brief, matey and contain a few jokes. It is difficult not to be serious in the face of things that are happening, represented by the figures of unemployment which are displayed in the hall and by flesh-and-blood people whom we meet throughout the country and on whom we shall continue to report. It is difficult to be jokey after the blanket remarks about the media.

I went on to say that I would not defend my report but pointed to the wide variety of media, from the *Morning Star* to the Tory-owned papers, and those like the BBC, obliged to reflect different shades

of opinion. 'Whatever was written about May 14th, the fact that it
was not the success that some hoped it would be was due not to
what was written in the media, but to differences of opinion within
the movement.'

The big story during the year, I suggested, had not been 14 May,
but the steel strike. I said that I could not remember when a union's
case was better appreciated and respected by the public. The reason,
I suggested, was that the union leaders had taken trouble to make
themselves available, to explain their position, and give frank answers
to questions. I ended: 'I had a pamphlet across my desk which carried
the complaint that the union's case was being put too much. That
came from Aims of Industry, and that does not happen too often.'

Two years later I found myself describing a situation that had
hardly changed. Now the Congress was preparing to join battle over
whether it should adopt what seemed the ultimate counsel of despair
– to withdraw from all involvement with government and the remaining tripartite bodies. In the event, it decided against a course that
seemed to play completely into the government's hands. But the
heat of the debate illuminated the way the movement still misunderstood the government.

I wrote: 'The $64,000 question – What happens if Mrs Thatcher
is returned to power in a year's time? – is not publicly aired. What
price then the current policy of opposition to the government, coupled with an expectation that union objectives will be secured by a
change of government?'

I asked what had gone wrong.

> Some would say it is wrong to expect forward looks from a
> movement under concerted attack from the government. Another
> answer is that the TUC has stuck too closely to old corporate
> strategies with which its members, as well as the government,

are out of tune. Another is that there is, tragically for a radical movement, an increasing reluctance among trade union leaders, certainly in public, to speak frankly or think hard, about the situation in which they find themselves. Massive support, solid backing is claimed on almost every occasion, regardless of obvious doubts and question marks.

There is a catalogue of union difficulty, yet to judge from what is said by one union leader after another, campaigns are succeeding, one more shove or industrial battle will topple the government. This time redundancy really will be resisted.

The lack of frankness not only blunts the effectiveness at the top but must be continuing to confuse the members.

I took as an example my experience at the two major Welsh steel plants where, in spite of their sense of achievement, workers were baffled that what was happening at local level was being officially spoken against by the national leadership.

Because, in the workplace, things were changing. The new realities were being recognised, as the steelworkers in Wales had made clear to me. Even Leyland was experiencing a brief revival as it successfully launched its long-awaited new Metro. British Shipbuilders was beginning to deal with the longstanding demarcation problems that had held it back.

New forms of organisation were being discussed. Central to these were single-union agreements where a plant would be organised by a single union instead of a variety, who would often compete against each other for membership or particular benefits.

Leading this drive were the big unions representing the more skilled workers, particularly the engineering and electrical trade unions led by what were labelled alternatively as right-wing or moderate leaders. For the engineering union, the chance of establishing themselves firmly in new plants was an opportunity to claw back the ground their skilled workers had lost in the motor industry to the generalised production workers represented by the Transport Union. The TGWU (Transport and General Workers' Union) was taking a principled but unimaginative stand against single-union agreements.

Key players in this development were foreign companies wanting to invest in Britain but wary of the industrial relations difficulties that had afflicted their UK competitors. They saw single-union agreements as a solution. The biggest prize was the Japanese car firm, Nissan. It was perhaps the Thatcher government's greatest industrial success to have secured the construction of a Nissan plant in the unemployment-ravaged north-east of England, agreed in 1984, on the eve of the miners' strike. The plant opened in 1986.

It was made possible by a single-union agreement with the Engineering Union, and the Nissan deal would be followed by the arrival of Toshiba and Honda to begin a rebirth of car manufacturing in Britain.

The electricians were also active, sometimes in conjunction with the engineers. Their leader, the combative Frank Chapple, had been involved in a bitter legal battle, to oust a Communist Party leadership in the late 1950s and early 1960s. A former Communist Party member himself, who had resigned over the invasion of Hungary, he took no prisoners and seemed to enjoy the hostile reception he received when he arrived at a Congress rostrum like some lightning conductor. But, in the new age of technology, electricians were a key group, while their industrial muscle most strikingly resided in their role operating the power stations.

Their most notorious decision would be to conclude a secret agreement with Rupert Murdoch for single-union operation of the new printing plant he was building at Wapping to produce a range of newspapers, from The Sun and News of the World to The Times.

With the operation of new technology, they replaced members of the traditional printing unions so enabling Murdoch to break a grip so strong that it had led to a year-long stoppage of *The Times* a few years before.

Behind this lay a bitter competition for members. The empire was collapsing. The number of people in trade unions shrank by 2.5 million, nearly 20 per cent, in the first five years of the Conservative government. It affected everything – finances, confidence and bargaining power. I had scandalised members of my local Labour Party some years earlier by saying that the biggest driver for the unions was membership. It was a huge factor in the inter-union disputes and rivalries, which too often had been blamed for the unnecessary stoppages, the demarcation disputes and the unwillingness to change established practice that hampered the country's economic progress.

Just how naked rivalry could be was demonstrated to me by the bitterness caused by Moss Evans of the Transport Union a few months before he was elected as General Secretary. His members worked alongside others in the building trade, which was organised largely by the Union of Construction and Allied Trades and Technicians (UCATT). He was invited to address its conference. UCATT, however, was making an attempt to become the main union for the industry, potentially absorbing the transport workers. Evans's speech was uncompromising. Let them not think, he said, that his union was ever going to get out of the building industry. They had better remember that it worked in the industries that produced the materials and drove the lorries that brought them to the sites. If they wanted, they could close any site down. It was a blunt reminder of the realities of union power.

His union had been the big winner in the motor industry. The division between general unions, representing a mix of largely unskilled workers, and craft unions, representing particular trades, was as old

as trade union history. Traditionally, the Transport Union had represented unskilled workers in the industry, while the Engineering
Union spoke for more skilled workers, such as the toolmakers, who
had served training apprenticeships. But many car workers fell somewhere in-between and the Transport Union had been most successful
in recruiting them. The question of differentials between 'skilled' and
'unskilled' was a continual issue. At its worst, it brought the toolmakers strike, which wrecked British Leyland's hopes of recovery in the
first months of 1977, when 40,000 people were laid off.

The difficulties were long recognised. The British trade unionists
who had helped establish an effective trade union structure for West
Germany after the war had planned a small number of industrially
based organisations. Now, behind the scenes, the patient executives in
the TUC's organisation department, who spent hours taking the steam
out of inter-union disputes, encouraged a merger process that chimed
with the ambitions of individual British unions to grow larger. This
would reach its apogee in the merger of the two biggest unions: the
Transport Union and the Engineering Union in 2007 to form Unite
the Union, covering an extraordinary range of industries and skills.

Unions sought a variety of ways to deal with the crisis. My desk
drawers filled up with recently invented video cassettes, cut by unions
to encourage recruitment. One union, the Iron and Steel Trades
Confederation, tried to reinvent itself by styling itself Community
and developing activities to appeal to a wider group around the plants
in which its members worked. Others sought convenient mergers to
share their costs.

In the autumn of 1982, I described union leaders as in a greater
state of disarray than at any time since the Second World War.

> Since the defeat of the Callaghan government undermined
> their foundation belief of working hand in hand with a Labour

government to secure economic and social changes, their empire has continued to crumble but they have failed to find a new role.

Such is the vacuum of new ideas or bold thinking at the top that this year's pre-Congress discussions have been dominated by two essentially negative debates: whether or not the time has come to adopt a guerrilla strategy, withdrawing from involvement with government bodies, striking by industrial action as and when possible in the hope of bringing the government down, and secondly a power wrangle over seats on the General Council.

The TUC did not withdraw from involvement but the guerrilla strategy – how far the use of industrial action by a powerful group of workers could shake the government – was about to be tested. Twelve months later, the National Union of Mineworkers, once memorably styled as the trade union movement's Brigade of Guards, began a ban on overtime working in a deliberate move to prevent coal stocks accumulating. In March 1984, it turned into an all-out strike.

Chapter Thirteen

The end of the empire of coal

The miners' strike and its consequences dominated my latter years at the BBC, as I charted, step by step, the end of the empire of coal and its dominance in British industrial and, often, political life. Aneurin Bevan had famously described Britain as an 'island of coal, surrounded by fish'. By the end of the '80s, it was no longer true.

I had written an account of the strike and the background to it, *The Miners' Strike, 1984–85: Loss without Limit*, together with John Lloyd, who had led the *Financial Times* coverage of the strike while I covered it throughout for BBC TV News. As a result, we were able to get the participants to speak frankly to us in the months just after the strike while most were still alive.

Significantly, there were two exceptions – Arthur Scargill and Ian MacGregor, who wanted to tell their own versions unmediated. In addition, David Hart, who had been MacGregor and Thatcher's sinister right-wing advisor, refused to speak to me, suspicious of my BBC connections, although he agreed to be interviewed by John. The book stands as our account of the strike, and benefits from the candour of many who were involved.

Now, more than thirty years on, the strike, an epic feat of endurance, seems increasingly portrayed in a romantic and rosy hue, with gallant miners taking on the brutal forces of a ruthless government.

That formulation is an easy shorthand, but it ignores how many working miners were browbeaten or picketed into strike action. It is common knowledge that the union never held the national ballot for strike action, which its rules and its custom and practice required. But few also remember that, for example, the majority of miners' lodges in south Wales, one of the most determined areas in the end, originally voted against striking. They, among others, were brought out by picketing which took advantage of the fundamental trade union shibboleth: never cross a picket line.

It is also worth remembering that the police response, massive and sometimes unnecessarily provocative and brutal as it was, was exactly that: a response. It was in answer to the attempts, particularly at first by Yorkshire miners, physically to prevent their Nottinghamshire and other colleagues going to work. The big Nottinghamshire area had refused to strike without holding a ballot. Mining is a very physical industry; picketing was too.

The battle at British Steel's Orgreave coking plant was brutal – on both sides. If it is true that police notebooks were later falsified, there is no excuse. But Orgreave was not a coal mine. It did not belong to the National Coal Board, and did not employ miners. It was a British Steel plant and the NUM strategy was to shut it down by physical force to prevent production by another industry – steel. The pickets were there to force it to close and, as the BBC cameramen on the spot on the climactic day of 18 June made clear to me, stones and bricks were being hurled against police lines before the police charged. There had been an informal agreement in some parts of Yorkshire between pickets and police: no stones, no horses.

Why was it that many other unions, while their members might sympathise personally with the miners' plight, refused to take supportive action? This was a contrast to the strikes of 1972, and particularly 1974, when Joe Gormley and his executive colleagues had reached prior agreement to support the miners so that picketing was scarcely necessary. This time, as the title of one of our chapters put it, 'there was no request for assistance' to the TUC. Arthur and the miners chose to go it alone on their terms.

Why was it that so many people, natural supporters of the miners' cause, the Labour leader Neil Kinnock among them, were so alienated by the conduct of the strike, the refusal to condemn violent methods, and the refusal to find a compromise, that they withheld their wholehearted support?

The strike began in March 1984 and occupied a year of my life. It is fair to say that none of us expected it to continue for so long and certainly to end without some compromise deal.

My role was essentially as an anchor and sometimes as a coordinator; covering the national picture – the regular meetings of the NUM executive at their headquarters in Sheffield, the meetings with other unions and the TUC, the position of the Coal Board and the government as well as other unions. On many evenings – as well as during the daily news bulletins – I put together and broadcast an overview of developments. It meant that I saw less first hand of what was going on around individual pits and communities, although I was privy to what BBC reporters were finding locally, and to the night-time struggles which intensified as men started to return to work in striking areas.

Covering the NUM executive brought its challenges. One of Arthur Scargill's first actions as president had been to move the union headquarters away from London, too remote, supposedly, from the coalfields, back to his Yorkshire base. It now occupied the top floors of a tower block in Sheffield. Now, instead of being welcomed into the executive room for a post-meeting briefing, we found ourselves corralled in an anonymous eighth-floor waiting room. As we set up our cameras, so too the NUM set up its own camera to film us, a potentially intimidating surveillance. Our chances of even a quick word with members of the executive in a nearby pub were torpedoed by Scargill's determination to prolong proceedings until after lunchtime closing times. After the strike I was given a set of executive minutes for the period. They said very little about the conduct of the strike.

I was at Sheffield on 12 April for the crucial vote on whether to hold a ballot. About 2,000 lobbying miners, fresh from the picket lines, surged around the base of the building and into its stairwells. As the *One O'Clock News* approached, I climbed onto the roof of an outbuilding to deliver a live report. As I was positioned and wired up with a microphone, the crowd realised what was happening and struck up a bawdy chorus. When the studio director in London, oblivious, switched over to me, viewers were treated to a swelling refrain of 'The BBC are wankers' as bricks and a flat cap were hurled in my direction.

Later as I came down in the lift from the long-delayed press conference together with pickets who had burst into it, I was kicked and knocked down before we reached the ground floor. For the record, the motion for a ballot was ruled out of order.

On the picket lines at pitheads, camera crews were often targeted and our outside broadcast van had a brick thrown through the driver's window. A chapter in our book goes into detail about the allegations of anti-NUM bias made by Arthur Scargill, particularly against news bulletins. In a debate with him at the Edinburgh Television Festival, at which I was asked to represent the BBC, he accused us of 'pure, unadulterated bias', a slight improvement to his description of the media as 'our enemies' front-line troops'.

In defending our coverage, which was so extensive that it was bound to be sometimes uneven, I was able to show that almost all the reported complaints which we had been accused of failing to report – pickets dragged from their tents, cars being stopped at long distances from the coalfield, police use of truncheons – had been covered by us. Then Arthur produced an issue of the union newspaper showing a mounted policeman apparently swinging his truncheon at a protester and accused us of ignoring it. I was able to give the precise date on which we had shown it on the *Nine O'Clock News*.

Some weeks later, at lunchtime at the TUC conference, a few of us were eating sandwiches at a conference centre bar. In came a solitary Arthur and, with the whole bar to choose from, opted to come over to chat to us and complain about the strain of the strike and how, particularly and improbably, he could no longer go to football matches. There was a symbiotic relationship between Arthur and the media.

As the strike lengthened and the return to work slowly gathered numbers, the scenes at the pitheads became ritualised. Towards the end of 1984 I spent a night with a BBC team in the Doncaster area, traditionally the most militant of militant Yorkshire. Here the smallest number of men had returned to work, with fewer working than the week before in some pits. The executive member for the area claimed to me that most were 'misfits', targeted by the Coal Board for their known vulnerability. He had a point. I described the atmosphere in the early hours in a piece for *The Listener* headed 'All quiet on the Yorkshire front':

> The road narrows. A taxi. Two lads hunched on their way home
> after a night out. Nothing for 20 minutes. Then three police vans

close together, moving slowly, mostly empty. A few hundred yards later, three more, one obviously carrying riot gear, led by a motorcyclist needlessly flashing his lights. We turn after them. Out of the misty blackness the dim silhouette of winding-gear over brick buildings, and two constables. They come from Sussex. All quiet.

3 a.m. Goldthorpe Colliery, and the strike can only be described as solid. Here a long, straight lane leads to the pit. At its mouth, two police vans, both full. We walk past the foundations of a toilet block demolished so that pickets can no longer use the bricks from it. A hundred yards down, another police Transit, engine running to keep the men inside warm. Another hundred yards and another van with a cluster of four tucked round the corner in the pit yard. Miners complain that it is the police who now control the pit yards.

Beside the van, a rusted shack of corrugated iron with a wood and canvas door. Outside, it could be something from a third-world shanty town; it is the picket hut. Inside there is a warm fug and a strong smell of socks. Four men stretch their feet to a breeze-block stove, its metal chimney poking through the roof. It resembles a wartime dug-out.

This is one of four shifts who man the hut 24 hours a day; their names pinned on the wall. Beside a girlie poster, a circular from Doncaster Social Services tells how to apply for fuel for children with special needs. A grill perches on top of a large blank-screened television set. We make a joke about collecting the TV licence. There's a story about someone unable to pay because of the strike. Everyone else, say the pickets, is going easy on pressing for repayments.

They are a mixture of ages, united in their belief that they are winning. 'Wait until the lights go out in January and businessmen start to put pressure on Thatcher.' One man talks bitterly about the drift back to work. 'Christmas is finished anyway. There is no money now even if you go back.'

Then it is on to endless beefs about the police. Talk of another picket hut being demolished and warnings that this could happen to them unless they keep numbers down and don't use cameras or binoculars. We ask if they see any difference between police forces. Well there were some Welsh police who they thought were sympathetic; they thought from mining areas. They speak of the difficulty of making complaints. They write off the police's public meetings as a waste of time. It is reminiscent of reporting race relations in Notting Hill 15 years before.

Then it's our turn. 'All your news is biased.' We disagree. My colleague Andy Taylor points out how he has already done one piece that week about how the number of working miners has fallen off. 'You say it's all about Scargill, but, me, I am on strike for myself,' says one picket.

3.30. As the cars move on, a phone call. A resonant police voice, 'It's as quiet as the grave.' Then, out of the mist, tall chimneys and angled pipes, puffs of smoke turned yellow under neon lights.

Askern pit and at nearly four in the morning, a crowd of dark figures, perhaps 100, with a police cordon holding them back. Across the road two empty vans, one with riot gear. A police inspector says the bus is due in three minutes. The group nearest are half a dozen women, a cheerful bunch, one joking that she has locked herself out and discussing how to get back without waking her husband.

Then suddenly a green bus, three or four men crouched at the front, a shout of 'scabby bastards'. The crowd disperse. The vans drive back into the pit yard. Another woman shouts out, 'You show some pictures and tell bloody lies.'

4.20. Traffic-lights and the main road past Pontefract race-course. In the centre of the road, a police van with lights flashing and what is altogether a bigger show. A big concrete enclosed pit, Prince of Wales. A huge drift mine which in normal times men enter through sloping tunnels to mine thick six foot seams. Pickets saunter towards it in twos and threes.

A confident West Yorkshire police superintendent maps out his strategy. 'We shall put a line across the road here. Then we shall sweep down the hill towards them in front of the bus. I don't expect trouble unless we have visitors. Last night we had some and there was brick-throwing.' He tells me that the previous night *Panorama* had filmed from the pickets' side. The question of a connection hangs heavy between us.

More pickets are arriving, stopping to chat, in knots of six or seven. A crocodile of police march out of the pit and up the hill. Relaxed, cheerful, one of the pickets tells us how he is due to appear in a Nottingham court in the morning. He looks up at the starry sky. 'Not a bad night for a shove.'

Then across the field by the pit, dark silhouettes, barking. Dogs leading men. They are there to discourage pickets leaving the road and heading into the field or the racecourse. Another crocodile of police, heading, Duke of York-like, down the hill again.

'I shall sweep down using ordinary uniformed police,' says the Super, 'And put up a line to keep this lot back. If they get through they are usually rather embarrassed and try to get back to their own side quickly. They are as good as gold really.'

The pickets start down the hill at a steady pace with the unseen police cordon pushing them on. Not tonight the dogs or mounted police which the pickets say have been used on occasion. A double line of police along the roadside watches them and a man moves forward. 'Can you stand back Inspector and leave them to their own devices,' calls the Super.

Then an ancient National Bus, screens hiding the men inside, an indicator declaring incongruously 'Blackpool'. A shout of 'scabs' and 'scabby bastards'; the police lines are shoved back, quickly reinforced and heaved back in place again.

It all takes about two minutes. Someone has seen a single brick thrown at the coach. Police and pickets disentangle from each other as if a whistle has blown to disperse a rugby scrum. They head off. No arrests.

'Might see you at Kellingley,' says a picket. The Coal Board policy of staggering the arrival of working miners to concentrate police resources cuts both ways.

We walk back up the hill past the vans – Mercia, Avon, Hertfordshire. The radiophone tells us that somewhere among Yorkshire's 60 or so pits four trees have been cut down across a road and an NCB van has had its windscreen smashed. A quiet night. No story.

Later I charted the aftermath of the strike. After the brave marches back, demoralisation and the closure of pit after pit, forty-two in two years, I went to one of the most militant Doncaster pits, Yorkshire Main at Edlington, where its miners had voted unexpectedly to close. It was clear the heart had gone out of them. Five hundred had applied for 300 redundancy places. As I sat in the sun chatting to them, the Coal Board was spelling out redundancy terms and investment advisors were offering to help them look after their money.

I told the detailed story of three of the miners and a pit manager in the book. Of the four, just one opted to stay in the industry. One bought a seaside off-licence; another, who had run an informal shop, pursued his retail interests while the manager worked with the investment companies. Over the coming months, I met people who had set up all sorts of small enterprises: garden supply, woodworking businesses, and one who had bought a fishing boat, although he would not let the boat be identified because of possible reprisals.

As for Arthur Scargill, months after the end of the strike, he resigned. But it was only to put himself up for a re-election, which he won easily. I went up again to Sheffield to make a feature. This time there was no eighth-floor waiting room. I was invited into Arthur's own office. He sat at the end of a long executive table. At the other end of the room, facing him, hung his own portrait. He agreed to do an interview and inquired what else we wanted. I explained that we would like to film an election meeting he was holding in the welfare (the miners' club) of a nearby pit. No problem.

There was some muttering when we turned up at the mine that evening but we set up our equipment at the back of the hall and filmed Arthur in full flow. There was to be more than a touch of a religious revival meeting. Abruptly he halted and pointed to us, 'There at the back of the hall is the BBC and Martin Adeney.' Puzzled faces craned round to take a closer look. 'It's all right, Martin, all you have to do is to come down here to the front and say you are sorry.' It was vintage Arthur. I smiled and we kept on filming.

When I went to America in the summer of 1985 on a US-sponsored visit to look at 'changing patterns of trade', I sought out the parallels. There were plenty of uncomfortable similarities in the traditional industrial heartlands, the so-called 'rust belt'. I visited communities along the Monongahela river near Pittsburgh where unions were setting up their own job centres in an attempt to help their members after the loss of their steelworks. Big plants were being replaced by more flexible 'mini-mills', which had sprung up in different parts of the country.

I visited American coal mines on the borders of Illinois and Indiana, owned by MacGregor's old company AMAX. Their production did not directly compete with British coal as it was committed under long-term contracts to US power stations; longer contracts than ours, providing more security. But it showed just what British miners were up against. Coal could be produced more cheaply from seams that were nine-foot thick and in the huge open-cast mines nearby, which boasted the largest draglines in the world. I thought of the British miners I knew who had worked seams just three feet high in pits running with water. One of Britain's best pits, Kellingley, with six-foot seams, was producing the same amount of coal but with double the workforce.

Worse was to follow for the British industry. Over the next few years productivity picked up but the oil price fell. However, the British coal industry was effectively destroyed by two new developments: 'the dash for gas' and the growing political awareness of climate change. For power generation, the cheapness of North Sea Gas and the ease and speed with which small gas-fired power stations could be constructed tipped the balance against new coal stations, which were far more expensive to build. The government, no friend now of the miners, declined to intervene.

Then, once the emissions of coal-fired stations had become a focus in the global warning debate, both construction of new capacity and the use of British coal became issues. British mined coal, it turned out, generally produced much higher carbon emissions than much foreign coal, available for import.

As a result, in 2016, the last deep mine in the UK, Kellingley in Yorkshire, closed. A hundred years before there had been 1 million miners – almost one in ten of working men. As for Bevan's description, most of the fishing industry had disappeared together with the plentiful fish, and there was no market for the coal.

The miners' strike was the most dramatic example of the 'guerrilla strategy' of responding to the Thatcher government that I had logged. But it failed. A few months later, another traditional union power-house, the national newspaper printing industry, saw a similar struggle end in defeat.

Journalists were all too aware of the restrictive nature of the union-isation of the printing industry. We saw the antique machinery in our offices, whose updating unions had opposed, and sub-editors knew the limits of what they were allowed to do as the paper was assembled. No touching of type, or there might be a stoppage. The Economist Intelligence Unit report of 1980 had exposed corruption behind the scenes where full pay packets were handed over for distribution to fictitious workers who were contemptuously labelled Mickey Mouse or Lester Piggott or other transparently false names. The lack of seri-ous industrial discipline was openly displayed in old Fleet Street, as obviously drunken workers sat about sunning themselves at midday.

Dealing with union leaders like John Bonfield of the National Graphical Association, or Dick Briginshaw of Sogat, was uncomfort-able. They made clear they could bring pressure on the paper or even prevent publication if they did not like what was written.

However, their successors had become more emollient and Bill Keys of Sogat took a more strategic view and played an important role in the TUC. He saw the need for change. His attempts to reform benefited from the tireless work of the TUC organisation depart-ment and, particularly, John Monks, later the TUC General Secretary.

In the summer of 1985, my colleague John Fryer went down to the East End to inspect the new headquarters that Rupert Murdoch was constructing for his newspapers, which included *The Times* and *The Sun*. He came back with a simple message, 'It's built like a for-tress. He is preparing for a fight.' So it was. Exasperated by lack of progress, Murdoch made a deal with the electricians to operate the new-style, although hardly new, machinery, and effectively locked out his printers. Numbers of my journalistic colleagues on *The Times* bravely refused to go to Wapping, but most did. For weeks on end there was nightly picketing, with struggles with the police as the delivery vans left down a well-defended ramp. It was particularly confrontational on Saturday nights. But, in the end, the guerrilla strategy was defeated again.

In the meantime, union membership continued to fall. By 1989, it was down to 10 million, 3 million less than ten years before. As I wrote in my final article for *The Listener*, 'It has been sheer survival. As their members have fallen, so my desk drawers have filled with union videos explaining themselves. Laws about balloting have concentrated union officials' minds on the message they give to members.'

And the nature of union membership was changing. In 1987, I wrote:

> Coal and steel employment has roughly halved; the union for skilled engineering workers has reduced from more than a million to 857,000. By contrast unions for white-collar workers have fared better. The union for town hall workers has lost few members while the National Union of Teachers, also a relatively recent recruit to TUC membership, has had a fairly stable membership. The TUC now has twice as many teachers as miners; nearly as many town hall clerks as skilled engineers.
>
> White-collar workers have in recent years been among those most given to industrial action, sometimes appearing to see it as having some intrinsic virtue. Arthur Scargill has proclaimed that the miners' strike passed on the torch to the teachers while the only national strike action during this year's election was called by two white-collar civil service unions. The miners' strike apart, the most working days lost through strikes since 1984 have been in public administration, education and health.

The extent of change was explained to me by teachers in the
North East when I looked recently at links between school and
industry. As traditional industries like coal, steel and shipbuilding
have decayed, parents, often victims of redundancy, are advising
their children to avoid industry and look instead to local councils and the Civil Service.

Later, one teacher would tell me how she watched the number of
shipbuilding apprenticeships reduced from 200 to ten.

In the past unions have been little bothered by the concentration
of members into large establishments, often seeing them as
universities of trades unionism. But what concerns them now
is the prospect of their bailiwicks being reduced to a few public
service redoubts within a sea of largely unorganised private
sector and often part-time jobs.

The unions have plenty of experience of organising part-
timers – the public services union, NUPE (now part of Unison),
has long had a majority of part-timers in school meals and hospital services. But it is one thing to organise them in a sympathetic
public institution and another in a private or privatised company.

And so it has proved.

Adversity, however, brought an unexpected development. In the
1975 referendum on continuing European Common Market membership, the majority of unions had campaigned against Brussels
regulation. Jack Jones of the Transport Union had been a particularly vociferous anti. I got some indication of the visceral distaste
for the Common Market as I sat in a Geneva restaurant with Harry
Urwin, Jones's deputy and confidante, during proceedings of the
International Labour Organization (ILO). As our group looked across

the wide street, we could see men on the other side queuing for what
was pretty obviously a brothel. 'Look at that,' said Harry in disgust.
'There is the Common Market for you!' None of us pointed out that
Switzerland was not actually a member.

But now, with Jones and Urwin gone, and the TUC blocked from
progress on workplace reforms by an unsympathetic government,
Europe began to seem rather more appealing – a backdoor to achieve
union objectives, particularly negotiations over the 'Social Chapter'.
The switch was signalled in dramatic fashion by the appearance of
the president of the Commission, the old French socialist Jacques
Delors, at the TUC conference in Brighton in 1988. He did not quite
come ashore from a landing craft on the beach, but the effect was similar. The TUC embraced him and Mrs Thatcher was furious. Only a
few weeks later she declared in her famous Bruges speech: 'We have
not embarked on the business of throwing back the frontiers of the
state at home, only to see a European super-state getting ready to
exercise a new dominance.'

The continuing importance of European legislation and direc-
tives for workplace relationships was indicated by the decision of
John Monks to leave his post as TUC General Secretary in 2003 to
become General Secretary of the European TUC.

As I took my leave of the BBC in the spring of 1989, I reflected on
some of the leaders I had met, and the effects they had had on events.

Standing head and shoulders above anyone else was the determined
and rather chilly figure of Jack Jones. Starting work in the harsh world
of the Liverpool docks, where no one knew whether they would have
work from one day to another, he was a veteran of the Spanish Civil
War who never forgot the international aspect of the union movement. Jones was not very clubbable and he did not do lunch.

He pursued his clear-minded ambition to give power to working people. Labelled by the columnist Paul Johnson as 'the Emperor

Jones', in the '70s he was the driving force behind the social contract. This traded wages deals for benefits for working people, but Jones also understood how vital it was to get runaway inflation down. He fell short of his dream of having elected workers' representatives on company boards but when he retired, there was nobody with the clear vision or muscle to succeed him, and the movement floundered.

One of his abiding achievements was permanently to improve the lot of pensioners. Until the '70s, support for pensioners had been a weapon deployed by Conservatives; with distressed middle classes in mind, they argued that they lost out as high wage settlements brought inflation. Jones turned the argument on its head. In one of the most forceful interventions I witnessed at any conference, he thumped the rostrum at the 1970 Labour Party conference to demand a 'massive campaign' to raise the level of pensions, promising his union would run off 1 million broadsheets in a week. He pursued the issue determinedly. For years after he would lead a pensioners' march on the day before the Congress, and from then on Labour never surrendered the issue.

Jones remained deeply suspicious of the TUC. He was always unsure how much the fixer Vic Feather had agreed or promised in his extensive private meetings with members of different governments. When Feather retired, he did his best to reduce the influence of the TUC, and of Feather's successor, Len Murray.

Len (Lionel) Murray was easily typed as a TUC bureaucrat. He had spent most of his working life in the TUC economics department, a key division under Woodcock and Feather, and he had a strong grasp of the possible. He was a patient negotiator with a realistic sense of what was possible. His lugubrious manner masked a fine sense of the ridiculous which came out in sardonic asides. He was a decent man, bitterly disappointed and ultimately insulted by the Thatcher government's cold shoulder. Just when he was rethinking attitudes and inching towards what came to be called 'new realism', the decision by the government to ban staff working in the security-sensitive GCHQ from belonging to unions was the bitterest of insults. It implication, hugely resented at all levels of the movement, was that trade unionists at best could not be trusted; at worst were incipient traitors.

Murray's misfortune was to succeed at a moment when two strong union leaders, Jones and Scanlon, were intent on their own agendas and, deeply suspicious of his predecessor, were determined not to allow a TUC bureaucrat a leading role. Murray was unable to find strong enough allies to counter the huge voting power of the two big unions. David Basnett, of the GMWU, who had ambitions for a stronger role, lacked clarity of objectives and his numbers were significantly smaller.

Murray, by dogged determination, gained in strength and Jones appreciated his commitment to industrial democracy, but he failed to assert himself sufficiently when the powerful figures retired, and I felt his reticence turned into caution after he had had a heart scare and the onset of angina. Inside the TUC, he encouraged and empowered his staff, who made particularly effective progress in union education and getting to grips with inter-union rivalries.

He moved the young Brendan Barber, himself later to become General Secretary, out of the organisation department, where he had gained a sharp insight into union realities, to head the press department. For the first time it became properly open and respon-sive, while Brendan's trusted links with his colleagues meant it was also informed. But somehow it seemed significant that the front row at Len's memorial service was occupied by senior figures from the Transport Union.

Murray's successor, Norman Willis, could do a fine rendition of 'The man who watered the workers' beer' and was a great source of self-deprecating union jokes. I used one about the fairground workers who decided to have a go slow on the wall of death in my TUC speech. But it did him no favours and led to him too easily being disregarded.

Norman had started as an office boy at Transport House and, after studying at Ruskin, the trade union college at Oxford, took on responsibilities for research and education. We knew him as a congenial but not particularly heavyweight source. When Murray became TUC General Secretary, however, Willis applied for his old post as deputy. Given the TGWU's clout and general reluctance to see the position as simply Buggins' turn for TUC apparatchiks, he got the post. He always maintained that he had not been put up to it by Jones (although Jones formally proposed him), but he was seen, unfairly, as the union's man.

Willis had the misfortune to succeed in the middle of the miners' strike and his period in office coincided with a steady reduction in union membership. You could make a case that his companionable style helped to hold together a divided movement and there was no doubting his principles and courage, on occasion, in pursuing them. His condemnation of violence at a Welsh miners' rally in an intimidating hall with a noose dangled above his head was the act of a brave and principled man.

Nevertheless, he found conference speeches difficult and disheartening, rambled and lost confidence. Although loyally supported by his staff, for a period he seemed to lose the plot and take refuge in drink. In 1988, on the eve of the Congress, I made a *Newsnight* feature laying bare the doubts about his leadership. In something of a coup, I interviewed the now-retired Len Murray, who admitted to disappointment about his performance. It provoked a bitter reaction against Murray for stepping out of line. Norman opted to retire in 1993. Somehow it seemed that he was once again selling himself short when he chose to pursue his interest in embroidery and contributed a regular column to *CrossStitcher* magazine.

Moss Evans, Jones's successor, was regarded by bosses in the motor industry as the best negotiator of his generation. But it turned out to be a poor qualification for a General Secretary. He was quickly sidelined because of aggressive cancer but, even when fit, had neither the temperament nor the conviction to lead from the front. He continued to take the feeling of the lads. Unlike Jones, who knew exactly what he wanted from every meeting, Evans could miss or be late for TUC committees and defer to his union's other nominees.

His friend and successor, Ron Todd, an East Ender who had come up through the ranks in Ford at Dagenham, was known for his honesty and directness. He took an unyielding unilateral nuclear disarmament line, resisted single union deals, challenged Neil Kinnock's Labour Party changes and was respected by all he dealt with. Determinedly loyal, he refused to speak to the BBC when, for a few days, some of us were suspended due to industrial action. He regularly reminded me of it.

Hugh Scanlon, the principled left-wing leader of the Engineering Union, had fought most determinedly against the Wilson government's industrial relations proposals. Then he carried out his union's decision not to have anything to do with Heath's legislation even though it led to the seizure of his union's assets. But when he retired, shortly before Jones, the union, which regularly shuttlecocked between right and left as all its major posts came up regularly for election, opted to go a different route.

Instead it chose a little-known Midlands official, Terry Duffy, after a right-wing caucus had preferred him as their candidate to the experienced Salvationist General Secretary, John Boyd, a Scotsman. I remember the moments before the result was announced. Duffy seemed as surprised as anyone, walking slowly as the last member of the executive into the room where the announcement was to be made. He stayed close to his Midlands roots, interested in industrial agreements and moves to harmonise pay and benefits between blue- and white-collar workers. He had less interest in the TUC and was more absorbed in internal battles against his opponents in the union, whom he insisted on labelling the 'Coms', in truth a mixture of local Labour left-wingers and card-carrying Communist Party members.

He had less of a grip on his union, and was blamed by Denis Healey for his failure to deliver support in some key votes on the Labour Party's future. However, while he might have been less artic- ulate, he had an underlying toughness and understanding of human nature. He was once invited as the guest to one of the regular lunches held by the then Director-General of the BBC, Ian Trethowan, a for- mer political journalist whom I much respected. It was not a great success, but at the end of it Duffy turned to a rising programme edi- tor and said in his Wolverhampton accent, 'Yow hasn't said much. Yow must be on the way up.'

Boyd, hardened by years of upholding an executive position at odds with the union's majority left-wing tendency, was a different character. He had been appointed to the BBC Governor's position normally held by a trade union nominee. I crossed swords with him during the same dispute that had caused Ron Todd to refuse inter- views while we were suspended.

The dispute had come about because a group of BBC journalists working on the *Nine O'Clock News* had held a chapel (branch) meeting when the programme was being prepared, and it had been seriously affected or even prevented. The following morning, another meeting was held, which a number of us who had not been present the previous evening attended to find out what was happening. In the middle of it, the personnel manager appeared and announced that we were all sus- pended. He invited us to hand in our identity cards and BBC car keys.

The dispute only lasted a few days but in the course of it I rang John Boyd, explaining that I wanted to fill him in with the details. He cut me short: 'I know exactly what is happening. You are over-paid. You want more and you have got what you deserve.' Moderate never seemed an appropriate description of him.

By contrast, no one could be more hail fellow well met than Joe Gormley. I first came across him when I covered a by-election in Merthyr Tydfil and he was putting the Labour case at a local pit. He was very drunk and I was not impressed. By the time he retired and welcomed me into his home on the day his peerage was announced, I had a different opinion.

Gormley had not started out as a union man. He had led his own gang of non-union workers down the pit. He was a 'puffler' who negotiated the rate for the job and distributed the money. But he was so successful that the union asked him to join and negotiate for them. It set the pattern for his career.

As he came up to his retirement, deliberately delayed so that the Communist Vice-President, Mick McGahey, would be too old to suc-ceed, I said to a senior member of the Coal Board, 'I suppose you will miss him?' He replied, 'The sooner he goes the better. He has been the only man to lead us into two national strikes in the last fifty years.'

Joe was shrewd and gregarious. His briefings after the monthly union executive meetings were unmissable. Suddenly, in the middle of a technical discussion of pay rates, he would deliver a judgement on the latest attempts by a government to agree a pay policy. It would work or it would not. He had his ear to the ground and knew what the lads were saying; what the market would bear. He would be right. He was the smartest weathercock.

He stayed close to his members. But, with his jaunty hat, his horse-racing, his back-garden swimming pool and his colourful scorn for the chances of revolution, he was an all-too-human trade union leader to whom the public could warm.

You could take different views about his negotiating skills. With an executive split roughly down the middle between right and left, either out of conviction or because he knew just how to utilise the blocking votes of the left, he rarely accepted a deal without tacking on extra benefits. He took the miners to the top of the pay league, managing on occasion to make 20 per cent pay settlements seem modest. Yet he could be over-confident about what he could sell to his troops and his advice to the Coal Board about what would happen was on occasions disastrously wrong. He was blamed by some for the onset of the 1972 strike and by others for the failure to squeeze through a settlement with Heath over waiting and winding time when he spilled the outline of a deal to Harold Wilson.

Mick McGahey, on the other hand, always dark-suited like some self-styled undertaker of capitalism, came from the same Scottish Marxist traditions that had seen the Glasgow socialist uprisings of 1919. He was determined and straight and true to his convictions. His gruff rendition of 'a man is a man for a'that' accompanied by a short bark of laughter over his pint and a whisky chaser hinted at his reputation for self-taught learning. He largely hid his discomfort with Arthur Scargill's leadership and famously prefigured the 1984 strike with his remark 'We shall not be constitutionalised out of action', an untypical stance that showed the way the current was flowing.

After the strike, his more thoughtful perspective reasserted itself. He reflected to my co-author, John Lloyd:

> I am not sure that we handled it all correctly. The mass intrusion
> of pickets into Nottinghamshire, I accept some responsibility for
> that and so will the left have to ... I reject, I have made it clear
> since the strike, that 30,000 Nottingham miners, their wives and

families and communities are scabs and blacklegs. I refuse to
accept this. We did alienate them during the strike.

In the aftermath, he was seen as something of an elder statesman
and at his last miners' conference at Rothesay, in the Firth of Clyde,
he talked nostalgically to me in a farewell profile of what the miners had achieved since the days when as a boy he took the paddle
steamer from Glasgow to the island where we stood.

Which brings us to Arthur Scargill. Arthur stood out from the
moment I met him at Saltley gates as different. He was and remained
one of a kind, focused and always wary. He found it difficult to trust.
His ability was unquestionable; his persistence obsessive. He was the
centre of his own universe. He was also a rarity in the way he was
able to combine a command of public speaking on a public stage with
a mastery of the intimate one-to-one interview. He made sure he was
well-briefed and could sense a moment's weakness or hesitation in
an interviewer. I remember a confrontation with Peter Snow over
one of the series of supposedly secret documents that Arthur had
a habit of producing. As Snow asked about some detail, Arthur
sensed a slight gap and was through in an instant – 'Have you read
the document, Mr Snow?' He had to confess he had not and Arthur
had triumphed.

Coal Board officials who negotiated with Arthur in Yorkshire did
not think him exceptional and struck deals with him. But when he
became national NUM president he seemed to take a vow never
to strike a deal, and a succession of wage negotiations were only
concluded when the membership voted by ballot to ignore his res-
ervations and accept. The strike, of course, ended in defeat with
no settlement.

I sometimes felt that those used hardest by Arthur were his political enemies and his friends. During the miners' strike, executive

members were scared of his ability to pillory them as well as his control, as president, of their pension arrangements and other emoluments.

It was a pity to see Jim, his faithful driver and effectively bodyguard, who had driven him for thousands of miles at all times of the day and night during the strike, and had worked with him down the pit, finally being alienated from him. And it was a sad end that Arthur should end up in legal battles with his own union over various expenses claims.

The miners' and Arthur's challenge was the climactic attempt to use industrial power to change national politics. But, by the end of the '80s, it was clear that political focus was shifting away from labour and industry. The number of industrial correspondents fell and John Fryer, my colleague at BBC TV, became a special correspondent for the *Nine O'Clock News*. He was not replaced. I decided that it was time to look for other challenges. As the new broom of John Birt swept in, I failed in my attempts to find a new senior job at the BBC so I looked to test my expertise outside. Like my colleagues, I had regularly been approached about communications jobs in different industries. I had not been convinced that I wanted such a move and the companies were not right for me. But, in 1989, I had the opportunity to join the country's largest and most respected manufacturer, whose imperial connotations were displayed in its name, ICI – Imperial Chemical Industries. It was time to put my beliefs about communication to the test.

Chapter Fourteen

The boxwallahs –
a failure to explain

In 1982, my colleague Ian Ross left the BBC to join the newly forming Channel Four News, where he continued his distinguished career. I was also looking for a new challenge and had applied for a foreign posting. I was then approached, however, by Peter Woon, the head of BBC News, to become BBC TVs first and only industrial editor, heading a business team which also included an economics and labour correspondent. It was an offer I could not refuse.

My new role focused my attention more closely on business and I set about trying to profile some of the key companies, taking the opportunity offered by their announcements of annual results – one of the few occasions when business heads were compelled to raise their heads above the parapet.

My approaches met with some surprise. I found, or rather confirmed, an astonishing unwillingness to communicate publicly. There was a particular wish to avoid television. It was exemplified, surprisingly, by Sir John Harvey-Jones, the chairman of ICI. It was then Britain's biggest industrial business, and one of the largest exporters and research spenders; its fortunes a key indicator of the health of the economy. It was nicknamed 'the bellwether of British industry', the leader of the flock.

ICI had suffered badly from the recession and its own slow pace of modernisation and at his press conference, the forthright Harvey-Jones described the results as 'lousy'. Before the meeting I had requested an interview, and had been turned down. Now I telephoned his office, pointing out how clearly he had answered questions and repeating my interview request. There was a debate at the other end for a minute or two but then the refusal was confirmed. I was left to repeat his words in my own piece to camera, perched on a milk crate borrowed from the newspaper-seller outside ICI's main entrance, bringing my head level with the company's famous roundel.

Months later, Harvey-Jones admitted that he had made a mistake and in recompense offered me an exclusive interview when ICI became one of the first British companies to list its shares on the New York Stock Exchange. Later, of course, he became well-known for his plain-speaking and had his own arresting television series as *The Troubleshooter*, an early example of reality TV. The camera tracked him as he went into problem companies and advised them on possible strategies. It provided a much better insight into business than *The Apprentice*.

But the fact that even a man like Harvey-Jones should shrink from the media revealed much about the attitude of British business. As I wrote at the time:

> However much trade unionists complain about the quality or
> content of coverage, they have, in recent years, become very

proficient in achieving large quantities of it. It is a lesson which business in general and companies in particular still have to learn. In a phrase which union activists use to complain about their treatment, they have learnt how 'to set the agenda'. Business is left to respond or, all too often, not to speak at all.

How often does one tune in to a trade unionist talking about his preoccupations; how rarely to industry talking about its achievements or matters which have nothing to do with industrial relations?

The lack of experience of business in putting its case in a combative atmosphere, where it might be subject to challenge, had been clearly enough illustrated by the CBI's lacklustre performance when confronted by the tripartite talks with unions and government under the Heath government.

It should have been no surprise. Businessmen – the rather contemptuous term for them in empire days was 'boxwallah' – were used to operating below the radar. Trade followed the flag. Unlike politicians, or campaigners like trade unionists, they were not public performers, but more used to getting on with their job. They answered publicly to shareholders, usually once a year, at a formal meeting, where they largely controlled the agenda.

There was plenty of discreet lobbying of government behind closed doors but the general line was to encourage as little government 'interference' as possible. From a Conservative government's point of view, it expected tacit support from industry while reserving the right to manipulate it, through control of lending and other means, most notoriously the 'regulator', which fixed hire purchase levels for the motor industry. It was used as a way of controlling the economy at the long-term expense of the industry.

When captains of industry did emerge blinking into the light, they expected still to be treated with a deference that was disappearing in other walks of life. But, in order to keep themselves from time-consuming sorties into industrial policy, they engaged a variety of bodies to do the representing on their behalf. The most all-embracing was the CBI, but every trade had its association, the Chemical Manufacturers, the Engineering Employers, the Newspaper Proprietors and so on. As one of their directors put it to me, 'We are the League of Gentlemen's Gentlemen,' the phrase traditionally applied to the personal servants of the aristocracy.

But times were changing. The impact of industrial relations crises compelled some businessmen to go agonisingly public. After Lord Ryder's disaster at British Leyland – an example of an important private sector businessman totally unprepared for the public stage – the savvy Michael Edwardes made his carefully planned public interventions with the help of his personal PR advisor. Nationalised industry chairmen had to cope with the public spotlight. Although, like Ian MacGregor, they might duck it for a while, it came with the territory. But their counterparts in private industry saw little need to do so and with a touch of schadenfreude often marked down those who habitually ventured onto the public stage as ineffective businessmen.

Someone who sensed the problem but dealt with it in a characteristically individualistic way was Arnold Weinstock. He had built GEC into an industrial behemoth encompassing most of what was left of Britain's heavy electrical engineering, with businesses from aerospace to power generation to domestic washing machines. Weinstock's takeover and subsequent rationalisation of the rival AEI in the '60s had been ruthless but effective. In fact, the adverse political reaction to his stringent downsizing was acknowledged to me by Donald Stokes as the reason that Stokes had failed to make the changes required at British Leyland.

Weinstock's increasing success was assisted by minute supervision of the company's finances and very close relations with the government departments responsible for major power engineering and defence contracts. But he was concerned about the lack of voice for business.

He dealt with this erratically. Every year or two, he would invite a group of journalists to dinner or lunch and expatiate on the way the business case was not being put effectively. On one occasion he floated the idea of a team of business spokesmen who could be called on at particular moments. At another, he declared that all his factories were open to us. We took him at his word and organised a feature about his Hotpoint factory, a small part of the empire, but about the only British washing machine maker left at the time. As for Arnold himself: after his interventions, he would retire into the obscurity of his spartan Mayfair office where he was accumulating a cash mountain that he appeared reluctant to reinvest in industry.

In the aftermath of the Heath debacle, however, a new Director-General at the CBI, John Methven, made a concerted attempt to rebalance the equation, calling on assistance from some other more thoughtful captains of industry. Coming into office in the last days of the Callaghan Labour government, making speeches in which he insisted that Britain was 'drinking in the last-chance saloon', he argued for a new attitude towards industry. In an attempt to even up the media score with the trade unions, in 1977 he instituted the first ever CBI conference. Held in the traditional party conference resort of Brighton, it had keynote speakers from major companies, resolutions and rather stilted debates, and achieved live television coverage, counterpointing the TUC.

In the years that followed, the CBI made a point of holding its conference in industrial areas such as Birmingham and even, briefly, introduced voting on resolutions. It was not popular. In the early years, three key themes dominated: the government's running of the economy, with interest rates a particular concern; the need for changes in industrial relations law; and the level of the pound. Here the problems of leaving matters to the gentlemen's gentlemen were apparent, as rival interests such as the oil companies and manufacturing industry took opposing views, and the CBI ended up sitting on the fence, as a third of British manufacturing industry disappeared.

In the wake of Methven's sudden death, the CBI turned to one of his key supporters, Terry Beckett, who had been an effective and articulate chairman of the successful Ford of Britain. It is tempting to argue that Ford's transatlantic perspective, and the very different behaviour of US businessmen at that time, had something to do with Beckett's more communicative approach. But the cerebral and rather soft-spoken Beckett, a welcome guest when he was announcing new investment or introducing Henry Ford to Prime Ministers, came up against the harsh realities of dealing publicly with governments when he made his famous 'bare-knuckle fight' speech at another Brighton conference.

It had been a pretty dreary conference and the night before it ended a group of senior businesspeople, including Harvey-Jones, reviewed the draft of the speech Beckett would deliver at the close of the meeting the following day. The consensus was that it needed strengthening. Subsequently, the threat of a 'bare-knuckle fight' with the government if it did not moderate its policies towards industry was written into the speech.

It may have come out rather unconvincingly from the measured Beckett, but the impact was immediate. Margaret Thatcher was infuriated and her most fervent supporter among CBI leaders, John (later Lord) King, announced that he was withdrawing his company, Babcock's, from the organisation in disgust. The conferences continued but gradually narrowed down. Today they occupy a single day at a London venue and are mostly composed of keynote speeches and guest speakers, including the Prime Minister or Chancellor.

But, just as reluctant business leaders were seeing the travails of Terry Beckett as a justification for keeping their heads down, they were becoming subject to other pressures for more public transparency; this time from investors. With the easing of financial regulation, the so-called 'Big Bang' in the City of London in 1986 brought with it as part of a greatly increased US presence in London a demand for clear and more frequent reporting of financial results, as well as pressures from increasingly powerful transatlantic investors.

A coincidental explosion in business news programming by both independent companies and the BBC with lunchtime 'results' programmes meant that company heads had to familiarise themselves with the techniques of broadcast communication. Even if it was confined to the narrowly financial details with which they were familiar, their presence in a studio could also evoke other questions, such as their company's effect on employees or the environment, or, most taxingly, their own remuneration. It was a process I would watch from the outside at the BBC and, later, from the inside at ICI. The adage that business people were interested in facts but unhappy about commenting on the issues that enthused the broadcasters was all too often true.

The attitude of the top was reflected down the line and I would argue that British business's failure to explain over many years helped its decline, prevented it addressing important problems and encouraged its remoteness from ordinary people. It had catastrophic results in the decline of interest in science and engineering, Even as late as 2014 the CBI was launching a programme to improve the public perception of business.

In 1983, in an article for *The Listener*, I put it like this:

> it is not simply a case of busy company chairmen having no
> time for the media. It is also industry's failure to maintain

regular bread-and-butter contacts, providing a broad range of information about what is happening instead of once and for all hyping a new product.

On numerous occasions, major export orders are announced suddenly and without warning and I have telephoned the company concerned to be told 'We didn't think that you would be interested', or given an explanation that no advance warning could be given because of some obscure reason like the timing of a foreign stock exchange.

Now there are, of course, some solid replies. As Sir Terence Beckett explains it, company chairmen are busy men with crowded schedules with strong priorities involving selling products and keeping companies in fighting trim in a highly competitive environment. Their job is not essentially a propaganda one in a way that a trade union leader's duties would include those of a politician on the stump.

At one CBI conference, the result of one of the life-or-death BL ballots was awaited. When it came (a return to work) I asked representatives from important Midlands component firms for their reaction. After consultation they nominated one of the CBI regional representatives to speak for them, 'because his firm is not involved'.

When I joined ICI in 1989, I discovered that the company had actually seriously considered engaging a working newsreader, Alastair Burnet, a former editor of *The Economist*, to represent them and put the company's point of view, apparently while still working as a journalist. It was an impossible idea but it showed how little serious attention even well-run companies gave to their public stance and media coverage. It was not a priority.

As I wrote:

It comes back to basic distrust of the media, apart perhaps for the narrow financial aspects ghettoed conveniently towards the back of newspapers or late-night programmes. It could be paraphrased as 'any publicity is bad publicity'.

Talk to those gentlemen's gentlemen and they will say how they are still regarded with resentment by executives whom they encouraged to appear before the press and now believe their careers were harmed by doing so.

I recently badgered the deputy chairman of a nationalised industry about obtaining coverage of a major new development. It was an amicable enough conversation until he suddenly turned on me and asked, 'Why does the BBC always ask the dirty question?' The illustration he gave was of the opening of an expensive extension to an old installation. He had reacted furiously to the reporter's final question, 'Why was it worth spending so much money on an old installation?' It is exactly the sort of question which industry should have no difficulty in answering.

I discussed these recurrent difficulties about filming British industry with one of our most experienced cameramen, responsible for some of the most eloquent pictures of industry. He brought up the comparison with the Continent; how relatively easy it was to get into major factories even at short notice. He said, 'The difference is that there they welcome you. Here they think that you are prying.'

In the Mercedes factory near Stuttgart I was fascinated to find that most German buyers prefer to pick up their new cars directly from the factory. It was not difficult to see why. Apart from the special guidance provided by mechanics, customers are offered a film show about the plant and regular guided tours throughout the day of the assembly lines and production facilities. What a world away from the closed world of British mass-production car plants!

To be fair, there are plenty of British factories where I have been welcomed and there are firms that are both energetic and straight about their press relations, but they remain in a minority. It comes down to a question of will. For all the talk of British industry being misunderstood, it still expects us to understand it without explaining itself. Companies can only blame themselves if they are regarded as something mysteriously apart from the mainstream of life and if, in the vacuum provided by their silence, it is left to others to set the agenda.

One of my more fascinating encounters came in 1986, when the business of the legendary inventor Clive Sinclair (on whose basic ZX81 our children had had their first taste of computing) ran into difficulty. The company was heading for bankruptcy but a deal was reached for it to be bought out by Alan Sugar of Amstrad, who was prepared to pay for the name and believed he could revitalise its Spectrum machine.

I went to the press announcement and interviewed both men separately. There was a staggering contrast. While Sinclair was fluent and explanatory, Sugar's answers were long-winded and woolly. He came over as wary and suspicious. When I came to edit the piece for transmission I gave up in despair of finding a short, coherent statement from him. Instead, I managed to make do with something just about passable from the formal press conference.

The lesson was that fluency could be misleading. In this deal there was only one winner, and that was Alan Sugar. But, if you had placed a bet on which of the two men would one day have his own television show, you would not have put your money on him.

Another successful businessman, who was very skilled at working the press but disliked press conferences and broadcast interviews, was the choleric John King, who had taken over as chairman of

British Airways after a long series of planted leaks in the Sunday papers. While his doings were mostly covered by the BBC's aviation correspondent, Chris Wain, I attended the announcement of BA's annual results at which the fruits of his cost-cutting were displayed.

King was pressed about a report that the company cars issued to airline executives had been downgraded. He was asked for examples. He turned grumpily to his head of public relations – 'What do you drive? You tell them.'

Afterwards, Giles Smith from ITN and I both interviewed him separately in search of that clear, thirty-second quote. As Giles finished, a press officer walked over to him and said, *sotto voce*, 'Please don't use any of those figures; he has got them all wrong.'

King was, however, much more comfortable when it came to the newspapers, and particularly the Sundays. He was adept at using what we called the 'Friday night drop', where companies and PR firms floated stories or previewed announcements in the Sundays without having to inform the stock exchange, which was closed for the weekend. His thoughts about BA and his possible chairmanship could be set out in advance. For other ambitious businessmen, a close relationship with a Sunday paper became a useful weapon, with a discreet Friday business editor's lunch a controlled way to get the publicity or test the water in the way they wanted.

Another of my interviews to remember was with an elderly and eminent Japanese businessman who had come over with one of the seemingly endless ping-pong of delegations between our two countries to deal with the growing trade gap. Japanese imports to Britain were increasing with no such movement the other way. At the end of the visit, the Japanese delegation offered us interviews. We pressed them on why the Japanese did not buy more from Britain. In a rather guttural voice, the delegation's leader explained to ITN that it was to do with the colour of the cars we sent over – yellows and reds, which were not popular with Japanese buyers. Then it was my turn and I duly posed the same question, expecting a similar reply.

At first my interviewee appeared to ramble, announcing to my astonishment, 'Japanese people have short arms and very thick necks.' When he paused I found it impossible to keep a straight face. Then he added, savagely, 'And you send us pullovers that do not fit!' As we packed up the equipment, he stumped across the room, saying clearly in English, 'I hate interviews like that.'

But, if the Japanese reaction on this occasion was not dissimilar to the aura of mistrust that came from so many British businessmen, it was noticeable how different European and American businessmen could be.

I had good relations with the big German shipping and shipbuilding company Hapag-Lloyd. I had first visited their Bremerhaven shipyard to film the conversion of one of the last great Atlantic liners, the *France*, into a Florida cruise ship. It was a symbolic end to the historic rivalries and romance of the transatlantic crossing. I delivered a piece to camera standing under the stern of the ship. Above me, you could see where they had amputated two of the four propellers originally installed in the hope of bringing back to France the Blue Riband for the fastest transatlantic crossing. The footage is regularly rerun as part of the BBC series on the great liners.

Thanks to these contacts, I was later able to break the story that the pride of Britain's merchant fleet, the *QE2*, was for the first time to have its annual refit outside the UK, at Bremerhaven. It was a story seen fit to lead the news, such was our preoccupation with Britain's imperial maritime heritage.

The yard provided us with every kind of assistance, including the use of our own tug for filming when the *QE2* finally docked in the early hours of the morning. It was indicative of a very different corporate approach. Its chairman made a point of coming to Britain every year to explain his company's performance in perfect English and answer any questions directed at him. It was an object lesson for his British counterparts.

So too when Roger Smith, the chairman of General Motors, then the greatest motor manufacturer on the planet, visited Britain at a time when there were big questions about the future of his Vauxhall manufacturing facilities in Britain, he made himself available. His company also provided us with access to make an accompanying film for *Newsnight*, in which we raised the questions about the impact of the increasing globalisation of car production and showed just how many of the parts assembled in Britain were actually brought in from sites all around the world.

This was important because at the time British companies provided very little footage of what was happening inside their factories. Not only did they discourage you, and by extension the public, from seeing for yourself, any pictures they did supply were usually as part of advertising promotional material, often with wording imposed on it. While occasionally there might have been processes so advanced that companies did not wish competitors to spy on them (and they did make that excuse), this was rarely the case, and there would have been ways round it.

When I later went to ICI, in 1989, one of the first things I did was to make sure that we had film, or tape, of our basic operations that was provided to broadcast organisations for use when the company was going to be mentioned.

By then, some practice was changing. Broadcasting training, often using working BBC and other reporters, had blossomed. In the same way that politicians like Norman Fowler had been put through their paces, with the results showing in the way they tried to stay on message and avoid engaging in serious debate, media training began to be part of some senior executives' training. But it was still confined to a very few and was liable to be cancelled or postponed if something else came up.

More seriously, it did not always encourage explanation and dialogue. The accepted pattern was to subject business people to ferocious questioning, often noticeably enjoyed by the interviewer, point out their shortcomings, and then show how they could do better. The problem was that some people were so shaken up by the process that they resolved never to have anything to do with the media if they could help it. Others, like my first chairman at ICI, Denys Henderson, a lawyer by training, enjoyed the cut and thrust.

Among the best examples of good practice in the private sector were Ford and BP. I don't think it was a coincidence that they were both international companies.

I have referred to Ford in the context of pay talks, where it made sure that it circulated its response to union demands as soon as possible after it had been provided to the unions, a reflection of a clarity of explanation and a willingness to make itself available not generally shared by other motor companies. BP, like Ford, had a press office which was always available and did its best to find answers to questions. It was also assiduous in providing access to its new oilfield developments and also to senior executives. But the case of Sir Robert Horton, chief executive from 1990 to 1992, is illustrative of the mismatch that can occur between good communication and business success. Unfortunately, it was too often seized upon as an argument against good communication.

Horton had been a rising star in BP as he headed its chemicals division and then its US operations. Confident and decisive, but also autocratic, he rose apparently unstoppably before being appointed chairman in 1990. He started with a major and necessary rethink of the company which only a few years before had been largely owned by the government and was still prone to a civil service mentality.

Under his 'Project 90', the most senior managers were brought together for a seminar lasting several days to rethink the company's direction and operation. The management editor of the *Financial Times* was given privileged access and produced lengthy and approving articles on the process. Empowerment workshops were arranged, the headquarters cut back and employees were urged to make suggestions.

In parallel, Horton made himself readily available to talk frankly about the business and his challenges. But his revolution came unstuck. In part it was the contrast between his apparent openness and autocratic style; in part it was too sudden a change. As his successor, John Browne, put it, 'BP needed to change but Bob's energetic style became out of step with the organisation.'[8]

The immediate cause, however, was that his bet on the oil price went wrong. He continued to spend on investment as the price BP was receiving for its oil sank. He believed that it would soon rise and was happy to brief me and other journalists on his reasons for thinking so. Unfortunately, it did not, and Horton was sacked.

In the aftermath, Horton was held up as an example of someone who had been too keen to communicate. His search for public profile, so the scuttlebutt went, had led him to take his eye off the business necessities.

I don't think that was particularly true, but the idea that somehow there is an inverse relationship between being good at public relations and running a successful business is dangerously pervasive. I found a frightening satisfaction, sometimes amounting to glee, among businesspeople who shunned what they called the limelight when one of their number did speak out and faced criticism or even abuse. It provided them with an easy excuse not to raise their own heads above the parapet. Always look on the downside.

---

8   John Browne, *Beyond Business* (Weidenfeld & Nicholson, 2010), p. 62

In a valedictory *Listener* piece as I left the BBC, I reviewed the changes in attitudes that had occurred since my criticisms of six years before. In truth, they were not as great as one might have expected, but I picked out two illuminating case studies.

The first was the attempt by the acquisitive and non-communicative BTR, a conglomerate of engineering businesses, to take over the world-famous glassmaker, Pilkington. Pilkington, whose headquarters remained close to its plants in St Helens in Lancashire, was a genuine world leader with a history of developing new technology. It also had a well-established community programme around its factories, which extended to sports facilities and the provision of meals to elderly pensioners.

The company played up its technical and community strengths and provided access for us to visit and film, as well as talk to local people. The reclusive BTR told us simply, 'We don't do television.'

In the event, the shareholders on whom BTR had been counting, given their previous run of success, rejected the bid. It was a scenario remarkably similar to one that would play out between Hanson and ICI a few years later, in which I would be centrally involved.

If it had just employed the community support argument, I don't believe Pilkington would have triumphed. But its all-round strengths tipped the balance. As I wrote, 'It was able to convince the City that even though it was headquartered in the unfashionable North West, it still had excellent prospects, research and management ability, and could inspire the commitment of its workforce.'

I added, 'It was significant that BTR refused television coverage both during the battle and after, and that Pilkington subsequently resolved to stay much closer to the City. With the CBI's encouragement, big companies are now spending much more of their time briefing analysts.'

For the record, neither company is any longer British-owned.

Twenty years later, in 2006, Pilkington succumbed to a takeover by a smaller Japanese company, Nippon Sheet Glass, but has continued to make glass in the UK. BTR became less popular with investors, was merged into a company called Invensys and needed debt restructuring before it was also sold – to a French company, Schneider Electric, in 2014.

The other example I gave was the Westland affair. On Friday 13 December 1985, at about 7 p.m., I received a call from the newsroom. The government was having crisis talks about the helicopter maker, Westland. Was it important enough for the *Nine O'Clock News*? 'Yes,' I said. 'I will do the story.' And so began an extraordinary couple of months that cost two Cabinet ministers their jobs and came close to bringing down Mrs Thatcher herself. It was a riveting experience as the companies and the banks involved went into overdrive to communicate, employing the growing tribe of PR companies whose expansion in influence and numbers as the century wore on would become a major story.

I wrote, again in *The Listener*:

In more than a dozen years of reporting many of the great political and industrial conflicts of our times, I cannot remember being subjected to briefings so remorselessly one-sided, often quite shameless in insisting that their own partial view was the one which must be reflected in the news, and then complaining that it was not. In a month of covering Westland, there have been more attempts to bend my ear from Whitehall and associated sources than in a year of the miners' strike.

Battle was joined on Friday 13 December when at a press conference supposed to put the lid on the uncertainty surrounding the company's future, Sir John Cuckney of Westland and Bill Paul, who is in charge of the American Sikorsky company for the

United Technologies Corporation, announced a recommended deal. Scarcely had they finished when the Ministry of Defence was briefing that there was no money and no requirement for the Black Hawk helicopter they proposed to license, and that although Mr Heseltine would not speak publicly, waiting by their telephones there just happened to be Admiral Sir Raymond Lygo of British Aerospace and Jim Prior MP, chairman of GEC.

In the days that followed, not only did the ranks of available admirals swell (Sir Raymond on one side, his contemporary Sir John Treacher on the other, with French and Italian officers coming over now and then), but so did the number of public relations companies.

It was not sufficient to telephone Westland or British Aerospace (the alternative suitor). The GEC man said frankly at one point that he was not being told anything. Instead there was a separate PR agency for Westland; another for the Europeans and another for the United Technologies–Fiat end. In addition there were separate agencies representing the city interests of the combatants and the merchant banks. When they were not available, there was likely to be one admiral or another to fire a broadside at the other side.

In the meantime lectures about the precise state of the European aircraft market were delivered to us by public relations men and bankers, who as some openly admitted, had known nothing whatever about it a few days earlier.

For me, the circus reached its ludicrous height when shareholders arriving to vote at the company's special general meeting at the Albert Hall were greeted by short-skirted cheerleaders with pompoms, hired by a PR company to promote the European solution.

The outcome, a victory for the wily Sir John Cuckney through votes whose ownership has never been satisfactorily explained, backed the original American deal. But, after the sound and fury quietened down, the dire predictions did not transpire. Ironically, European cooperation continued while little of the projected American work materialised. Westland was bought by the British company GKN, and later sold to the Italian helicopter maker, MV Agusta, in a European solution.

The pattern demonstrated by the Westland battle became more established as the century wore on. Businessmen were faced with the need to communicate more directly with their shareholders as business channels opened up. Particularly important was Bloomberg, the American company that placed an outlet it seemed on every analyst's desk and expected to broadcast interviews with chief executives or at least finance directors on the morning of their results.

I wrote in 2000 in *Sunday Business* (a whole new newspaper that had appeared, reflecting the growth of business reporting):

> new imperatives, particularly the need to explain to financiers and analysts in the interests of shareholder value, have kicked in. Under these pressures, business leaders have learnt to do their bit. Sit by the bagel-and-coffee stands in the lobby of Bloomberg's Finsbury Square offices – an aroma of Manhattan in EC2 – and you brush against one after another of the crowned heads of quoted companies arriving before the cameras to put the best gloss on the financial figures they have announced minutes before.

And with them were the ubiquitous PR companies to whom they had turned in order to shape their message for journalists, but above all for the financial analysts.

As a result, business and industry became increasingly seen simply through the prism of financial numbers and potential deals. Progressively less attention and less explanation was provided about the way they were run and the consequences of their activities. So when, for example, attention shifted to the huge increases in pay for senior executives, the so-called fat cats, there was no balancing narrative about the importance of their jobs and what the real achievements of their companies were. They had, in a sense, chosen to appear outside the fabric of society.

So, having missed its opportunity to explain as a matter of course, business was more and more channelled down the lines of what came to be called 'shareholder value'. Journalists followed. It was a very popular concept in the City in the early '90s, but it became increasingly flawed as shareholders became increasingly transitory. Marks & Spencer's defeat of a takeover by Sir Philip Green was a rare example of long-time small shareholders defeating a financial grab. Most companies could no longer call on them. Businesses became increasingly subject to the whims and wishes of investors simply out to maximise their profits quickly. Small wonder that the interest in business switched to short-term performance and there was increasing reluctance to engage in long-term capital investment.

When I made a film for *The Money Programme* in 1989 which questioned how much business would invest as the economy recovered, the result was hopeful if ambiguous. The same film in the 1990s would have produced a gloomier verdict.

By the time I left ICI in 2000, my slightly optimistic mood of 1989 had changed. As I continued to argue that firms must explain, the battleground had become more entrenched. Business had emerged from its tent under growing media pressure but had been bruised by the experience; journalists had grown increasingly scornful, and less receptive. A piece that I wrote for *Sunday Business* was headed

'What makes business and the media hate one another?' I quoted a PR advisor I respected, saying:

> Senior executives are aware of the need to communicate with the media and have been prepared to spend time on it. But they are increasingly frustrated by the tabloid nature of the coverage and of the ignorance of those interviewing them. Some are starting to question the wisdom of doing it.

I also quoted a respected company chairman, who said, 'In the old days journalists would usually phone me up and we could say this or that is happening. They might interpret it but they would write it. Now they don't often bother to ring and the story is a kind of gratuitous shooting from the hip.'

I wrote:

> On the other hand business leaders still come to major positions inadequately prepared for the rough and tumble of dealing with the media and the public. Learning on the job can leave indelible scars which discourage communication in the future.
>
> So what can one say to persuade them to keep communicating? Funnily enough, I think the answer begins with their single biggest beef. They routinely contrast what they see as the culture of envy in Britain with the admiration for business success in the US. Reporting of pay increases for executives – 'the fat-cat syndrome' – raises clouds of righteous steam on both sides. Yet their rising standard of living is fact.
>
> One headhunter told me bluntly, 'Lots of executives are earning millions with opportunities to pass Go and collect more. Ten years ago an executive director might be expected to earn £250,000 a year and, if lucky, a bonus. Today he will make double that.'

The same person describes business leaders as 'the new film-stars ... if you make it in the business world, you have superstar status. They all have houses with pools and jet-set around.'

With this goes an obligation to give an explanation of the importance of business achievement. It is here that there remains a pool of silence. The result is a gap in our public understanding. Writing in 2000, the late Dame Mary Warnock, a pillar of the intellectual establishment, talked of business as 'this rather mysterious world'. But why? Is it just that it has explained itself less well than other major institutions?

To open up that mysterious world means business holding its nerve and not faltering in the drive to explain. For the media it means listening and not simply following the kneejerk reaction of 'big deal good, big pay-out bad'.

That was 2000 and the change in status and rewards to something more transatlantic, which I charted, has grown exponentially since then. I think it strengthens my conclusions.

Chapter Fifteen

Politics and politicians

My time in journalism spanned the administrations of four Prime Ministers: Wilson, Heath, Callaghan and Thatcher. Wilson had been in office for about a year when I joined *The Guardian*. Mrs Thatcher departed a year after I left the BBC. During that time I found myself at close quarters with all of them, as well as with various departmental ministers who came and went more rapidly.

My strangest and saddest encounter came with Edward Heath. I had come across him often enough on official business, on platforms and at walkabouts, but in the middle of his premiership, Westminster Council, on which I sat, arranged to give a party for the Queen. I suppose it was to celebrate the first twenty years of her reign. She graciously lent us Marlborough House and the good and the great turned out in full fig, including Mr Heath.

My wife Ann and I found ourselves waiting for friends in a large empty downstairs room. At the other end of the room, having a quiet drink – solitary, totally on his own – was Edward Heath, at the height of his powers but a Prime Minister all too obviously short of friends, a graphic indication of what was to come. It was a contrast to the relentless lobbying that came with close coverage of a political party – in my experience Labour, but no doubt true also of the Conservatives.

All four Prime Ministers had their different and distinctive ways of dealing with the media.

Wilson professed a chumminess which was allied to a know-all attitude, suggesting that he always knew better. He took great delight in teasing the press in his annual conference speech. I had various close encounters with him; a double-edged occasion was his opening of the vast Russian Trade Delegation complex on Highgate West Hill at the height of the Cold War, when vodka flowed freely and great friendship was professed. The building was used, as it turned out, as a base for Russian spies who were later expelled.

After the elections of 1974, those of us who had followed Wilson on the campaign trail were invited to Downing Street for a social gathering. Wilson, who liked to be among journalists and show off his knowledge, was in expansive mood. He encouraged us to ask questions. Somehow we got round to who should be the next leader of the Conservatives as it was clear that Heath would not long continue. If they were sensible, he suggested, they would select Richard Wood, the little-known former Minister for Overseas Development. We were baffled. He invited us to guess why. Was it perhaps because he was a war hero who had two artificial legs? No. His answer was that he was a decent, patrician figure who reflected the traditional values of the party and would elicit respect. In the event, of course, they chose almost the opposite in Margaret Thatcher.

Wilson's successor, Jim Callaghan, took a more wary and suspicious line. He was a bruiser. In any interview you knew he would challenge your questions almost immediately, particularly if he was

on difficult ground. When he launched the Bullock Report on industrial democracy, which we both knew was a dead duck, he was very
quickly on the attack.

Margaret Thatcher, by contrast, went out of her way to be charming. I once attended a reception for the press at Downing Street at
which both Denis and Mark Thatcher were also present. Mark was
particularly agitated because, as he told his father, he believed there to
be someone there from *Private Eye*. The event was primarily for political journalists but Bernard Ingham had sent me an invitation as I was
the current chairman of the Labour and Industrial Correspondents
Group. Mrs Thatcher greeted me and Ann warmly over the quail
eggs, although I represented the group her ministers regarded with
the gravest suspicion.

Some months later, on a tour of the north-east, she arrived at the
Sunderland shipyard, which had just launched one of its last-ever con-
structions, a sophisticated North Sea survey ship. As we stood on the
deck, local journalists asked the routine questions, standard in
the manufacturing north: what was the future of the yard? Would
there be more redundancies? She drew herself back, in an imitation
of her famous response to the Falkland victory, 'Rejoice, Rejoice.'
'This is no time to talk about that. We are here to celebrate this marvellous ship!' She was comfortably in charge.

The Labour beat took me into political coverage, and particularly
the internal workings of the Labour Party, both its National Executive
Committee (NEC) and the Transport House staff who served them.
I had come across some of them in battles to get the issue of race
relations into the agenda of the 1970 party conference. But now my
specific brief was to cover the party's monthly National Executive
meetings and all that flowed from them. The general secretaries
of the biggest trade unions sat on the TUC General Council, while
their deputies or number threes competed for election to the

Labour NEC. In the same way, the labour correspondent of *The Guardian* took prime responsibility for the General Council, while I, as the number two, looked after the party.

At the time, it was still a tenant of the Transport Union in Transport House in Smith Square in Westminster. Conservative Central Office stood on the opposite corner. Apparatchiks from both used the expansive bar of the adjoining Marquis of Granby pub.

In those days, think tanks were few and far between. The ideas and fledgling policies for the Labour Party were largely worked on by the small staff of the research department at Transport House. Serving Labour Prime Ministers could be exasperated by the suggestions thought up by some young researcher, but it did not prevent the committees of the NEC discussing and often approving them. Tensions between the party machine and a sitting Labour government over policy were never far away and mammoth joint meetings would be held to try to resolve differences when a party manifesto was required for an election.

As a result, party documents often made good copy. In fact, a leaked document often got rather more attention than the same, often dull, paper would have received when it was officially published. My greatest coup was to get hold of a copy of Labour's draft election manifesto in 1974, a couple of days before it was due to be discussed. *The Guardian* published it as its front-page lead.

Labour's newish General Secretary, Ron Hayward, was trying to be more open about the party's proceedings than his predecessors. In the afternoon following NEC meetings, we would gather in the same Transport House boardroom as the executive had met, for him to describe what had gone on that morning. But the official version only went so far. Afterwards, we would phone up our sources to try to find out what really happened, or we would already have some inkling from lunching an NEC member.

I had a variety of sources, not always the most prominent, but sometimes surprisingly ready to share information, in some cases deliberately to discredit some initiative. I was frequently surprised by the willingness of my sources to provide detailed information, apparently for no particular advantage. As with the trade unions, both sides knew the other leaked but that did not diminish the glee and feigned horror they displayed when a rival was caught red-handed.

The favoured dining place for Labour Party leaders was the Gay Hussar, a narrow Hungarian restaurant in Greek Street in the heart of Soho. It had been set up in the 1940s by Victor Sassi with help from various Labour worthies including Bill (later Sir William) Richardson, who had been the editor of the Labour-supporting newspaper *Reynolds News*, later to become the *Sunday Citizen*. In consequence, it had now become almost a Labour Party canteen, although there was also a strong representation from the nearby film industry.

Now, arranged along tables divided by a single central aisle, could be found MPs, ministers and trade unionists as well as lobbyists and journalists. Indeed, at one bizarre moment, a defendant in an East End murder trial gave as his alibi that he had been at a party at the Gay Hussar at which Michael Foot MP had been present.

Victor Sassi was no Hungarian. He was the son of an electrician who had worked in the Vickers shipyard in Barrow-in-Furness. But in the '30s he had taken advantage of a government catering industry training scheme. He had then found his way to Budapest where he had worked in the kitchens of the Esterházys and other great families in the days when three-day banquets were still on the menu.

I was in good odour with him as I was a friend of Bill Richardson and his energetic wife, Lady Gladys, who happened to live in the same Peak District village as my mother-in-law. But I made a point of avoiding the restaurant's ground floor, where Victor prowled the aisle because everybody could see who was dining with whom.

It might be good for a story, but it compromised your sources. Instead, I preferred the first floor, supervised by an impeccable Hungarian, the charming Albert, away from the badinage of downstairs.

So it was that one executive day I was lunching Tom Bradley, an MP who was a close supporter of Roy Jenkins. At the end of the meal he left, but suddenly reappeared, ashen-faced, at the head of the stairs. 'I can't possibly leave. Judith Hart [a left-wing Labour minister who sat with him on the National Executive] is here. She will know that I have been talking to you.' I suggested that she would not notice me if I left first. I paid the bill and slipped away unnoticed.

The irony, of course, was that I had lunched Judith Hart myself at the Gay Hussar more than once as she was chair of the important Home Affairs Committee of the party. She was a cautious briefer but she gave me one story of immense long-term constitutional significance that led the paper one Monday morning. It predicted the birth of a new political species. Labour was planning to introduce special advisors drawn from party loyalists, to assist ministers. Forty years on, Spads, as they are now known, are ubiquitous and in 2015 both the Prime Minister and the Leader of the Opposition had started their careers as special advisors.

The climax of the party year was the political conferences in the autumn usually held at a seaside resort, most commonly Brighton or Blackpool. The theatricality of the occasions was particularly enhanced by the gilt and red plush surroundings of the Winter Gardens in Blackpool, my favourite venue.

At the time, conferences were still a celebration of the spoken word. But the wheel was turning. It was Bill Richardson who told me of attending a Ramsay MacDonald rally in the north-east in the 1920s. MacDonald had spoken from a platform of farm carts pushed together but the crowd was so big that it was impossible to hear what he said. People knew that would be the case but still turned out.

Now the leader's speech (on a Tuesday afternoon for Labour and at the end of a conference for Conservatives) sucked in trainloads of Fleet Street editors and industrial lobbyists.

Conferences were revealing places where you could easily rub shoulders with people with whom you would usually have to book interviews, as well as watch the parties at play, and identify coming figures. It was an opportunity to buttonhole politicians as the swelling numbers of lobbyists demonstrated. But I also found the prolonged exposure put you off whichever party you were covering.

By the '80s, the significance of the big speech was being reduced to a collection of sound bites. But there were still epic debating battles. We treasured some of the high-blown language, particularly when it went wrong. My favourite was the delegate who, in a misremembered rallying cry from *Henry V*, urged the conference to 'stiffen up your nostrils'.

For Labour, the issues had usually been laid out much earlier in the year but were now coming to a head. They were usually decided by the votes of the big unions who controlled by far the largest percentage of the votes; the rest being divided between 600-odd constituency parties, MPs and some small affiliated organisations.

This made our union contacts priceless, and thorough lobbying and subsequent calculation often enabled us to predict outcomes in advance. At one historic Labour conference I predicted the results of two important votes later in the week on the Sunday evening news. I was right on one, but on the second – a crucial amendment to the Labour Party rules – the vote turned out differently. The key member of the boilermakers' delegation, who was supposed to cast the vote in line with the decision which I had monitored, had left the conference hall to go to the lavatory. Another delegate took over the voting card and cast it for the opposite view. A cautionary lesson about making advance predictions.

I particularly enjoyed the days leading up to the TUC Congress when the General Council gathered to prepare. It was a relaxed time and an opportunity to chat informally to contacts with less pressure than usual. It was very useful in the long run although it did not necessarily produce any short-term news. Sometimes it also illuminated how stories got into the papers.

I was at breakfast one morning in Blackpool when the correspondents of *The Sun* and the *Daily Star* discussed the dearth of news. It was the time of the Northern Ireland Troubles. 'Well,' said the first, jokingly, 'I suppose we could always run the IRA story that we ran last year.' 'What's that?' said the second. 'You remember the one about the navy keeping a watch in case the IRA target the conference.' 'Oh, yes. But we haven't seen any ships.' 'Well of course not, they would not want to be conspicuous; they could be using a submarine.'

Later that day, the *Daily Star* correspondent filed the story, only to be taken by surprise when he was sought out by a photographer sent from Manchester asking him where he could photograph the submarine. A moment's thought and he explained that naturally that was impossible because it was submerged. The story duly appeared on page two of the *Star* the next morning, complete with a stock photograph of a submarine 'of the type believed to be' monitoring the waters off Blackpool, and it was followed up by the *Daily Mail*.

We would get an early sniff of the forthcoming controversies at the spring conference of the Scottish TUC. It was an agreeable occasion, usually held at a pleasant resort and so attached to the left-wing line that voting on resolutions was scarcely necessary. No cliffhangers here. But its significance was its use by trade union leaders like Jack Jones to try out the arguments they would deploy as the year progressed.

The faded resort of Rothesay on the island of Bute was a particular favourite. The bay curved with the conference hall at its centre while a grand Victorian hotel, the Glenburn, terraced gardens step-ping down to the water, overlooked the channel through which Royal Navy ships passed to anchor. One year the conference was furiously debating nuclear disarmament and the sale of a British submarine to Chile, then under the dictatorship of General Pinochet. Suddenly into the harbour, tying up at a buoy, sailed a submarine. For many delegates it simply had to be the supposedly Chilean-bound ship.

In the evening, as trade unionists gathered in the bars of the Glen-burn, a boat put out from the submarine and approached the hotel jetty. Led by a bearded commander, his tie studded with Polaris mis-sile patterns, the sailors entered the bar. It turned out that they were actually part of the Perisher course, which assesses the abilities of would-be submarine commanders to react in difficult situations. There was no Chilean-bound submarine. But it did not prevent the earnest discussions and arguments that broke out as the two groups mingled. It was a classic meeting of opposites. A good time was had by all.

Political party conferences attracted an often bizarre range of onlookers and participants. I watched the progress of Robert Maxwell, the ultimately disgraced newspaper and magazine publisher, through the prism of the Labour Party conference. It had interesting politi-cal lessons. Maxwell had been elected as Labour MP for Buckingham in 1964. Party supporters at conference were notably wary of him as he was already a suspect businessman with a Department of Trade inquiry over his financial dealings and a history of confrontations with unions over his printing businesses. Delegates gave him a wide berth and when he lost his seat in 1970, they seemed to breathe a sigh of relief. Maxwell continued doggedly to attend the party conference but cut an isolated figure as he drank alone at the bar. Meanwhile, the Department of Trade had declared him 'not a per-son who can be relied on to exercise proper stewardship of a publicly quoted company'.

Then everything changed. In 1984, Maxwell bought Mirror Group newspapers. The group was a long-standing supporter of Labour. It backed it with its editorial line and also provided practical assistance at elections and other times. The company's executives had privileged accommodation in the conference hotel and their evening party was a magnet for politicians. Maxwell had purchased respectability and influence for £113 million.

I watched as he glowed in the lobby of the Imperial Hotel at Blackpool that year, greeting significant party members and lapping up their lately resumed attentions. At his elbow was Terry Duffy, the engineering union president, helping him to identify the people who mattered.

As a figure emerged from the bar, Duffy whispered, 'Do you know who that is?' 'No,' said Maxwell. 'That is Sandy Feather, son of Vic.' Without a moment's hesitation, Maxwell paddled forward on his huge feet with a shameless greeting, 'Sandy, my boy, how good to see you. I know your father – and your mother too.'

Ministers had a curiously uneven relationship with businessmen. It was inevitably coloured by the endless search by the chronically underfunded parties for more cash. In the 1970s, it was still almost routine for large, publicly quoted companies to make regular donations to the Conservative Party; a practice which is now rare. Labour were always on the lookout for sympathetic business people who would do the same for them. None of the parties were as choosy as they might have been.

They were also endlessly searching for an ingredient that would help them manage the increasingly intractable problems of British industry and provide some insight into a business world few of them claimed, or indeed had previously much wanted, to understand. They could arrive at some strange choices.

Harold Wilson, for example, famously wore a Gannex raincoat

manufactured close to his Huddersfield constituency by its inventor and maker, the multi-millionaire Joseph Kagan. Kagan became part of Wilson's circle and was called on for advice. He even got a peerage in Wilson's final resignation honours list, the infamous 'lavender list' in which Wilson included a strange assortment of business people including the ultra-Conservatives Jimmy Goldsmith and James Hanson. Kagan himself was jailed for stealing from his companies in 1980.

Wilson also had his close links with the Mirror Group, the party's cheerleader. But these too turned out to be problematic. Cecil King, the boss for much of the earlier Wilson years, ended up plotting against him. Lord Ryder, who subsequently took King's place, became Wilson's industrial advisor in his second term and became chairman first of the National Enterprise Board and then of the great albatross British Leyland, with disastrous results.

Another candidate for setting the industrial scene to rights was pressed on me by John Silkin, briefly a Labour spokesman for industry. His advisor, bizarrely, was the current owner of the prestigious, but financially challenged motor company Aston Martin. I must, he said, meet him; he had such clear ideas. Silkin did not retain the portfolio long enough to test them out.

In her long reign, Margaret Thatcher had a range of favoured businessmen and acolytes – not always the same thing. She prized the business experience of David, Lord Young, who had been brought in to head the Manpower Services Commission and later became an Industry Minister and chairman of the Conservative Party. Perhaps her most devoted admirer was another King, John, Lord King, a vociferous champion who took his company out of the CBI when it dared to criticise the government.

She was initially charmed by the transatlantic good manners of Ian MacGregor, who turned round the fortunes of British Steel before the disaster of his Coal Board chairmanship. But particularly to her liking was Graham Day, the no-nonsense Canadian who tried to make a go of British Shipbuilders and then succeeded in stabilising British Leyland, renaming it Rover. He subsequently sold it off, to the Prime Minister's immense satisfaction and relief. The clear-minded Day saw himself as essentially a hired gun. He was given a job and did his best to fulfil the brief.

From the reverse perspective, I was always puzzled by the willingness of senior business people to become involved with the government when most of the evidence showed it almost always ended in tears. If a hard-worked report did not find public favour then governments seemed comfortable in dumping publicly on the very person who had done them a favour by taking it on. Richard Greenbury, who had spent his life within the comfortably successful walls of Marks & Spencer, was particularly hurt when his report on executive pay was conveniently savaged.

A year or two later, at ICI, I was surprised by the willingness of my apparently clear-headed chairman, Ronnie Hampel, to take on a successor committee to head off more criticisms of 'fat-cat salaries'. Hampel handled the assignment prudently and, unlike Greenbury, understood media relations, briefing journalists at the start to manage expectations. He got away with a deliberately cautious report.

But that was not the case with another senior ICI manager, John Lister, who became the final chairman of British Shipbuilders. Lister had headed a significant ICI business, its fibres division, which had attempted to dominate the UK textile market only to be caught out by fast-changing foreign competition. By the time he was prevailed on to take over the rump of British Shipbuilders, the government, under pressure from Europe, was already planning its demise.

To an observer, it seemed that he had been chosen deliberately so as not to cause trouble. Not a political animal, past his best, with what seemed an obvious drink problem, he was not going to sustain much resistance. But he was still shocked to find how much of the industry the government had committed to close down without taking him into its confidence.

For some it was the lure of a gong, especially a knighthood. If you scan the business people in the honours lists, they are more likely to receive a decoration for helping the government than for success in their day job, for which awards are distinctly limited. I remember the dismay of one hard-working businessman who had striven to make a success of a knotty government enterprise when he found he had been awarded a CBE and not the hoped-for knighthood.

In the daily passage of business, the politicians we most frequently encountered were the Secretaries of State of the departments we most dealt with – Employment and Trade and Industry, and, when they had their own ministers, Energy and Transport.

When I first began, the Secretary of State at Employment was Maurice Macmillan, another to be spied as a solitary drinker at party conferences. The son of Harold Macmillan, he had been bequeathed the nigh-impossible job of trying to make the 1971 Industrial Relations Act work once it had been passed. Bernard Ingham, his loyal director of information, declared him to be the best Employment Secretary he had known. But Macmillan's understated presence provided little evidence to back up the claim.

His dramatic replacement by Willie Whitelaw, the great conciliator fresh from Northern Ireland, in the middle of the 1974 miners' strike, proved a flash in the pan. Great hopes, intense activity for a while, but then it proved that the remorseless logic of Heath's statutory pay policy, with its three stages and its relativities boards and enquiries, had left too little room for realpolitik and political solutions.

Michael Foot's appointment, on the other hand, as Labour's rather surprising replacement, was all to do with political balance and realpolitik. As the bearer of the left-wing banner in the Commons, and with a personally conciliatory manner, he already had the respect of senior union leaders and became a key figure in the negotiations over the social contract. Much of the technical details in unpicking the legislation could be left to his painstaking civil servants and his loyal deputy, Albert Booth, who eventually succeeded him.

A committed left-winger and unilateral disarmer, Booth had been Foot's choice as his Minister of State, and stayed close to him. He eventually lost his seat at Barrow-in-Furness, where the UK's nuclear submarines happened to be constructed, after leading a CND protest march there. Booth was diligent in seeing through the details of the government's labour reforms, including the introduction of workplace safety representatives, but came over as very dull. A former engineering draughtsman, he was just the person to give his chauffeur a hand to fix his car but not to hold his listeners spellbound with his rhetoric.

I remember his appearance at one Scottish TUC to deliver a speech about the government's achievements. It became so long and detailed that parts were still being written when Booth had already begun to speak from the rostrum. New pages kept on being handed up. Unfortunately, as we filmed it, the fraternal delegate from the Irish TUC was sitting, plumb in shot, immediately behind the rostrum in his braces. As the speech failed to engage his attention, he drew a small penknife from his pocket and proceeded to clean his nails. Job done, and speech still continuing, he unfurled his newspaper and spread it wide before him. It was unfair but it seemed to sum up the decent Albert.

Thatcher's first Employment Minister was Jim Prior. His inclusive style was well summed up by the introduction of an annual cricket match between the industrial correspondents and the Department of Employment, in which he and his ministers took part. Usually held in a country setting in Oxfordshire, it was a much more serious event than the more traditional but rather knockabout annual fixture between ourselves and the TUC, which took place on the Saturday before each Congress.

Prior's 'softly, softly' approach to legislation, which he described as 'keeping just behind the public's demands for more action', and to speak 'quietly but firmly', became less and less acceptable to Mrs Thatcher and her supporters. In 1981 he was moved to Northern Ireland and succeeded by Norman Tebbit, whose combative behaviour in the House of Commons had led him famously to be described by Michael Foot as a 'semi-house-trained polecat'. His handling of industry had not been helped by a widely reported remark querying whether we needed so much manufacturing.

Tebbit was a hugely political animal, a mercurial character who could suddenly lurch into cutting put-downs and confrontation, but he had a very sharp intellect and instinctive common sense. His civil servants were wary of his snap but respectful of his intellect. I remember his shrewd observation in a newspaper feature that a politician usually had no more than three years at the top. He himself managed slightly more before the IRA Brighton bomb left him with terrible injuries and crippled his wife.

Tebbit's determination had been on view for all to see at the annual cricket match. No cricketer, he still insisted on playing. When he went out to bat, he found himself facing our fastest bowler, Michael Cockerell, a BBC journalist renowned for his programmes about political figures. Tebbit made clear he would not be intimidated. As Cockerell appeared to bowl his fastest, Tebbit put himself in the line of fire. Crouching slightly, holding his bat tightly in front of him, he lunged forward at almost every ball. Some struck him; some were deflected off the bat; a few whistled harmlessly by. He knew little about it. For four long overs he stuck it out without wavering until he was finally dismissed. He shook hands with Cockerell before he left the pitch.

Tebbit was just as unyielding in defending the government's record. He became Employment Secretary at one of the grimmest times in its term. Under the impact of recession and uncompromising industrial policies, unemployment was rising sharply and reached the dreadful 3 million level. Yet, as we charted the rise month by month at briefings on the figures at the department, Tebbit would rarely refuse to be interviewed. Truth to tell, there was little he could say to offer much hope. But he insisted that the process of rebuilding the economy would take time. Things would not turn around quickly, but the pain had to be endured.

The only occasion I heard of Tebbit being nonplussed was during the miners' strike. It was at one of the apparent turning points in the strike. Miners were trying to stop coal supplies reaching the big south Wales steel plants, a bitter confrontation that led to a taxi driver's death when pickets dropped a piece of concrete from a motorway bridge onto his car. At this point the miners' attempted blockade was being frustrated by the lorry drivers who brought in the coal.

Special camps had been set up to cater for the large number of lorries and their drivers involved, but the drivers made clear they wanted more. The chairman of British Steel, Bob (Sir Robert) Haslam, who told me the story, found himself explaining to Norman Tebbit that the drivers were demanding that a brothel was established before they would agree to continue. I don't believe the request was granted.

The Conservatives put a lot of faith in their belief that they had a large amount of unspoken support from ordinary trade unionists, which was true. But it was certainly not reflected in the Conservative trade unionists organisation that they had established. It had a very small conference every year but ministers turned out in force. For a couple of years I carried out platform interviews with the

Employment Minister, first Prior then Tebbit. It was an interesting experience as both took it as an opportunity to engage in point-scoring which the audience could applaud. But the numbers who turned out were derisory. As a demonstration of union support for the Tories, it was an abject failure, although it made the point, as intended, that the Conservatives were not opposed to trade union-ism in principle, however much it might feel like it.

On the other side, we dealt with a succession of Labour spokes-men on employment, most of whom passed through without leaving very much trace. One of them briefly was Tony Blair. Until he came along, it was routine for Labour spokespeople to make the ritual promise that they would restore the trade union rights that the Tories had legislated away. Blair, in an indication of what was to come, warned the unions that they should not expect all the Thatcher reforms to be repealed. He was soon reshuffled to another portfolio.

In the last days of the Callaghan government I dealt with Tony Benn as Energy Minister. I had been impressed by him when we were campaigning over race relations law. He showed a willingness to lis-ten and he put himself out to speak at a hastily arranged conference meeting in 1970. But that was his natural element. Now battered by his tussles with Harold Wilson and his ministerial experience, he was a cagey and suspicious interviewee, an early adherent to the school of managing the interview. He would put his watch on the table, draw out a small pocket recorder, ask 'how long do you want' and then seek to give an answer of approximately that length. However, when you continued the questioning, he would reproach you afterwards, complaining, 'but you said that you only wanted twenty seconds'. He knew, of course, that we were unlikely to take a single answer and would want to probe deeper, but it was a good try.

Benn, a fan of technology, also took his own cine pictures, chron-icling his encounters at places like the ill-fated Meriden motorcycle cooperative. But his technical skills were sometimes found wanting and the results once famously played backwards in a session at his Holland Park home.

I interviewed him once after a meeting of a short-lived body he had established called the Energy Commission. It was supposed to bring together the heads of all the energy industries, but met only a handful of times. After one meeting I said to him, 'You don't seem to have decided anything.' His reply should be pasted into every politician's handbook. He looked at me rather pityingly and said, 'In politics, meetings come frequently; decisions come rarely.'

Benn's enthusiasm for technology was matched to a degree by Kenneth Baker, an Industry Minister before he became Education Secretary. Again, I had known Baker previously. I had covered the 1968 by-election at Acton in which he had first been elected to Parliament and he had been interested to understand how we journalists worked. We kept occasionally in touch.

Now when we had lunch he was interested in talking about business successes, and business concerns, with the usual complaint that we did not tell the good stories. I made my usual challenge: it's all very well talking about them but where are they and can we film them? To his credit he came back with concrete examples. In consequence I made two features. One profiled a successful clothing business which had become a major supplier to the then highly successful Marks & Spencer. A second drew attention to the dearth of robot machinery in British industries, compared with Japan or America, and the government incentives to invest in them. It was a rare example of someone getting the point.

Another person who got the point in a different way was John Smith, then Labour's industry spokesman. As we broke stories about new developments, potential closures and mergers, he could be relied upon to make himself available. Often it would be late in the day and I would find myself interviewing him down the line where he would be shut into a small remote television studio at which he had arrived at short notice.

When we did have time to talk at length he insisted that the recipe for resolving Britain's economic and other problems was to devolve power to the regions. We talked of the power of different industrial centres in Germany and the contrast with their counterparts in Britain. It was a clue to things to come although I suspect that devolution has not worked out in quite the way he envisaged.

By and large, as correspondents, we were not subject to heavy pressure from ministers. We kept up continuing relationships with their press offices which varied from the highly professional, like employment and energy, to the frankly awful, like trade and industry, who never seemed to know what was going on and were not much interested. We talked to ministers more rarely, over an interview or occasionally at lunch.

The lack of full-on lobbying was the case even in the miners' strike, although it may have been influenced by the deliberate decision of certain ministers to direct their briefings away from informed industrial correspondents to generalist, and often less-informed, members of the parliamentary press corps.

But it was emphatically not the case with the 1986 Westland affair. The controversy led ultimately to the resignation of both the Industry Minister, Leon Brittan, and the Defence Secretary, Michael Heseltine.

Somehow Michael Heseltine became obsessed with supporting the European position. The issue came to a head over a prime ministerial letter to the company chairman to clarify whether, as the European consortium was suggesting, a US deal would mean an end to Westland's European contracts. The letter left it to Westland to decide but promised that the government would 'fight to the best of its ability' to oppose any discrimination.

Downing Street guidance was that it was 'neutral'. In my live *Six O'Clock News* report I suggested that it strengthened the Westland board's hand. Scarcely had I returned to my office when the phone rang and Michael Heseltine's voice came on. My report was wrong, he said in an agitated tone, the letter was 'a disaster, a disaster' for the Westland board. I heard him out but did not change my mind.

By the time I left the BBC in 1989 this move to intensive lobbying, evident in the Westland affair, was spreading to more bread-and-butter politics. By then Peter Mandelson had taken over as the Labour Party's press relations chief. That autumn, as the BBC's *Nine O'Clock News* team sat down at their desks in an attic at the Blackpool Winter Gardens, scoping out the evening's bulletin, I was shocked and amazed to see Mandelson regularly sitting beside the responsible editor, arguing the toss. Politicians and the media have a symbiotic relationship, feeding off and sustaining the other, but this seemed to me to have gone too far.

Chapter Sixteen

Industrial empires

When I joined BBC Television News in the spring of 1978, I was regularly asked how it differed from reporting for newspapers. I talked about immediacy, about the wider impact, about the need to keep things clear and simple. I might have mentioned how certain reluctant contacts suddenly became more friendly. But for me perhaps the most striking and most liberating feature was simply the necessity to go and look, and bring back pictures of what was happening.

Over the next twenty years or so, with the BBC and later working with ICI, I had an extraordinary opportunity to visit factories and plants all over the UK and sometimes abroad. I saw coal mines, steelworks, shipyards, motor works, chemical plants and oil refineries and just plain places of work, large and small, too often at the point when they were about to disappear into history, but also as they began and flourished.

These days working in a factory is something youngsters are keen to avoid. The old images, Blake's 'satanic mills' or Lowry's desolate landscapes of noisome pools and polluted land in the shadow of gaunt chimneys, still wield their power. My Birmingham experience was scarcely enticing. One of the great achievements of trade union-ism has been its concentration on safety and working conditions. The health and safety reforms of the 1970s, with the empowerment of workplace safety representatives, were an important milestone. If today we shake our heads over examples of bone-headed recourse to ''elf 'n' safety', it is worth remembering where we came from.

At school in a delectable Somerset valley in the '50s, I had my first experience of a satanic mill. Its dark silhouette crouched beside a brook at the bottom of the valley. Overalled women workers, scarves tied round their hair, vied with its smoking chimney as they sat in the adjacent field, puffing on cigarettes in a break from stuffing mattresses with what looked like old rags. Later, crossing England for a week of voluntary work in Leeds, we marvelled at the clouds of smoke and steam that hung over Burton-on-Trent as our train rattled by.

Starting work in Manchester in the '60s, I was shocked by the condition of the rivers, reeking and steaming as they flowed past blackened churches on their way to discharge into the sea. And after driving from Leeds to Sheffield in a damp and smoky fog, I was able to report with some relief how the Clean Air Act, only passed in 1956 but embraced with enthusiasm in Sheffield, was making a measur-able difference. On the same journey, I passed early efforts finally to landscape the disfiguring foothills of waste and slag excavated from the local mines over years.

The external face of industry is rarely inviting, although it can pos-sess a kind of dramatic grandeur. Leaving aside smoking chimneys, steaming cooling towers and miles of unfolding pipes, the great slab-sides of modern factories give little indication of what is happening inside. Few outsiders have much chance to enter.

But once past the enclosing doors, the world of work has its own fascination. I can think of little to challenge the extraordinary atmosphere of a major steelworks. It is difficult to avoid comparisons between industrial processes and domestic cooking. In the case of steel, in the dark shadows of a huge cathedral-like interior, a giant cooking pot, several metres high, is suspended, its liquid contents glowing red and yellow. At a signal the cauldron is tilted and, in a burst of white light, its burden pours flaming and steaming into the moulds and channels prepared for it.

Even more dramatic is the exit of molten iron, a vital ingredient in the recipe for that giant cauldron, pouring out of the base of a blast-furnace, so hot that its rivulets can only be contained by banks of sand, guided through by helmeted blastfurnacemen in fire-resistant coats. It might be a medieval wall painting of the doom to come, a fancy encouraged by the naming of control stations as pulpits.

In smaller works, so-called mini-mills, where the steel is made from scrap metal, the process could be even more dramatic. As the waste metal was dumped into another cooking pot, the contents banged and crashed amid noisy showers of sparks as an electricity charge was applied.

By contrast, the great power stations where the electricity was generated were halls of silence. Outside the merry-go-round coal trains, relentlessly circling from pit to power station and back, might clank and shuffle outside the walls as tractors stacked their coal. But within the station, turbines positioned with geometric precision across the vast concrete floors went about their business of generation in eerie quiet.

Coal mines came in all shapes and sizes. In a small valley in south Wales I filmed one where men in leather gaiters still pushed small wooden trucks by hand across the pit top towards the stock piles. It was no surprise to find it threatened. At the other end of the scale, the biggest Yorkshire pits were highly mechanised. At the coalface, huge rotating cutters smashed along the seams as miners controlled them beneath a metal roof of interlocking hydraulic supports.

One of the strangest places was and remains Sellafield, on the bleak Cumbrian coast. It is about as far away in England as you can get from London, or from the flight-path of the German bombers in the days when it was first established as a weapons factory. In the eighties, its sprawling acres still contained Calder Hall, the world's first commercial nuclear power station, opened by the Queen, when nuclear power was being described as 'cheap as chips'. But the buildings that surround it now have a different, if related purpose. Their role is to store and, as far as possible, to reprocess the residues of the fuel that has powered Britain's nuclear programme.

Inside great concrete walls, down generous corridors where sensors monitor for any change in radioactivity, you peer through armoured glass. Used fuel rods brought in special stainless steel canisters are stored for cooling in what looks exactly like a giant swimming pool. After many months, they are moved remotely to another chamber where they are unpacked and the ingredients treated with heat and chemicals in a process that is still difficult for many countries to replicate.

Finally, small quantities of the irreducible remains are stored in fresh containers in a honeycomb of labelled cavities beneath the floor of another hall, like a giant gym, across which one can walk in safety.

That is the good side. But the processes have been dogged by engineering failures and run millions over budget without reaching their targets. Outside the more modern facilities are a network of storage sheds containing other forms of waste packed into drums and other containers. There are more pools, some open to the sky, in which residues from other power stations have been dumped and are now difficult to retrieve. Not far away stand the towers that were the scene of the catastrophic 1957 fire, when the complex was known as Windscale. In the '80s they were still seen as too dangerous to demolish.

Many of the problems at Sellafield go back to laxer attitudes to safety and the environment, which prevailed even in the recent past. In the course of writing an obituary of a nuclear industry pioneer, I talked to Lord Flowers, who had led the inquiry into nuclear power for the Royal Commission on Environmental Pollution in 1976. He told me that when they confronted management over their discovery of mud caking the passage between the two retaining walls of the Windscale plutonium store, they were shocked to be told 'you can't expect laboratory conditions in a factory'.

Sellafield was a pioneer in opening up at least some of its works to public inspection, but sadly security concerns have meant the closure of its visitor centre and the end of bus trips around the site.

Chemical works, too, are constructed to portray little of their internal alchemy. Again, the cooking comparisons bubble up as different ingredients are mixed together and heated or cooled in a variety of processes to produce the desired-for result. The essence of a chemical process is that it should be safe and contained. In my forgiving moments at ICI, I would put down the reluctance of some executives to speak to the media to the nature of the industry we worked in – everything should remain shut away – if a process becomes visible, it means there is trouble.

With even control rooms sometimes positioned some distance from the plants themselves, chemical works could be remote, windswept places. I once went with a London-based producer to Billingham on Teesside to cover a government small-business initiative. ICI was using a cleaning agent developed by a local supplier to cleanse its railway tank cars. As the wind whipped about us, we stood beside rail tracks on the Tees dockside. She clasped her fashionable but rather skimpy coat about her and declared, 'I didn't know such places existed.'

Shipyards were even bleaker. British shipyards were slow to modernise and the old ways of building – laying a keel on a slipway, building it up piece by piece in the open air until the time came to slide it into the river, completing the process with the ship moored in the open – contrasted with yards in the Far East or some other parts of Europe where ships were constructed in covered dry docks. Sometimes I thought things had hardly moved on since my meeting with the newly redundant shipyard workers of Blyth in 1966.

On one visit to Scotland, I went to the Clydebank yard of John Brown, which had built the Queens of which Southampton was so proud. The yard was derelict but the lofty workshops where the engines for the Queens and their predecessors had been constructed still remained. Inside, the additions to the supporting columns told the story of proud industrial progress. They had literally raised the roof step by step as the engines, and the ships, grew larger and larger. Only a few miles away stood another monument of British industry, where pride in manufacture had been celebrated. At the old works of the Albion motor company, its classical front and bronze angels rivalled the heroic shipwright statues flanking the entrance to the Govan shipyard of Upper Clyde Shipbuilders. There was pride and ambition in what they were building.

The old way of doing things made for dramatic moments. At a launch a ship would slide down a newly greased slipway, slowly gathering speed until it arrived in the water. A great splash of wave would be almost blotted out by a giant cloud of rust from huge dragchains that checked the vessel's progress, slowing its descent and preventing it crashing into the opposite bank. It was a strange experience to stand on a platform watching the ceremony, overshadowed by the beetling brow of the vessel, suddenly to find empty space and blue sky where the ship had been.

Ritual pomp and circumstance accompanied it. Special trains or aeroplanes brought the guests. Afterwards the yard would put on a grand lunch with speeches. At Harland and Wolff in Belfast, where the White Star line had built its famous liners, the *Titanic* among them, they still used a building that had been built specifically for dining. In the evening, the shipping line would respond with its own dinner.

The government kept Harland and Wolff separate from British Shipbuilders. As the major employer in Northern Ireland, it was a very sensitive site and it had received millions in investment. The result was a vast dry dock built for supertankers which were no longer being ordered, serviced by two overhead cranes, Gog and Magog. They dominated the Belfast skyline and their summit could be reached by an internal lift. During these years the energetic figure of its chairman, John Parker, himself an Ulsterman, was seeking to fill the gargantuan dock with work, successfully building smaller tankers for BP, refitting cross-channel ferries, and constructing some of the last Blue Star liners to carry the refrigerated meat of the great Vestey empire.

Parker became a successful chairman of Babcock, acquiring the naval yard at Rosyth on the Clyde as well as being appointed chairman of National Grid and Anglo American and a member of the court of the Bank of England. He had flourished earlier on the banks of the Wear at Sunderland, where in private hands Austin & Pickersgill had developed a basic cargo ship, the SD14, a kind of replacement for the wartime Liberty ships, of which 2,700 were turned out for the Allied war effort. Parker helped sell or license over 200 SD14s around the world, later becoming deputy chief executive of the nationalised British Shipbuilders.

The A&P yard had been one of the earlier British yards to adopt pre-fabrication techniques, with much of the work taking place under cover. But by now it had become less competitive and another yard across the river had been modernised under the private ownership of the Court Line. In the Pallion yard ships were built in a dry dock that was totally enclosed, a giant shed from which the finished vessel could be floated through huge doors. Both enterprises became part of Sunderland Shipbuilders, a subsidiary of British Shipbuilders.

But modernisation had come too late. The Labour government had proposed the nationalisation of the shipyards in 1976 with a tough Canadian, Graham Day, who had had success at the Birkenhead yard of Cammell Laird, as its chairman. But a parliamentary defeat delayed the project for a year and Day resigned. It was not until 1983 that he was persuaded to return by the Thatcher government and found, in his view, that the necessary labour reforms and marketing plans had not been put into place. His job became to privatise what he could.

At the beginning of 1984, Day invited me to make a promotional film about North East Shipbuilders in an attempt to sell some ships. We filmed the yards and the fitting out of two ships for Hong Kong owners. One was the old established imperial firm of John Swire & Sons and the other a Chinese millionaire ship-owner who had studied in the north-east. I accompanied Day as he made presentations to the owners and we did interviews. I don't think it led to a single order, but it gave me an insight into the determination and marketing focus that Day would take to British Leyland.

Shipyards with their lack of cover were matched by the barrenness of the docks. The deep distrust of employers felt by men, like Jack Jones, who had started work on the docks, went back to the days when dock employers simply picked the men they wanted from a waiting pool of men. It was little different to the hiring fairs of another century.

The facilities provided on the bleak and windswept docks were minimal. It was only when the London docks were in terminal decline that under one new scheme, changing and recreation facilities were finally provided. I can remember sitting in the sun drinking tea with Hull dockworkers just outside the port boundary.

There were no catering facilities and poor toilet arrangements on the docks themselves.

In Southampton, the wharves were flanked by bleak sheds with refuse dumps labelled 'No offal'. Even transatlantic passengers had little comfort before they tramped up open gangways to reach their 'luxury liners'. They were processed in echoing sheds before the Ocean Terminal was built in the 1950s. It was not a great deal better.

Shipbuilding was always on a knife-edge, only as safe as the next few orders. The key ones were usually the subject of competition from other countries, where the level of government subsidy, acknowledged and disguised, was a key factor. By the 1980s, big passenger vessels were no longer built in British yards, and they were scrabbling for small orders.

Instead, early in 1984 I had to travel to Finland for the introduction of P&O's new flagship, the *Royal Princess*. No launch here but a dramatic floating out from a covered dry dock into waters so cold that icebreakers had to weave back and forth to create a passable channel. Later in the year I was in Saint-Nazaire in France to inspect construction of what was then the largest liner in the world, the cruise ship *Sovereign of the Seas*. I contrasted that with the best that Britain could do, a North Sea passenger ferry less than half her size being built at Govan. She turned out to be the last serious passenger vessel built in Britain. A hopeful tender to construct a ferry for Brittany Ferries failed as the French government ensured it went to France. Soon the yard was sold off to Norwegian owners to build gas carriers.

The decimation of the shipyards brought consequences for the wide variety of trades that supplied them. In the days when Cunard was building the *QE2* at Clydebank, a shipyard manager could offer to assemble '1,000 electricians in the morning' and many other craftsmen, like carpenters and plumbers, would be employed in the elaborate fitting out of cabins and public spaces.

As for the ships themselves, the British-owned fleet was shrinking steadily. Throughout the '80s I charted the decline as first one vessel after another was sold and then whole shipping lines disappeared. P&O and Orient merged and were combined with a building and transport group; Cunard became part of a property and newspaper conglomerate. Ellerman and its remaining ships were sold to the Barclay brothers, who were property investors. Court Line, who had modernised the Sunderland shipyards, diversified into the travel business and went bankrupt.

While some companies like P&O persevered, developing a successful cross-channel ferry business and joining with rivals to establish a world-class container consortium, Overseas Container Lines, they were exceptions. Even then, in the event, OCL was sold to Dutch partners and then P&O to Dubai largely because of the value of the docks it owned around the world.

The fleets of the great industrial empires were also disappearing. When, as children, the Isle of Wight ferry from Southampton took us past the newly built Fawley oil refinery, we would count up the number of Shell tankers with their yellow funnels and distinctive shell symbol and the red funnels of the BP tankers, each with a name that began with 'British'. Now I attended an announcement at BP's Britannic House that it was reducing its fleet, placing them under the Bermuda flag, and would no longer man them with British crews or train officer cadets. Next I found myself at Douglas in the Isle of Man, where a Shell captain was registering more than twenty tankers at an office on a wooden pier at which none of his ships could ever call. It was the latest example of companies seeking to cut overheads, and sometimes supervision, by registering their vessels outside Britain.

At that point, as I wrote, the British merchant fleet had all but vanished. It had been cut by a third, from 15 million to 10 million tons, and now another 3 million was destined to disappear to the

Isle of Man. Ten years before it had been five times as big. Back in Southampton, I stood in front of a laid-up supertanker and reported to the *Six O'Clock News* that this single ship now represented one fifth of all UK-registered tonnage.

On the bridge of a still British-registered container ship, the master, brought up in the traditions of British imperial seapower, told me in puzzlement as much as anger, 'We are an island nation, yet our trade is falling away. We don't have any merchant navy presence left in the world.'

The changes were much to do with trying to reduce the cost of crews. There was no way that British crews with North European pay and conditions could get close to the rates accepted by crews from places in the developing world like the Philippines or Taiwan. But, as I wrote in *The Listener*:

> The principal cause of the decline is the drop in world trade which began in the '70s. Idle ships swinging at anchor have been unable to repay the huge borrowings required to build them.
>
> Their numbers have been increased by new vessels subsidised by governments in an attempt to keep another failing industry – shipbuilding – alive. Many have been sold to Far Eastern and Third World countries who have been building up and subsidising their fleets to earn foreign currency and have run them at rates far below traditional European agreements.
>
> In the face of that, British lines have sold ships, gone broke or diversified out of shipping altogether. Now a new drive is on to trim costs among the fleets which remain.

The shipping industry continued to lobby successive governments. Eventually, in 1999, more helpful tax arrangements were announced. Since then the fleet has grown once more. It recently stood at

30 million gross tons, double what it was at the low point in 1987, but nothing like its peak. It now ranks tenth in the world behind Malta and the Bahamas but ahead of the United States and Germany.

Shipyards and docks were among what seemed a preponderance of large industrial complexes employing hundreds and often thousands of workers. Stand outside one of the large works and you risked being knocked down by the torrent of bicycles that would pour out when the shift changed. In the pubs across the road from the Glasgow shipyards they would line up the pints on the bar in anticipation of the lunchtime rush.

The works provided all sorts of facilities. Some even had their own guest houses. They served visiting engineers or accommodated their customers, often from the old empire, who came to supervise the construction of generating plant and other heavy equipment which took months to construct before being shipped abroad. Within the sites, the divisions on which British society had once prided itself clung on, with the sharp difference between blue-collar and white-collar workers, reflected in their terms and conditions of their employment. 'The workforce' was paid weekly in cash in brown-paper envelopes, for which they might queue up, and 'staff' more often by monthly transfer. The distinctions were most vivid at lunchtime, with separate canteens not just for white- and blue-collar but also for different ranks of supervisors and management.

At Cowley at one point there were no fewer than seven canteens with obvious progressions: foremen had salt and pepper pots; supervisors knives and forks; while directors were served by waiters. It was not until the early '80s in some cases that the divisions were broken down. Japanese companies insisted on everyone eating together, and British companies began to merge their catering arrangements. We began a film on the changing workplace in 1982 in which we filmed the partitions being shifted at Vickers headquarters and the introduction of work-group brainstorming under the influence of the Industrial Society, which attempted to bring together staff and workers.

However, in the '80s the big complexes were being remorselessly whittled down in the interests of economy and also as a result of new technologies – and in some cases because of industrial failure.

Many of the best known have gone. Trafford Park, a centre for engineering firms through much of the twentieth century, is now known for one of the huge shopping complexes that have replaced industry as the biggest sources of employment. At Longbridge in Birmingham, where Herbert Austin established the biggest Midlands motor complex with a workforce touching 25,000, the old factories are mostly being replaced with housing, shopping and educational facilities in a wholesale redevelopment.

Today those kind of employment concentrations are rarely to be found. Airports are one exception, with Heathrow accounting for perhaps 40,000 people. And in industry, it is a sobering thought that Sellafield, with over 10,000, confronting the problems of nuclear waste and keeping the Cumbria economy going, is perhaps the most populous industrial site.

Nowhere was change and crumbling empire more obvious than in the motor industry. Car factories were the big beasts of industrial Britain, and their success or failure were the stuff of politics. Like it or not, we were drawn into making assessments of how well they were functioning. Comparative figures were hard to come by. Ford, with its far-spreading European operations, could compare production factory by factory, but conditions and ways of operating were different in different countries. Where labour was cheaper, as it was in Britain at certain times, more might be employed.

Visiting the factories, as with other plants, it was difficult for the unskilled eye of a journalist to evaluate how well run they were.

There was one obvious marker – housekeeping. How clean or orderly a site was, industrial managers advised me, was indeed a useful if not a sufficient benchmark. Sometimes you got a rapid insight. When visiting Jaguar's Browns Lane plant in Coventry for a story about a new model, we had to wait for an hour before an electrician could be found to accompany us. So we were not surprised when Ford threw up their hands in horror at its inefficiencies when they bought it.

The factories really did sprawl, as the production line, rather like a tram track, fed slowly round what was essentially a single-floor building. Key parts, stacked beside the track or brought by circling conveyors overhead, were gradually fitted on as the line continued its relentless progress. Unions would complain particularly at Ford about the speed of the line. Operatives, including an increasing number of women, moved rapidly to bolt or screw and, before robots were generally employed in British factories, to weld metal parts together. As computerisation gathered pace, each vehicle began to carry its own specification with it.

In other parts of the factory, other processes took place to prepare the parts or increasingly just to marshal supplies constructed elsewhere. When we filmed construction of the Cavalier in Vauxhall's Luton factory in the mid-1980s, we found hardly any major items still being made in Britain. The engine came from Australia, the manual gearbox from Japan. The distributor and many of the body pressings came from Germany, the carburettor from France while the oil filter, some glass and the wheels, but little more, were British.

There were visible differences. At the Rover plant in Solihull, recently established, there were markedly more women. At Ford in Dagenham, there were many West Indians on the line and management had allowed some to fix up their own stereo systems to play while they worked, sometimes flat on their backs. When Ford compared the performance of Dagenham with its continental plants, it was sometimes unkindly said that it was comparing the performance of one group of immigrant workers with another. (Ford in Germany relied heavily on Turkish workers.)

Cultures differed even in neighbouring plants. The most extreme case was at Cowley in Oxford. The body plant made the car shells which were fed on a moving belt to the assembly plant over a covered bridge that spanned a main road. There seemed little other connection.

The factories had once belonged to two different companies and it showed. While the body plant, the old Pressed Steel, had relatively orderly industrial relations, the management at the assembly plant, keen to keep unions at bay, had given local shop stewards their head and then found them dominated by Trotskyists with a revolutionary agenda and an interest in avoiding outside union supervision.

The legacy of the past weighed heavily. Car factories had not been comfortable places to work. Noisy, often dirty, with constant pressure to keep lines moving, their chief appeal was the relatively high level of wages they offered. Past practice had encouraged seasonal work with workers being laid off when sales fell off in the summer. It had been compounded by successive governments' use of 'the regulator', the fixing of the hire purchase rate so that it encouraged or discouraged sales to stimulate or slow the economy. The motor industry was the prime target and victim. The result discouraged loyalty to the industry.

When I interviewed Rover workers at the newish factory at Solihull in 1977, at a moment when 23,000 workers across the Midlands were laid off because of three separate strikes, I found a similar pattern. There was a mixture of long-serving men and those who worked in casual jobs, for example as milkmen, during part of the year and sought factory work at other times, depending on conditions, weather and pay rates.

When I came to write my history of the British motor industry, *The Motor Makers: The Turbulent History of Britain's Car Industry*, I was struck by the historic insularity of the industry and how long it clung to the imperial 'British is best' mantra. As foreign industries rebuilt and redesigned after the war and protective tariffs, which continued until as late as 1977, were steadily dismantled, the British industry remained self-satisfied. It was most sharply brought home to me when I interviewed John Barber, once finance director at Ford of Britain, who later did a similar job at the British Motor Corporation. Barber, a motor enthusiast, found a striking lack of interest in competitors' cars and at one stage lined up a selection of foreign models outside an executive meeting for his colleagues to inspect. Asking one, 'What do they do about this at Volkswagen?' he received the reply, 'I don't know. This is what we do at Longbridge.'

Similarly, those who came from other industries were also shocked. Geoff Whalen, later to become chairman of the Society of Motor Manufacturers and Traders, came to Cowley as an industrial relations specialist from the coal industry. He contrasted the well-drilled professionalism of miners' negotiators with what he found, and he did not spare management either in an interview for my motor industry book:

> The mixture of paternalism and autocracy continued after the war and they carried on managing ineffectively and inadequately. Then the unions became stronger. It was as if the management had restrained the unions completely and then once the floodgates were open and the militants were strong, the result was difficulty and strikes. On average there were two and a half strikes a day, over 600 in a year.[9]

9   Adeney, op. cit., p. 261

Whalen and his colleagues fought a long fight to improve relations in the industry; a major feature being the struggle to replace the piece-work system, which entailed endless renegotiations as processes and models changed and inflation bit. They were not helped by years of lack of investment. At Ryton in Coventry where Whalen later kept a Peugeot operation successfully functioning for years, the plant had been built as a 'shadow factory' in anticipation of Second World War requirements for military production.

By the '80s, many in the industry knew what needed to be done but were constrained by history in their efforts to achieve it. The lessons they had learnt came to be applied most successfully to the new arrivals, particularly the Japanese firms like Nissan, Toyota and Honda. They benefited not just from the practices they brought but also the hard-won experience of the British managers who joined them, men like Ian Gibson and Peter Wickens at Nissan and Whalen and George Turnbull (who had established Hyundai in Korea) at Peugeot, which took over the old Rootes and Chrysler plants.

Even Leyland had a brief renaissance. One morning in 1986 I received a call from Graham Day at British Shipbuilders. He wanted me to know, confidentially, that he was being appointed as chairman of what was now called BL that afternoon. I arranged to interview him. It was a surprise.

Day had agreed clear objectives with Thatcher – stop haemor-rhaging money, become profitable, return the company to the private sector; it was a tall order. When I asked him if there was a role for a British motor company, he replied, with typical frankness, 'I don't know. We have to demonstrate that we can perform better, and then the answer moves to maybe. If we can consolidate that then maybe moves to yes.'

Astonished by the bureaucracy, he cut paperwork and 10 per cent of white-collar staff. He played tough, sacking top managers who he saw as disloyal but working to build morale with less of a command-and-control culture, encouraging younger managers to speak up.

As a salesman, he beefed up marketing research. He changed the group's name to Rover, after its upmarket car, and planned new models. Noting the continuing popularity of the Mini abroad, he revoked the plan to end production and successfully rejuvenated it while huge resources were put into a new middle-sized Rover to establish a reputation for quality and good value.

Helped by a debt write-off, Rover had returned to precarious profitability by 1988 when, again to general surprise, Day achieved his third target when British Aerospace agreed to buy Rover and take it private again. Later it would be sold to BMW.

It was the arrival of the Japanese that captured public attention. Die-hard union leaders objected to their single union deals and what they labelled 'Japanese practices', which included company uniforms. When Ford and its unions clashed in 1988 over changes inspired by the company's concern over the strength of Japanese competition, pickets paraded with banners that read 'We're Brits not Nips'. It seemed all of a piece with the insular Midlands managers who had so shocked Barber. Imperial attitudes were classless.

Ford had launched a crash programme to improve productivity in 1982, labelled 'After Japan' or 'AJ'. By the mid-'80s it started to make some progress, and the average number of cars produced per worker doubled, although it was still short of the company's European plants.

About the same time I had visited the new Nissan plant. I wrote in *The Listener*:

> It is no coincidence that Nissan's most senior executives come from Ford. It shares Ford's dedication to keeping the line moving and hitting schedules. But within that framework individual responsibility is encouraged in a way unfamiliar, if not actually

alien, to traditionally managed British plants. Workers have a say in the arrangement of machinery on the lines and get time and opportunity to carry out agreed modifications in workshops.

At tea-breaks lines are stopped rather than kept going, to encourage teams of workers to sit down together and encourage cooperation, which is also the target of the now-famous five-minute discussions every group has before the morning start. Clocking-on has been abolished; workers are paid salaries and trusted (with certain safeguards) to be on time. As Ian Gibson, Nissan's most senior manager, puts it, 'that has not been the approach of mass production industries in the UK. They have tended to want to withdraw individuality in order to feel in control.'

The advent of the microchip and computerisation changed the scene again. Car production became much more flexible. Individual vehicles could be fitted with microchips allowing them to be customised on the production line. I found myself filming laser-guided machine tools and robot machines of different varieties, from those replacing humans in the paint booths that sprayed sometimes toxic paints through to the tiny trucks that fetched and carried engine parts remotely in giant warehouses.

Decline was balanced by the advent of new industries and the rejuvenation of others. Pharmaceuticals became a success story while the chemical industry, continuing to benefit from innovation, maintained a strongly positive trade balance. As I came to appreciate in my study tour of American industry, defence spending made a big difference. The warship building yards and their suppliers survived, with the isolated mudflats of Barrow-in-Furness becoming the centre of nuclear submarine production, while the merchant yards disappeared.

In the aerospace industry I watched the careful wrapping of layers of carbon fibre to form the rotor-blades for Westland's new helicopters and inspected the precision engineering and the testing rigs in Rolls-Royce's Derby plants where they fired frozen chickens into their new engines to test their resistance to bird-strike.

Meanwhile, a whole new industry was created in the North Sea, and the servicing and supply of the oil and gas rigs stretched down the east coast from the Shetlands to Suffolk. British ships and seamen found new opportunities and challenges in the process and the supply industry drew on those remaining in the declining trawler fleets.

A visit to the huge oil rigs, with whole communities planted in the middle of the most stormy of waters, was an awe-inspiring experience, both for the scale and the effrontery of the effort. Sitting in a familiar kind of works canteen, admittedly with rather a good menu, a hundred or so feet above the restless North Sea, watching videos, seemed frankly bizarre.

But if travelling out to the BP's productive Forties Field, muffled in life-saving gear in a powerful helicopter, was a dramatic insight for me, it had become standard routine for thousands of workers. The testing conditions demanded a whole new level of precision engineering and management that Britain struggled to provide. Under largely American tutelage, the industry met the challenge and the skills and experience developed were exported across the globe.

Even the motor industry became once more a world leader, if on a small scale. From its beginnings, the British industry had prided itself on its technical skills, although they were often over-elaborate and too individualistic for effective mass production. In the '70s and '80s, as the big companies laboured, I reported on the advent of small specialist consultancies which developed ideas of engineering and styling and came to advise the major manufacturers. At the other end of the scale, Ford recognised British skills in engine manufacture and established a key plant to serve its European operations in south Wales and later expanded its facilities at Dagenham too.

In 2016, the company assembles no cars in Britain but bases most of its European engine manufacture here.

The most spectacular example of specialist motor engineering is in the rarified world of motor sport, where almost all the Formula One racing teams have established their technical centres in a small area of the Thames Valley.

The new technologies were beginning to create new kinds of industry. While the internet was still some way off, the electronics industries were heading into new fields. Racal was an electronics company that had started by providing radio equipment for the armed services and had then expanded into radar and other fields, absorbing companies like Decca. But in 1983 it won the licence to provide cellular phones and in 1984 it gave the name to its new baby of Vodafone. It was the birth of what would be a world-beating company that spread across the globe.

Encouraged by growing confidence but also by a feeling that business abroad might prove less encumbered and provide more opportunities than in Britain, UK enterprises were increasingly looking overseas. For some like the engineering company GKN, it was an opportunity to expand on the basis of its patented motor joint technology; for others like ICI it reflected the falling away of its traditional customers for paint or fibres in the motor or textile industries, and the search for new technologies; for James Hanson and Gordon White and their Hanson Trust, whose advertisements proclaimed that there was a British company 'who is over there and over here', it was the realisation of the rich pickings from joining the 'barbarians at the gates' in the break-up of old-fashioned US conglomerates.

These trends were starting to be in evidence at the end of the 1980s and they were assisted by the unmistakable signs of economic recovery. It was at this point that I decided to take a look at an industrial empire from the inside.

Chapter Seventeen

Imperial transitions

At the end of 1980s, British industry, smaller and chastened, was beginning to recover due to a worldwide improvement in trade and the radical changes it had been forced to make. When the American business magazine *Fortune* ran a cover story 'Britain is back', they chose to put the chairman of ICI on the cover. The company had posted the first billion-pound profit to have been achieved by any British company.

ICI was a national institution. Formed in 1926 as Imperial Chemical Industries by merging four British chemical companies, its stated aim was to provide a British champion strong enough to stand against the might of IG Farben in Germany and US rivals such as Dow and Du Pont. When its name was challenged, its founders declared to the president of the Board of Trade: 'We are imperial in aspect and imperial in name.' No other combination of business activities could be so important to the empire, they argued.

These aspirations were set in stone with the construction of a monumental headquarters on Millbank, a couple of hundred yards from the Houses of Parliament, which framed the approach to Westminster from Lambeth Bridge. The façade of Imperial House was decorated with busts of the great chemists alongside the company's founders. A pair of twenty-foot-high bronze doors displayed cast bas-reliefs illustrating the progress from primitive man to modern scientific discovery. A brochure did not shrink from comparing them with the doors to the Baptistery in Florence. Within the building, directors presided in offices panelled with limed-oak or, in the case of a former Viceroy of India, Lord Reading, Indian laurel.

The company made explosives in Scotland, fertilisers on Teesside, chlorine and pharmaceuticals in Cheshire, paint in Buckinghamshire, textile fibres in Yorkshire, dyes in Manchester, pesticides in Kent and metals in the Midlands. It operated its own salt mines and limestone quarries. Its activities spread across the empire through India and China as far as Australia, where many of its activities were replicated. Over the years its scientists invented Perspex and Polythene, trademarked Terylene, built up a successful drugs business, introduced betablockers and played a significant wartime role in the development of the British atom bomb.

Its supply of materiel to British industry was so significant and such an indicator of the industrial weather that it had gained its 'bellwether of British industry' nickname. When *The Times* ran a survey of the company in 1962, listing over 100 sites in the UK, the ICI chairman, Sir Paul Chambers, wrote of a 'public duty to go on making the essential, basic chemicals even though the sales may appear to be less progressive and less profitable. ICI cannot withdraw from the production of industrial explosives, soda ash and caustic soda without giving the public many years' notice of its intentions.' Imperial duty.

This was the company that, in the spring of 1989, I joined as its first international media manager. In the ensuing years, it had of course undergone major restructuring. It had shuffled its operations, exchanging plants with BP Chemicals and floating off its metals interests. But it had not made any substantial closures in the UK and was still recognisably the same company. It was no longer a grace-and-favour enterprise, bestowing its products on a grateful public and even rationing the supply of some commodities, although sometimes it seemed that the mindset lingered.

Part of its appeal to me was that it had a genuinely international perspective. When Britain's first efforts to join the Common Market had been rebuffed, ICI set up its own European operations with a headquarters in Brussels and it had also expanded into the United States.

In the pre-war years, the great chemical enterprises of the United States, Germany and Britain had divided the world between them in a convenient cartel. It was business imperialism. ICI stayed out of the Americas and left Europe effectively to the Germans. It went unchallenged in the empire while establishing operations in areas such as China, where another imposing Imperial House was constructed in Shanghai. Following Germany's defeat and antitrust legislation in the United States, the 1950s saw a sharpening of worldwide competition, and the company moved into the US and Europe. As other British industries faltered in the '70s and '80s, chemicals remained a mainstay of British exports.

ICI's resurgence in the mid-'80s had been associated with its chairman, Sir John Harvey-Jones, whose ebullient manner was matched by outrageously colourful ties. He had gained a reputation for speaking his mind and was no longer afraid to appear on broadcasting discussion programmes to make his, and industry's, point of view. After our initial stand-off in 1982, he had become a confident performer and a friendly and helpful source of information.

Part of his appeal was that he seemed to speak his mind regardless of possible consequences. When asked at one point on a visit to Germany why the recession was deeper in Britain, he had blamed government policies and been quoted as saying 'because we have Mrs Thatcher'. In the ensuing commotion, he could not be found and the press department struggled to cope.

In a sense he had been ICI's PR department, and now he was gone ICI's communications structure struggled to fill the gap. Denys Henderson, his successor, keen to communicate but lacking the casual verve of Harvey-Jones, saw the importance of marketing and commissioned a successful television campaign about ICI's industrial prowess under the slogan 'ICI World Class'. But he was also looking for more day-to-day support, and I was asked if I would be interested.

Like many of our generation, I had admired ICI from afar. I had noted its reputation for taking the best graduates and absorbed comments on the radio which compared the creaking shambles of some nationalised industries with the efficient way ICI ran its operations ('ICI would never have allowed something like this to happen.') But my contacts with the company had been limited. Apart from the Harvey-Jones forays, the company did not seem to be communicating about its basic operations and when it did so, its rambling press releases might run to an extraordinary five pages.

So the challenge was intriguing. I had recently featured Henderson in a *Money Programme* which questioned whether, as economic fortunes improved, companies would now invest. We got on well and I said that I would be prepared to join the company if he agreed to operate as open a communications strategy as possible. He did so and, I must say, was as good as his word.

It was an absorbing transition. I found enormous goodwill within the company towards the project of communicating better based on a feeling that it had not been doing enough to put its case. But goodwill could run quickly into the tyranny of process. I brought with me a request for the European operations to participate in a planned BBC programme. The response of the manager concerned was to ask whether such an interview had been factored into the annual communications plan. We seemed to be working on a different timescale to the newsrooms I had just left.

Immediate or rapid communications response was a difficult concept for carefully plotted businesses to grasp. It was a contrast to the politicians whom I had been used to. Swimming in the media sea, they grasped it best. Ultimately they overdosed on it to the extent that Gordon Brown, when Prime Minister, set up his office to resemble a newsroom with himself as a sort of editor-in-chief.

And then, of course, there was the jargon. Every profession has its own code. The BBC management engaged the greatest profusion of acronyms I ever came across, from the DG (Director-General) down to a character who went by the initials of CAND, which roughly translated as Chief Assistant to the Assistant Chief. The minutes of the weekly news and current affairs meeting started with half a page of alphabet soup describing the attendees. Business liked the acronyms too but in addition it had invented or mangled a language all of its own.

In pride of place was 'pro-active', the essential quality for any manager – the opposite of reactive, from which it had been derived. But what was wrong with 'active'? Companies no longer 'ended' years; instead, with a sensation of urgent activity, they 'exited' them. 'Bull points' had long been transmogrified into 'bullet points', with a much greater sensation of movement. While the pervasive American influence meant that we no longer failed to see the wood for the trees, it was the 'woods' we missed on our way to discover about not 'speciality', but 'specialty' chemicals.

I had, of course, to start with a plan, to be presented to the ICI board. I prefaced it with a wonderful quotation I had found in Anthony

Sampson's classic, *Anatomy of Britain*. In 1962, Sampson, himself the son of an ICI research scientist, had described what he called the company's 'smugness'. He wrote, 'anything less than unqualified praise ICI is liable to regard as a stab in the back and their public relations still has an old-fashioned blustering, threatening character'.[10] Times had changed in the intervening twenty-five years but the company still seemed grand and remote to many.

I made my familiar pitch, arguing that in the 1970s other interest groups had filled the vacuum provided by business's unwillingness to make its case, to state their particular concerns, and the public had broadly bought their line. I pointed to developments in the 1980s which had seen a multiplication of broadcasting channels, including the first satellite channels, and more business programming.

I identified a realisation by major institutions that they must explain themselves more fully. Here I picked out changes made by the army in Northern Ireland and the police in the UK. I explained how relatively junior officers directly involved in incidents were now expected to speak with authority and given training. The implication was that local managers on ICI's vast sites should be in the same position.

I suggested that politicians 'are even more accessible than they were and increasingly adept at getting over their messages almost regardless of the questions they are asked'.

As for the City: 'Any programme on business can be assured that an approach to a financial analyst to appear will succeed and that they will cross London to give the benefit of their advice, publicise their own companies and give their judgement on other companies, however badly informed.'

Finally, I looked at the globalisation of information occurring as a result of the arrival of electronic and satellite transmissions. 'For

10 Anthony Sampson, *Anatomy of Britain* (Hodder, 1962), p. 448

companies, it means that any section of their activities, however far-flung, can impact on the view of the company as a whole, or any of its parts.' We would have plenty of experience of that.

My paper theories were quickly put to the test. I had picked out concern for the environment as an issue that had accelerated very sharply over the previous couple of years and was now 'probably the largest single topic of non-specialist media comment on the chemical industry'. I highlighted the green movement as one of the key pressure groups.

The company already had plenty of experience. In the mid-'80s, the damage that CFCs – a relatively inert gas used for refrigeration in domestic appliances and car air-conditioning systems – were causing to the ozone layer was a major issue. ICI had queried the science relating to the effects, insisting on more precise proof. Eventually the chairman had stepped in to tell the business division concerned to accept that public perception was overwhelming and that CFCs must be phased out.

Another issue faced me as soon as I joined. ICI's acrylic works at Billingham on the Tees, one of whose products was Perspex, was loading chemical waste from its operations into a tanker which was then discharging it out in the North Sea. The operation had already been targeted by Greenpeace who had attempted to disrupt it with activists in dinghies. Now the company was building a new plant that would treat the waste. Sea disposal would end. I found managers nervous about how this would be received, worried that it would be seen as a victory for their critics.

I persuaded them that we should take a positive view and make a virtue of the fact that we were taking action to stop our discharges. But I made clear that we would not get our point across unless we cooperated with the media, and one aspect of that might be to allow them onto the tanker so they could explain what the change meant.

We brought the relevant managers down to London to agree what would be said and provide media training. We took them to a nearby restaurant in the evening where it so happened that the local Teesside MP, Mo Mowlam, was sitting at the next table. We were obliged to bring forward the briefing for her we had planned for the next day.

The announcement went well. The Teesside managers did more than required, one of them even giving assistance to the BBC radio correspondent heading for the ship when his car ran out of petrol. The story ran prominently on the flagship BBC *Nine O'Clock News*.

The company was delighted. But Greenpeace were not pleased and cooperated closely with the investigative programme *World in Action* on a very different sort of feature, which was screened late that year. A camera crew travelled systematically around ICI's UK sites highlighting examples of pollution of local water-courses and neighbouring countryside from the discharges into the Tees from the Wilton plant, to areas in Cheshire affected by salt discharges, across to the plants at Runcorn where chlorine was the principal manufacture.

The programme disturbed me. It might well have been ICI that was responsible for some of the polluted rivers I had been so struck by in the north-west. It also shocked employees in the company, who traditionally had been proud of where they worked. We had to make urgent attempts to rebut what accusations we could, highlighting any mistakes and emphasising the remedial action we were already taking, for the benefit of our own staff. It was an early example to me of the wide spread of concern within an institution that media coverage can stir and of which journalists are often blissfully unaware.

But how to respond? The first intimation of the programme came with a fax to the press office, informing us that the footage had been shot and asking for an interview at short notice. It was a pretty standard media tactic for awkward stories. Sunday newspapers, for example, tended to ask for comment on a Friday afternoon, providing the minimum time before they went to press. It was quite common for companies to decline and just issue a short written statement to the programme, but I thought that it always looked as if the company was hiding.

After serious discussion, Henderson agreed that we should put up a spokesperson and that it should be a director of the chemicals and polymers division, which ran the big northern English sites with the responsibility for environmental matters. We knew it was likely to be a poisoned chalice and Mike Brogden, a laconic, hard-driving manager, was understandably not pleased to be selected.

I went to Runcorn to prepare background material and to refresh his media training. Experience had taught us that this kind of programme might confront him with some undisclosed piece of evidence. We rehearsed a response: to accept whatever it was, refuse to comment, explaining that we did not know its provenance but offer to investigate. It was a difficult interview and the camera was placed intimidatingly close to Mike's face for a close focus, but he stuck to our agreed line and when the surprise came – a sample of river water with supposed high concentrations of waste material – he refused to comment but offered to investigate.

Afterwards the cameraman said, 'Your man did well.' But the cut interview took the weakest replies and the company was shaken by the programme. I was worried that the experience would dissuade others from speaking out and Denys Henderson agreed to send a message expressing his appreciation to Mike. He would later become an ICI director. As for myself, I felt the poacher really had turned gamekeeper. But the programme and its treatment of the spokesman brought home to me just why businessmen were reluctant to put themselves in the firing line.

Environmental issues came increasingly to the fore. One press officer was traditionally a specialist in scientific matters. Now Dr Dick

Robson explained to me that more and more of his time was being occupied with environmental queries. So we moved Dick, who had a strong commitment to the improvement of the environment, into a full-time environmental manager role in which he supported busi- nesses around the globe.

At a board level, environmental responsibility had been allocated to a director, Chris Hampson, equally committed to improvement. Hampson insisted that the way forward was for the company to produce an annual environmental report in which it openly stated its emissions and through which progress to reduce them could be publicly assessed.

So ICI became one of the first UK companies to publish an envi- ronmental report. The initiative was matched at local level where major sites, particularly on the river Tees, regularly published their emissions data. Measurement and disclosure allowed the company to set clear targets for improvement and punctured the argument about unknown or secret discharges. At the same time it was in a sense only buying time. It depended on the company cleaning up its act as it was endeavouring to do.

While dealing with the environmental challenges, we were also establishing a programme of closer relationships with journalists. We identified the major business journalists and at the chairman's suggestion invited them individually for an off-the record chat over an early evening whisky in his office. We included some economic commentators as well. It would pay off handsomely.

This informal arrangement supplemented an established sched- ule of results announcements and rather formal lunches held for the editors of the major papers with the chairman and some board mem- bers. My fondest memory of those was of a lunch with Max Hastings, the *Daily Telegraph* editor, and of his horrified reaction when he was refused a gin and tonic because ICI headquarters had recently gone dry. He froze in mid-grasp with his hand outstretched. I heard later that he had resolved never to attend again. Our answer was to move the lunches to a private ICI residence in nearby Smith Square.

In parallel, a Government Relations department maintained regular contacts with MPs local to ICI's plants and those with a particular interest in the industry, as well as with relevant Ministers. They were all invited to an annual reception. Such was ICI's position and reach that an invitation to the permanent secretaries of all government departments and their partners to a similar event every two years was welcomed. Some said it was a rare opportunity to meet each other. Concerns from civil servants about being seen to receive hospitality, however, would lead to its cancellation in the late '90s.

The company gained credit for having its finger on the pulse of the economy. In an early briefing I had arranged for industrial correspondents by the chairman, he announced that he had told divisions to cut back on spending because of a downturn in orders, accurately forecasting the recession that followed. At the time it was seen as a significant announcement, a first indication of the early '90s recession. To my recollection it did not move the share price hugely. Reflecting on it some years later, Sir Denys considered that such frankness had since become much more difficult because of the tightening of stock market regulation and the increased emphasis on share price trading.

Everywhere the industrial landscape was shifting. With the backing of financial institutions, both in the UK and the US, aggressive takeover activity was targeting long-established companies, conglomerates in particular. They were then dismembered at a considerable profit, with the juicier parts sometimes retained. The practice was known as a 'leveraged buy-out' because it was largely financed by borrowed money, or more bluntly as 'asset-stripping'. It was highlighted in a celebrated book, *Barbarians at the Gate*, which described the takeover of RJR-Nabisco in the US in 1988. Its proponents argued that, apart from the benefits to themselves and their shareholders, the process made businesses more efficient.

ICI was well aware of the activity. In fact it had bought Glidden Paints, an American company, from the most active British proponent, Hanson Trust, after it had taken over its parent company. Some ICI and Hanson directors were friends. But the general view was that ICI was too big for any predator.

That changed in 1990 when another British entrepreneur, Jimmy (Sir James) Goldsmith, with two associates, launched a bid for the huge British American Tobacco company. The bid was unsuccessful but it set alarm bells ringing in Imperial House and the company's rather pro forma 'defence plan' against hostile takeover was reviewed. There was a list of possible predators. It included the big oil companies, but top of the list was Hanson. Following our review, we hired a financial PR agency for the first time. We chose a relatively recently created agency, Brunswick, headed by Alan Parker, the son of my old acquaintance, Sir Peter Parker, whose presentational skills had been so much in evidence at British Rail.

In August 1990, the Iraqi invasion of Kuwait, and the ensuing First Gulf War, upset everyone's calculations, increasing the oil price and deepening the recession. I spent a month that autumn on the Civil Service Top Management Programme, which brought together senior civil servants and managers from private business. It was a valuable experience and we got on well. But my colleagues included a senior Hanson manager, Stephen Park. We treated each other with circumspection.

On 14 May 1991, out of the blue, an announcement was made by the stockbroker Smith Newcourt that it had bought 2.47 per cent of the shares of ICI, for 'investment purposes'. It looked like the preliminary to a takeover bid. Smiths did not name its client and speculation ran wild in the press. ICI had little doubt it was Hanson and this was confirmed the next day. The ground had been well prepared and both the *Daily Telegraph* and *The Times* published major pieces lauding Hanson's business record and querying ICI's. An accompanying cartoon showed Hanson as a nimble swordsman, rapier in hand, advancing on a lumbering ICI.

It was an image we needed to shake. But the next few days and weeks would stretch everyone to the limit. It was not strictly a takeover bid, but we treated it as such. Tellingly, Hanson refused to rule out a bid.

The usual advice in these situations was to keep quiet and say as little as possible until advisors from the banks had looked at the numbers and a detailed response had been agreed. At first it seemed from the shocked and frozen faces round the boardroom table that silence might prevail.

But Henderson and his closest colleagues, with my support, determined on a robust response. Alan Parker announced characteristically, 'If Hanson wants to bid for ICI he is going to have to take his clothes off.' In other words, we would carry the fight to Hanson. If he wanted to control Britain's leading manufacturer, a top exporter and a leading research spender, he would have to prove his credentials.

The robustness of the company's response was demonstrated the next day. Some of the most brutal transactions in the City of London were carried out under the guise of silky good manners. As it happened, Denys Henderson was due to make a presentation about the company's performance the very next day to none other than Smith Newcourt, who had bought the shares. The oily tones of its boss, Sir Michael Richardson (who years later would be banned from City trading), came down the telephone. He would quite understand in the circumstances if Sir Denys wished to cancel. No, said Sir Denys, he would not. I travelled down with him, advising him to look as cheerful as possible. As cameras whirred he walked confidently in with a warm good morning. Inside the meeting a patronising Sir Michael publicly complimented him on his courage.

Back at ICI, Henderson formed a small war cabinet with half his team which met at eight every morning to review the situation – and the media – and decide on an action plan.

It was an uncomfortable beginning. The Hanson image – nimble entrepreneur versus lumbering company – still had some way to run. We needed time for our examination of his business and also to agree the key strengths of ICI on which we would rely. We had to mobilise our supporters in business, in politics, the trade unions and our own employees.

In the meantime, while radio silence had its benefits – we could analyse what Hanson's arguments were from what was appearing in the press – we needed to start to contribute positively in the media. In particular we were facing a demand from our own employees for information; they wanted reassurance that the company was going to put up a fight. But this also provided us with an opportunity. While our advisors frowned on public statements, I argued that there was no reason not to communicate with our employees – in fact we had a duty to do so. So Denys and I prepared messages directed to our employees which we then provided to the Sunday papers – a key battleground – on a Saturday, issued as close as possible to publication time to prevent comment from the other camp.

We had no illusions about what we were facing. When I rang one hard-working Sunday business reporter, he told me, 'You should know what you are up against. We had two PR agencies working for the other side here in this office the other night checking our copy.'

On our side we just had Brunswick. But we benefited from Alan Parker's energy and his decision to put David Brewerton, the former City editor of *The Times* and *The Independent*, who had recently joined Brunswick, on our case. David brought judgement and credibility to the task, and the friendship we forged in those testing days has lasted more than twenty years.

In the early days, I and individual directors were approached by a number of agencies hoping to get in on the action. Inevitably I was asked the question – do we need more than Brunswick? My reply was emphatically not: we wanted clear advice we could interrogate, not a stable of competing advisors of varying quality. Fortunately the key directors agreed.

The story of the Hanson affair can be summed up briefly. ICI rallied its friends, made progress on convincing the world of its strengths in effective management as well as scientific research, and exposed Hanson's lack of transparency. Most tellingly, a detailed examination of Hanson's finances, to which journalists were led, raised questions and revealed that the company was using its shareholders' funds to buy racehorses without declaring it. Hanson and his close associate, Gordon White, were known as keen racegoers and owners. Later, *The Observer* would publish a note from James Hanson to his PR advisors in which he declared that he was disappointed with the press coverage: 'I think we are entitled to better results … Alan Parker shows himself to be running circles around us…' The turning point came on 25 July, when ICI declared an unexpected high level of profit. Months later, Hanson sold his shares – at a profit. He sent Henderson a handwritten note in advance. But his glory days were fading – his company was never the same again.

ICI had done a good job at mobilising support. The scientific establishment had come out on its side. Employees had supported it and their worries about Hanson's treatment of their pension funds – a lucrative target in his previous takeovers – had been assuaged by transferring supervision to an independent body. ICI's local MPs had rallied round. Trade unions had voiced open support and I even received an invitation for Denys to address the annual TUC Congress, a rarity for any businessman. We turned it down in case it gave the wrong message to the shareholders who would determine any bid battle.

Perhaps the biggest secret was that at one point Denys had a private meeting with Mrs Thatcher. At the end of it, she told him, 'We have a few shares, they are yours if you need them.'

Picking the bones out of our experience, there was no doubt that a key factor had been our PR activity in which Henderson's willingness to front up had been vital. We had had an active programme of background briefing about ICI, an extension of our previous early-evening chats. Alex Brummer, the *Guardian* City editor at the time, described it as 'intimate, forward-looking, carefully targeted and hard-nosed briefing at its best. It was a relatively relaxed technique which James Hanson, put on the defensive, found hard to match'.[11]

We also made sure that our public interventions were limited and disciplined; only made in a proper context and for obvious reasons; in letters to employees, in formal analyst briefings, and in the case of MPs, making use of a formal meeting of the established All-Party Group on the Chemical Industry.

The date for this was set well in advance and publicly known. We saw it as a chance to make our considered case. Denys was due to travel the short distance to the Houses of Parliament in the afternoon and his speech was carefully prepared. That morning James Hanson agreed to allow filming in his office for an item, pegged to the speech, which BBC News was preparing. Its business correspondent, Iain Carson, accompanied the cameraman, and Hanson unexpectedly agreed to a short interview. In the course of it, he complained that his intentions had been misunderstood. Alan Parker and I watched the

---

11 Alex Brummer and Roger Cowe, *Hanson: A Biography* (Fourth Estate, 1994), p. 223

exchange on the television in my office, realising that it would form the context in which Denys would speak – and be asked questions.

We discussed our response and came up with the line, 'If Lord Hanson is unhappy, all that he has to do is to say four little words, "I will not bid."' We coached Denys. I went in advance to the St Stephen's entrance to the Commons where camera crews were waiting. To forestall a mobbing rush, I told them that Denys would stop and talk to them. He arrived, paused as arranged, was asked the inevitable question, 'Lord Hanson says...' and delivered the 'four little words' reply, before entering to make his speech.

But while ICI might have triumphed for the time being, the affair had raised uncomfortable questions about the old imperial assumptions. To the board's surprise the company's boast that it was one of the country's biggest research spenders had not impressed some of its critics in the City. The question they asked was 'What return was it getting?' This was not always so easy to answer.

Similarly the prospect Hanson had raised of dismembering ICI, selling off parts and keeping the more profitable businesses renewed questions the company had asked itself in the previous decade. It was obvious that its big traditional chemical operations were only satisfactorily profitable in the good times, and then less and less so. The great discoveries had now become commodities that others could make cheaply, particularly in Asia or the Middle East with its cheap supplies of oil. The Harvey-Jones switch away from heavy chemicals to more modern and consumer materials had not gone far enough.

More fundamentally, just as the days of conglomerate companies that bundled together businesses from different industries were fading under the attack of the asset-strippers, might the time for single industry conglomerates like ICI also be passing? The synergies between businesses based on their common chemicals expertise had not been so easy to find. Was management time being spread across too many interests? Add into this the increasing cost of building huge plants, which took years to come on stream, and here was a serious argument for the board.

It was fuelled by a changing atmosphere in the City of London as the effect of the Big Bang of 1986 worked its way through. Increasingly the phrase on everyone's lips was 'shareholder value'. They were not words that were old ICI currency, and the City advisors during the bid had chided Henderson for his reluctance to use them. In the end he did.

Now he turned to those advisors for help in meeting the new industrial realities. While Ronnie Hampel, seen as the most demanding of the directors, was appointed chief operating officer to drive the company harder, Henderson asked Sir David Scholey, the chairman of ICI's lead merchant bank, for the services of one of his sharpest young financiers. John Mayo arrived in the Millbank offices to prepare a plan for the company's next step.

John and I, both creatures from outside the company, would sometimes lunch together in the canteen as John stared with some amazement at the six-storey atrium with a huge designer carpet, knitted when ICI's textile fibre business was significant, and the stained-glass windows above it dating from 1926. His language was rougher than traditional ICI managers, closer to my journalistic remembrances, and he spoke of 'cutting off the tail' of ICI's older non-performing businesses.

The version of his plan agreed by the board envisaged a split of ICI into two parts, an unusual although not unprecedented step. Into one half would go the bioscience industries, principally the successful pharmaceutical business that ICI had developed from scratch and whose drugs had included the first betablocker heart drugs and the breast cancer treatment Tamoxifen, which is still relied upon today.

The agroscience business, principally pesticides and seeds, would be included as well as the dyes business (from whose chemistry the pharmaceutical business had grown) and the speciality chemicals business.

The other half contained the heavy chemicals, paints, polyurethanes, explosives and other divisions perhaps more generally thought of as ICI, most of which ranked, regionalised heavy chemicals apart, in the top few in the world.

The question of which twin would continue to bear the world-famous ICI name came down to how easy it would be to unscramble the various agreements and patents connected to them. In the end it remained with the older businesses, which ultimately led to its demise. But it is interesting to consider what would have happened if the decision had gone the other way. Would we have a pharmaceuticals giant called Astra-ICI?

Amazingly, the complex process of splitting the company was carried out in secret, although hundreds of people were involved. It was announced to an unsuspecting world in July 1993 at a pre-arranged results announcement. Some months later I arranged a press conference at the Royal Society of Arts, at which the name Zeneca was announced for the new bioscience company. The name was greeted with some derision. One journalist described it as sounding like a Japanese camera.

Our original long list of names had been reduced to two. David Barnes, the chief executive-elect of the new company, had spent a nervous few days over the final choice as, concurrently, a Bosnian town of a similar name, Zenica, was under threat in the war that was raging and risked tragic notoriety. David made his decision and I was able to persuade him not to use the analogy of Siamese twins when launching his new baby, pointing out that their fortunes were not always happy.

The wisest advice we were given was that, whatever the name, its value would be imparted by the performance of the business. And so it proved. Under Barnes's cool direction, Zeneca became a success story.

ICI, however, struggled. Under the firm direction of Hampel, who became chief executive, some business performance improved. But, without the assured profits that pharmaceuticals could bring in, there were too many businesses requiring funds to take them from world class to top of their class. ICI was good, but not good enough.

And the outside world continued to exert its pressures. In about 1994 a group of churchmen linked with local sites asked to do a study of ICI's worldwide working practices. A senior director agreed to talk to them. In the speech I wrote for him, we emphasised that however much it might seem that corporations like ours dictated events, from the inside it seemed that we were always reacting to outside pressures, and were often a convenient target.

One such unexpected intervention came when a Texas court delivered a ruling over alleged anti-competitive activity by an explosives company we had purchased, which had taken place prior to its sale. I received a call from one of our North American PR staff in the early hours of the morning. 'You know that case where we thought that the worst could be a $30 million fine – well it's over $300 million.' It was the only time I got the company's chief lawyer out of bed. In the end it was settled for considerably less.

Then, in 1995, the American right-winger Timothy McVeigh blew up a government building in Oklahoma, killing 168 people in the deadliest act of internal terrorism before 9/11. It turned out that fertiliser used to construct his truck bomb had been made by ICI. Another phone call from the States informed me that Johnnie Cochran, the high-profile Californian lawyer who had successfully defended O. J. Simpson, was proposing to sue ICI for not taking the same steps to make its fertiliser safe as it had in troubled Northern Ireland.

Although we issued a strong statement deploring any attempt to switch responsibility away from the perpetrators, this was a matter for intensive legal activity. At one stage, the company staged controlled explosions in the American desert to demonstrate to members of Congress that even with the addition of chalk (the method used in Northern Ireland) the fertiliser would still have been powerful enough to have caused the explosion. Eventually a judge threw out the case.

Both in America and farther afield, the company had not forgotten its imperial roots and took confidently to globalisation. In the '80s and '90s it was acutely aware of the growing importance of Asia, and invested hundreds of millions. I visited two recently built plants in Taiwan producing the necessary chemicals to feed the insatiable market for plastic bottles. In Japan, ICI turnover was already over £1 billion a year, although the ICI factory there making plastic film was held up as an example of over-optimistic investment in our management training sessions. I attended the opening there of a joint venture for CFC replacements with a ceremony where a Shinto priest cast a blessing over cans of the product.

Then there was China, which was just beginning to open up again. Travelling on the train to Guanghzou from Hong Kong in an industrial smog, I visited the site of a new Dulux paint factory in a muddy field beside a river, being built in conjunction with the old Hong Kong imperial business of John Swire. Labourers in suit jackets and gym shoes pushed wheelbarrows to move the first earth. At an evening dinner, 1,000 guests were treated to a dozen courses and a hastily composed company song played by the band of the People's Liberation Army. Among the guests were used car repairers who already depended on ICI paint.

Later I would attend the announcement in Shanghai of a polyurethanes plant costing hundreds of millions. The first question from

local journalists was: 'Are you building this plant here because environmental regulation will not let you build it in Europe?' We had a good
answer: that we were constructing a similar plant in heavily regulated
Holland. But it showed the growing spread of worldwide concerns.

In 1995, Hampel moved from chief executive to chairman. He was
succeeded by an outsider, Charles Miller Smith, a relatively recent
recruit to the ICI board as a non-executive. He had spent his life in
Unilever where he had been finance director and enjoyed a formative period in India. I recalled the remark of a Unilever director
to Anthony Sampson in the '60s: 'People talk about us as a sinister
Anglo-Dutch concern but they regard ICI as part of their patriotism,
as if it were the army or the navy.'[12]

Now Miller Smith's appointment was meant to signal change and
it did so. Here was a chief executive who had not been reared on the
imperial presumptions of ICI. He admitted to being surprised when a
fellow member of his Belgravia church congregation had urged him
to 'take care of ICI'. His lens was Unilever, another company with
global operations, but Anglo-Dutch and so more international and
concentrated on consumer products.

Miller Smith's review of ICI reflected this. He identified a lack of
diversity with no women in the most senior jobs and a limited range
of nationalities, although most of ICI's country managers were locals.
At the same time, he saw the business future in lighter, more consumer-
based chemicals, sometimes called speciality or specialty chemicals.

Unfortunately the ICI specialities business had been packed
off with Zeneca. The company's planning team had been looking
unsuccessfully for alternative purchases. But Miller Smith had a possible answer – he knew that Unilever was considering the sale of
its own speciality chemicals as it concentrated instead on products

12   Anthony Sampson, op. cit.

sold directly to the customer. The old ICI planning department had run the rule over them but had not been convinced. Now under a new planning manager, Rona Fairhead, later to become chair of the *Financial Times* and of the BBC Trust, they looked again.

In due course, I was asked to report to Rona. I found her fair-minded. But ironically, given what came later, she showed little close interest in media relations, preferring to attend ICI's presentations to analysts rather than to journalists.

In the early months of Charles's term, profits were good, but then an economic downturn began and the big Taiwanese plants and their fellows slipped swiftly into heavy losses. It was a classic demonstration of the sharp swings of the chemical cycle. The decision was made to move out from heavy chemicals and attempt to buy the Unilever plants instead. But the deal was concluded before ICI had sold its own plants and it became effectively a distressed seller. As the businesses were eventually sold for less than hoped for, more operations had to be put on the block to reduce what had become an uncomfortably high level of debt.

I worked closely with Charles to help him explain his new vision. At short notice we arranged a two-day session for 200 or so managers throughout the world in London. It was based on a Unilever model and was new to ICI. I toured locations round the world to make short films about good practice in subjects like innovation, environmental management, marketing and safety. Then we took over ITN's London studios to carry out two satellite broadcasts to centres all around the globe, with Charles making his presentation and answering questions live.

It made a powerful impression and we repeated it, but when improvements did not come through strongly enough and the questioning got more difficult, a new chief executive, Brendan O'Neill, decided not to continue the exercise.

Meanwhile, the challenge of improving environmental performance remained and the legacy of the past still had surprises in store.
Cheshire in the north-west of England had been one of ICI's most
historic locations. ICI's forefathers, the German immigrants Brunner
and Mond, had established themselves there in the nineteenth century with a new process for making soda-ash, an important industrial
component. Later, the Mond division had mined salt from its own
reserves to make other chemicals, chlorine in particular, with a manufacturing base at Runcorn beside the Weaver canal.

In 1917, Brunner Mond bought two local quarries from which the
stone for Liverpool Cathedral had been cut. Over the years all kinds
of miscellaneous waste materials, some contaminated, from demolished buildings to old railway rolling stock, had been dumped into
them. By the 1970s, the dump was full and it was covered over and
turfed. But, with concern for the environment increasing, in the 1990s
ICI decided to check the condition of the dump and the possibility of
chemical pollution. The first step was a lengthy research process to
establish what had actually been deposited. Then it was decided
to sink exploratory boreholes to test for any leakage of aggressive
chemicals. Initial studies showed that it was not interfering with the
water table. But, in late 1999, boreholes on the edge of the site found
a chemical called HCBD, a by-product of dry-cleaning fluid that had
been shown to cause kidney damage in rats.

The site, at Weston Village, was ringed by houses and a pony club
exercised on the turfed-over quarry. The residents included some ICI
staff and pensioners. The company understood that it must notify
adjoining residents and also drill in their streets to see if the chemical detected on the edge of the site had spread.

It was not a situation to be proud of. One weekend early in 2000,
trained staff members went from door to door in the village explaining the situation. Hotel accommodation had been booked for those

who wanted to move out, health checks arranged and contact and advice lines set up. In due course the company bought houses in parts of the village at market price from those who wanted to sell. Some were demolished where the pollution was found to have spread; others were resold when they were found to be clear. The chief executive of the business apologised and explained the situation at a crowded public meeting. Press coverage took a while to get going but we monitored it in detail, identifying issues as they arose.

Some weeks in, *The Guardian* ran an article in its *G2* supplement headed 'The Village of the Damned' and *Panorama* featured it in a wider piece about new government legislation on historic pollution. But the company and its local management, who had inherited the situation, behaved in what seemed to me an exemplary fashion.

As far as I know there were no serious health consequences to anyone. But there could have been. What was apparent was that clear commitment to communicate and the unflinching acceptance of responsibility made a major difference. It was in line with ICI's reputation as a company that understood its commitment to local communities, one of the reasons that I had been pleased to join it.

But at corporate level the focus was shifting. As ICI had struggled to reinvent itself from demerger onwards, the question of incentives for improving managerial performance was a recurring one. The company had long given share options to its senior executives, which allowed them to buy shares at a price that was expected to turn them a profit. But, with the share price stubbornly refusing to reach the required levels (none of my options ever paid out), new ways of incentivising were increasingly being sought.

When I first joined ICI, its personnel department was staffed by experienced industrial negotiators whose forte was dealing with the unions and keeping good relations with the union national officers. ICI was known as a model of harmonious industrial relations – again

something that had attracted me. Every year the chairman and directors had attended a two-day gathering at Harrogate, at which they
set out the company's aims and achievements, heard questions and
comments and mingled with workforce representatives at meals
and meetings.

It had proved its worth during the Hanson episode and good
relations were reinforced by support for local communities in areas
where the company's plants were situated. In one example, when
Middlesbrough Football Club in ICI's Teesside heartland was in danger of bankruptcy, ICI stepped in with a loan. Now this central staff
conference was abandoned and the central personnel or human
relations department was reshaped. In came experts on executive
remuneration to devise cleverer ways to ensure executive effort was
more richly rewarded. It was a shift in focus that was becoming apparent across British industry.

As remuneration – salaries and bonuses – had risen in the City
under the impact of Big Bang, which brought in US institutions and
bankers encouraging easy comparisons with the very much higher
payments in the United States, so aspirations spread. If you sat with
bankers, as I did, arguing none too cleverly among themselves about
the wording on proposed stock exchange documents for a sale or a
purchase, it was difficult not to reflect on how much more they were
being paid. So corporate lawyers, for example, started to measure
themselves against the bankers, and so did business executives. The
result was a gathering explosion of executive pay.

Journalists are rarely well paid and are highly sensitive, not to
say envious, where pay is concerned. There is an old joke about the
three most essential journalistic questions – when, where and how
much? We knew that the one section of our annual report which
would be seized on unfailingly was the report on the remuneration
of the directors. Now, as reward levels in British business rose sharply,

the argument about fat cats grew more bitter. Chief executives found it began to dominate questioning, as I described in my valedictory article in 2000.

As for ICI's subsequent fortunes, it was soon recognised that the company had paid too much for the speciality businesses, and contracted too much debt. Although less volatile, they did not produce the big profits made by heavy chemicals at the top of the economic cycle. But there remained a good case for getting out of heavier chemicals, particularly when it was recognised that they were increasingly subject to the same forces that were affecting other British industries, such as shipping, steel and the motor industry.

Two factors, particularly apparent in my visits to Asia, were combining to limit imperial pretensions. The City and financial institutions were increasingly unwilling to finance, and insure, the huge sums that were required to build and operate the major plants required to compete on the world stage. Those who had the money to spend were often private companies owned by rich men who operated on longer timescales and did not have shareholders requiring instant returns above a particular percentage. They were particularly prominent in Asia, where much of the new investment was taking place. Governments in Asia and elsewhere were also prepared to back investment in order to realise their industrial ambitions, and sometimes to support local companies. The world was changing.

ICI's history in India, for example, had been one of decline and disappointment. Well-established at independence it had major operations that included textiles and paint. But when I visited in the '90s it was still headed by a manager sent out from the UK. The company retained its own guesthouse in the grounds of his house in New Delhi, but it saw its textile strength steadily emasculated by Indian rivals, particularly the Reliance Group run by the Ambani family. It ended up selling its remaining textile assets to them.

Its paints business was also losing ground to Indian rivals. Charles Miller Smith saw the country as a promising market, as it was for Unilever, but then found an attempt to buy another paints business to increase ICI's reach blocked by the Indian government.

So, as ICI was progressively dismembered in an attempt to reduce its debts, it was often to companies in private hands or connected to foreign governments that its assets were eventually bound. The private American Huntsman group and the private British-based Ineos company bought many of the northern English and European plants, while the Teesside cracker went to a Saudi operation. Most have continued to operate.

The main business that still remained in ICI was its paints empire, which had been expanded under the Miller Smith changes. But in 2008 ICI was sold, to a Dutch rival, the paint company Akzo, which then disposed of the speciality chemicals businesses that had remained. Today the ICI roundel is only to be found on cans of Dulux paint.

By then I had left the company. After I had worked with three chairmen and four chief executives, in 2000 the latest chief executive, Brendan O'Neill, who had come from Guinness, another consumer company, decided he wanted a different approach.

Epilogue

As I reflect on what I have written, I am struck by how much the narrative of empire is still with us, and how many of the issues that preoccupied us in the late '60s and early '70s are still the daily currency of our political discourse. Immigration and community relations (once intimately related to empire but now much less so), suitable education, housing provision for all levels of society and the place and importance of industry are still central issues of political debate.

At the same time, the way we engage with them has changed extraordinarily. Perhaps the biggest changes of all have been in my own trade of communications.

Back in the '50s, suspicion of journalists was nothing new, as the old Southampton joke about the perils of New York reporters showed. During the emergency in Cyprus, relations between the beleaguered government and the British-run *Times of Cyprus* were perhaps indicative. Apart from the moments when troops searched the offices, communication was by lengthy paper press release, which the paper was invited to collect from the secretariat offices without further comment. A brief appointment of the novelist Lawrence Durrell as government information officer brought no discernible improvement.

I had my own taste of traditional imperial control when the Pakistani Army overran Dacca in 1971. The censorship rules that were promulgated were scarcely altered from the days of the Raj and even covered the possession of typewriters.

Government supervision was still evident back in Britain, particularly in broadcasting where the Post Office policed and restricted the supply of wavelengths. BBC output was closely monitored and the World Service was funded by the Foreign Office. I was asked to sign the Official Secrets Act twice in my life: once when I became a temporary civil servant to report for the Colombo Plan, and once when, to my amazement, it was required of me when I joined the BBC as a correspondent in 1978. The Corporation had a misleadingly avuncular MI5 officer on its senior staff.

In my early days on *The Guardian*, almost every story was described as 'from our own reporter', with an assumption of authority. It took about six months until my first personal byline, as fashions started to change. The *Times* front page was still given over to advertisements only. News was confined to the inside pages. Paper press releases, posted out, remained standard communication and were often reproduced with little comment. The early years of the *Times* business section depended heavily on reproducing them, until business coverage started to find its feet. You got what you were given, and there could be complaints if you asked for more.

One of the very early videos I was ever sent came from a British Telecom executive, who had once been a well-known broadcaster. It was headed 'From your waste-basket; press releases you may have missed'.

Out on a story, you still searched for a public telephone box and your small change to dictate your copy. At the BBC, we had the use of our first mobile phone, a heavy, boot-like contraption as an experiment during the 1984 miners' strike.

Working in Asia in the late '60s, the growing reach of the electronic media was becoming obvious. Not television: the spread of electricity supply which has allowed it to become such a powerful force in the remotest villages today had not happened. Instead, I found Nepalese farmers with radios strapped to their ploughs.

News was only part of the picture. News bulletins – the word was indicative – were confined to a few very specific times of the day. The *One O'Clock*, the *Six O'Clock* and so on. When I joined BBC Television in 1978, we had our first news bulletin, lasting about twelve minutes, at around one o'clock. It was moved around to accommodate broadcast cricket and other events, and often followed the test card – the non-moving picture, like an early screen-saver, which filled the screen for most of the morning. A second, twenty-minute or so, bulletin came along at 5.40 p.m. and then our most important, the 25-minute-long *Nine O'Clock News*. Almost all our reporting was on film, which had to be biked back to a television centre, put in a tank to be developed and then physically cut into shape. So much for instant news.

By the time I left eleven years later, everything was electronic and regularly transmitted by satellite. We were being required to service breakfast television, news bulletins on every hour and *Newsnight*. Twenty-four-hour news was beginning. But as yet there was no internet, or Twitter and no outlet for 'citizen journalists' or pictures from the public's mobile phones. Media studies, which now claim far more undergraduates than there are possible journalistic openings, were in their infancy.

The now ever-present world of PR spin was different, too. In the '70s, a few organisations had a PR advisor, usually rather urbane and upper-class with a penchant for lunches at the Dorchester or the Savoy. Company press officers were distinctly down the scale and the title of press relations manager, an interesting idea, was common enough. And management was what it was about; even, or maybe especially at supposedly radical organisations like the TUC. There, until things changed under Len Murray, information was decidedly rationed.

I have charted business's too-frequent failures to explain but also the way that, particularly in the hard-pressed nationalised industries, people started to use public relations to advance their business aims.

But then, in the '80s, as business belatedly started to get its act together, the results of Big Bang, the loosening of City regulation and the requirements of selling the Thatcher privatisation issues switched the focus more narrowly onto the stock market. As business coverage and business broadcasting grew, regiments of PR men, working for rapidly growing outside consultancies, were brought in to do the job that business people felt ill-equipped to handle. And that financial and stock market coverage is where much of business coverage has stayed.

In the '90s, I first sat on a panel that decided the annual Wincott awards for broadcasting coverage of business alongside the more famous awards for the written word. We viewed some remarkable programmes, made by enterprising journalists, but as the twenty-first century unrolled, there were fewer and fewer of them, and fewer that dealt with what was happening in the real world of industry. Business seemed to be summed up by the success of the BBC television programme *The Apprentice*, copied from America, essentially a business-themed game show and depending on manufactured confrontation, not a serious attempt to portray how business really works. In parallel, the daily business programmes that sprung up in the '80s have disappeared and even the venerable *Money Programme* is no more.

Journalists, meanwhile, are increasingly chained to their computers, communicating with their Twitter followers and seething with resentment about the way in which their access to companies (and even more to sports people) is filtered through outside PR and marketing agencies.

The old imperial monoliths of the newspaper industry no longer control the agenda in the way they once did. But, marching beside the explosion of different voices has come a depressing attempt towards standardisation and control of what is being said, which in some ways matches the grip that imperial government sought to impose on communication.

It is depressingly ironic that just when the necessity to communicate for which we argued over the years seems finally to have been accepted, the nature of that communication has been distorted. Just as we watched the politicians in the '80s move from sometimes disarmingly frank discussion simply to repeating sound bites and staying on message, so other institutions and the rest of the world have learnt to do likewise. Like some everlasting election campaign, we are caught up in a cacophony of an accelerating output of supposedly 'key messages' from a growing number of media outlets which more and more drown each other out.

And what of the issues that have remained with us? The argument over immigration and community relations continues and has become stronger. In the days when I was reporting on immigration, we could still highlight individual cases of apparent hardship and unfairness in the pages of newspapers. Today, although local newspapers sometimes highlight local campaigns, the immigration numbers are now so large that it is difficult to pick out individuals – the argument is still about numbers, but much bigger numbers, and their nature has changed, with the focus shifting to Eastern Europe, and now, of course, Syria.

As for community relations, I have little recent involvement, but again the debate has shifted from the discrimination against the black community which we highlighted in the '60s to the engagement of the Islamic communities. Concerning as this is, it is a tribute to those who argued for an effective Race Relations Act that, although the Act itself is now rarely mentioned, its effect has been far-reaching. Too many people from ethnic minorities remain unemployed but cases where people are routinely refused jobs or housing simply because of their colour as they were in the '60s now seem extraordinary, particularly in multiracial London. The kind of experiences, and tortured explanations, that we highlighted in Leeds or London or Manchester really do seem like something from another age.

Planning and the provision of affordable homes has become even more of an issue than when the first queues formed on the streets in the 1970s.

And then there is industry. For people of my generation there remains the great unresolved question: 'Could the decline of British industry have been prevented, or at least reduced?' And, nagging just behind it: 'Does it really matter?'

This account finishes in 2000, when I left full-time employment. Afterwards, although I continued an involvement with industry and public affairs through my own PR consultancy, I was a more distant observer of the broader landscape.

Over those years, British industry and British ownership of industry continued to decline, although there were positive developments too.

A drum-roll of top-ranking companies were taken over one by one by foreign owners, although their operations did not necessarily disappear from Britain. Along with ICI, which went Dutch, British Oxygen and Blue Circle Cement became French and RMC building materials went to Mexico. P&O, an imperial talisman if there ever was one, had its worldwide operations taken over by the small Gulf state of Dubai, past whose desert shores its great white liners had once sailed with scarcely a passing glance. The commanding giant of the engineering industry, GEC, meanwhile, sold its defence businesses to British Aerospace, changed its name to Marconi and shrivelled away after its investments in new high-tech businesses proved duds. My old acquaintance, John Mayo, the architect of the ICI split, was its finance director. Now even Cadbury is American-owned.

On the other hand, many of the operations continue under different names. Since 1998, Jim Radcliffe of Ineos has built a huge petrochemicals business from the cast-offs of BP, ICI and others, and is planning new investments. His company is the tenth biggest chemical company in the world. Significantly, it is a private company.

There are, of course, successes. James Dyson's continuing achievements show what a bold pursuit of engineering excellence can achieve. Vodafone has grown and grown, while the Bamford family continue to spread the name of JCB around the world.

At the other end of the scale, there are the lucrative triumphs of a mass of smaller enterprises in sectors like music and entertainment, fashion and the video games industry.

But, perhaps the most indicative story remains that of the motor industry, whose travails once seemed never-ending. Put bluntly, it has been saved by foreign ownership. This should not be too much of a surprise. For much of the twentieth century, the most effective motormaker in Britain was the American-owned Ford. Today that place has been taken by the Japanese manufacturers: Nissan, Toyota and Honda, German BMW and, most recently, the Indian Tata company, owner of Jaguar and Land Rover.

In the 1990s, the crumbling Rover empire, formerly British Leyland, was steadied sufficiently for British Aerospace to sell it to BMW. The German company then developed a highly successful new version of the Mini, something the old management had failed to do. But then, despairing of future success, they gave up on the rest of the company and disposed of it.

Their successors, eagerly seized on by a government desperate to prevent large redundancies in an election year, paid themselves handsomely, but demonstrated the old British failings of hopeless optimism and incompetence. Five years later, the redundancies duly arrived and the rump of the company was sold to Chinese buyers, who started to ship the engineering equipment to China. A few MGs have been produced since but most of Longbridge has been redeveloped for housing and shops. Meanwhile, the German-owned Mini roars out from a modern factory at once-strikebound Cowley.

Not far away in Coventry, the long battle to keep car production ended when the French firm of Peugeot finally withdrew from its outpost at the ancient shadow factory at Ryton and Jaguar work was switched to Halewood in Liverpool. Soon after, Ford gave up on Land Rover and Jaguar and sold them on to the Indian Tata company. Since then, rethought and reorganised, they have had great export success.

It is a gratifying, if a rollercoaster, success story, particularly as most of the cars produced are going for export. At the beginning of 2012, the British motor industry exported more by value than it imported – for the first time since 1976.

It remains, however, a brutally competitive industry, with fluctuating exchange rates and individual countries continuing to promote their own industries. The concerns that decisions made by foreign owners in foreign countries will not have British plants in front of mind and over the concentration of research at national headquarters remain lively.

Government support appears to have been damned for ever by the expensive failure of British Leyland, but Rolls-Royce, which was rescued at about the same time, has been a major success and remains a beacon of high-quality engineering. The difference, perhaps, is that Rolls got into trouble financing a genuinely world-beating family of engines; it had a product of excellence. BL did not and failed to find one. Rolls was also in the defence industry.

There is also a view that maybe British industry just lost ambition. Back in 1974, it was not just BL in trouble; it was also Volkswagen in Germany, struggling to replace the gap left by the Beetle. But for VW it was the beginning of renewed success as the imagination of its research and engineering allowed it to introduce the ground-breaking Golf.

Government support was crucial for two of the most important investment decisions made by the industry: the arrival of Nissan and Ford's decision to site a major engine plant in south Wales. Both followed major lobbying efforts and government incentives by the Thatcher and Callaghan governments respectively. There are other factors, too – the fact that Ford now builds its sophisticated engines here although it no longer chooses to assemble cars here says something about the skills and traditions of British workers.

But the worries remain. The difference between what we buy and what we sell abroad – the balance of payments figures about which we used to agonise monthly, in the days when the purchase of a single jumbo jet might distort the figures sufficiently to threaten a government – now goes largely unremarked. Yet we are in the red each month, by billions rather than millions, kept afloat by the transaction fees of the City and the purchase by foreigners of our property and companies. A crumbled empire indeed.

And what of the trade unions? Many of today's widely shared concerns, about low pay and equal pay and the importance of the minimum or living wage, reflect the earlier campaigning and rhetoric of the trade unions and their allies. The huge advances in workplace health and safety over the period are major achievements.

In the '70s, trade unions' cooperation in the social contract helped to pull the country back from hyper-inflation. But they ran ahead of themselves and their members. Self-interest and their ability to stop changes happening, coupled with a romanticism about the intrinsic virtues of resistance and revolution, combined to prevent them realising the magnitude of change needed as the old industrial empires crumbled. Nor were they immune to the old imperial belief that 'British is best'.

In the '80s it became clear that many of their members recognised that things had to change. The success of new initiatives, such as Japanese manufacturing practices or a revolution in dock work at the huge new port of Felixstowe, resisted by much union leadership, showed an understanding by the workforce, as well as battle-weary management, of effective and more collaborative approaches.

Against this, of course, stood the struggle of the great miners' strike, and the question of whether the miners had any choice, except taking protest action. Leaving aside the questions of how they were manoeuvred by their own leaders into the strike, my answer would be yes. The coal industry had for years been accepting steady contraction. In the end it was competitive forces – the availability of cheaper oil and foreign coal, the comparative cost of building coal-fired as against oil-fired power stations – and finally the environmental disadvantages of British coal that did it for the industry.

Nevertheless, the final rundown could have been more gradual and more could have been done for the old coalfields. Throughout the '70s, Joe Gormley's guile had ensured the industry had special treatment and the miners had got used to that. The defeat of Arthur Scargill and his refusal to accept any settlement meant that the victorious Conservative government had no reason to shield the miners as those competitive forces tore the industry apart.

Looking at the trade unions from my distanced position today, two thoughts occur. The first is the question of size. Throughout my reporting on the trade unions, the received view was that there were too many unions – unlike Western Germany, where a trade union structure with a smaller number of larger unions, largely industrially based, had been set up following the advice of British trade unionists after the war. Much of the TUC effort was put into encouraging mergers and resolving inter-union disputes within industries like shipbuilding or printing. The process, tortuous as it was, was largely successful. But today I wonder if it has gone too far as a few huge unions dominate the scene.

The second thought is simply this: as you look around the increasingly fragmented landscape of work, with increased numbers of small businesses, widespread outsourcing, exploitative work placements (not least in my own media industry), and the ambiguities of zero-hours contracts, wouldn't you have had to invent the trade unions to try to do something about it?

This narrative has roamed across a range of sometimes seemingly unconnected areas. What of the thread that connects, if not binds, them together: the baggage of empire?

In part it is the experience and indeed the expectation of dealing with decline, and of disappointment. We share a perception that, for all the astonishing material prosperity that most of us enjoy, things were somehow better in the past, and we, the British, were taken more seriously.

But along with that recognition, there remains a remarkable self-confidence, often an over-confidence, nurtured by our imperial successes, that we can indeed stand out from others, seen clearly in the 2016 Brexit debate. Whether it is the example of our institutions, exported, if temporarily, to other shores, our industrial flair or the strength of our culture enabling us to absorb and persuade whoever is fortunate enough to set foot on our shores.

The hangover was apparent wherever I worked – on both sides of industry, among both sides of the argument over community relations, in the press, in the old empire itself in its immediate aftermath. It has been weighty baggage.

For my generation, it was reasonable to suppose that we would have had difficulty freeing ourselves from the associations and attitudes with which we were brought up. But it is curious how strong the nostalgia remains among today's very different generations, whether it is the endless relaying of Indian railway programmes about the line to Shimla or the tabloid ferocity surrounding England–Germany football games, the never-being-able-to-commit to a Europe that we don't dominate or the continuing belief among politicians that we should and do punch above our weight in world affairs. The baggage of empire remains plentifully strewn about.

Acknowledgements

So many people have contributed to the experiences that shaped this book. The responsibility for the remembered facts and opinions in it is all mine, but I am particularly grateful to three wise friends who read early drafts, made important suggestions from their different points of view and encouraged me to publish. To David Brewerton, Michael Herlihy, and especially Ann Shearer, thanks.

Index